DEDALO AGENCY

SPAIN & PORTUGAL
TRAVEL GUIDE

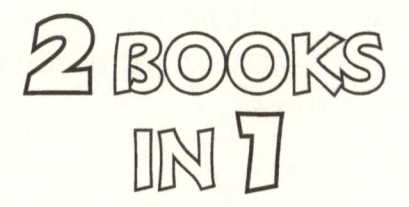

2 BOOKS IN 1

Edited by: Domenico Russo and Francesco Umbria
Design e layout: Giorgia Ragona
Book series: Journey Joy

© 2024 DEDALO SRLS
Spain & Portugal Travel guide
THE ESSENTIAL BOOK TO DISCOVER ALL THE BEAUTY
OF MEDITERRANEAN EUROPE

www.agenziadedalo.it

Index

SPAIN TRAVEL GUIDE

INTRODUCTION	15
CHAPTER 1: MADRID	21
The Prado Museum	22
Retiro Park	23
Madrid's Royal Palace	24
Gran Vía	24
San Miguel Market	25
Santiago Bernabeu Stadium	26
Almudena Cathedral	26
Madrid Nightlife	27
Thyssen-Bornemisza Museum	28
Day Trip to Toledo	28
Madrid Cuisine	29
Final Thoughts	30
CHAPTER 2: BARCELONA	35
Sagrada Familia	36
Park Güell	37
Gothic Quarter	38
Barcelona's Beaches	39
La Rambla	39
Picasso Museum	40
Casa Batlló	41
Barcelona Nightlife	42
Day Trip to Montserrat	42
Camp Nou	43
Barcelona Cuisine	44
Final Thoughts	45

Chapter 3: Seville — 49

- The Alcázar — 50
- Seville Cathedral and Giralda — 51
- Plaza de España — 52
- Triana District — 52
- Metropol Parasol — 53
- María Luisa Park — 54
- Seville Bullring — 54
- Day Trip to Jerez — 55
- Flamenco Show — 56
- Torre del Oro — 56
- Seville Cuisine — 57
- Final Thoughts — 58

Chapter 4: Valencia — 63

- City of Arts and Sciences — 64
- Valencia Cathedral — 65
- Central Market — 66
- Turia Gardens — 67
- La Lonja de la Seda — 67
- Bioparc Valencia — 68
- The Albufera Natural Park — 69
- Day Trip to Altea — 69
- Fallas Museum — 70
- Valencia's Silk Exchange — 70
- Valencia Cuisine — 71
- Final Thoughts — 72

Chapter 5: Bilbao — 77

- Guggenheim Museum — 78
- Casco Viejo — 79
- Bilbao Fine Arts Museum — 80
- Artxanda Funicular — 80
- San Mamés Stadium — 81
- Day Trip to Gaztelugatxe — 81
- Plaza Nueva — 82
- Bilbao Riverside Walk — 83
- Azkuna Zentroa — 83
- Bilbao's Bridges — 84
- Bilbao Cuisine — 85
- Final Thoughts — 86

Chapter 6: Granada — 91

- The Alhambra — 92
- Albayzín — 93
- Sacromonte — 94
- Granada Cathedral — 95
- Royal Chapel of Granada — 95
- Day Trip to Sierra Nevada — 96
- Generalife — 97
- Granada's Street Art — 97
- Hammam Al Ándalus — 98
- Carrera del Darro — 98
- Granada Cuisine — 99
- Final Thoughts — 100

Chapter 7: Santiago de Compostela — 105

- Santiago Cathedral — 107
- The Legendary Camino de Santiago — 108
- City of Culture of Galicia — 109
- Mercado de Abastos — 110
- Alameda Park — 110
- Day Trip to Cape Finisterre — 111
- The Old Quarter — 112
- The University — 112
- The Way of St. James — 113
- Hostal dos Reis Católicos — 113
- Santiago Cuisine — 114
- Final Thoughts — 115

Chapter 8: San Sebastián — 121

- La Concha Beach — 122
- Old Town — 123
- Monte Igueldo — 124
- San Sebastián International Film Festival — 124
- San Telmo Museum — 125
- Day Trip to Pasaia — 126
- La Bretxa Market — 126
- Peine del Viento — 127
- Miramar Palace — 128
- Tabakalera — 128
- San Sebastián Cuisine — 129
- Final Thoughts — 130

INDEX — 5

Chapter 9: Córdoba — 135

- The Mezquita — 136
- Alcázar de los Reyes Cristianos — 137
- Medina Azahara — 138
- The Roman Bridge — 138
- The Courtyards — 139
- Day Trip to the Sierra de Hornachuelos — 140
- The Jewish Quarter — 140
- Córdoba Synagogue — 141
- Calahorra Tower — 141
- The Flower Street — 142
- Córdoba Cuisine — 143
- Final Thoughts — 144

Chapter 10: Spanish Cuisine — 149

- The Tapas Culture — 150
- Seafood — 151
- Olive Oil — 151
- Traditional Dishes — 152
- Spanish Wines — 153
- Spanish Cheeses — 154
- Spanish Desserts — 154
- Spain's Food Markets — 155
- Vegetarian and Vegan Options — 156
- Sustainable Food Practices — 156
- Final Thoughts — 157

Chapter 11: How to Travel Spain on a Budget — 163

- Budget Accommodation — 164
- Eating on a Budget — 164
- Public Transport — 165
- Free Attractions — 166
- Budget Shopping — 166
- Cheap Flight and Train Tips — 167
- Discount Cards — 167
- Off-Season Travel — 168
- Final Thoughts — 168

Chapter 12: 10 Cultural Experiences You Must Try in Spain — 173

- 1 - Flamenco Show — 174
- 2 - Spanish Fiestas — 174
- 3 - Bullfighting — 175
- 4 - Spanish Art — 175
- 5 - Wine Tasting — 176
- 6 - Traditional Crafts — 176
- 7 - Spanish Language — 177
- 8 - Spanish Sports — 177
- 9 - Spanish Music — 178
- 10 - Spanish Architecture — 178

Conclusion — 181

INDEX

PORTUGAL TRAVEL GUIDE

INTRODUCTION	189
CHAPTER 1: LISBON	195
The Tower of Belém:	196
Jeronimos Monastery:	196
Alfama District:	197
LX Factory:	198
Baixa District:	199
São Jorge Castle:	199
Fado Music:	200
Tram 28:	201
Lisbon Oceanarium:	202
Day Trip to Sintra:	202
Lisbon Cuisine:	203
Final Thoughts:	204
CHAPTER 2: PORTO	211
Ribeira District:	212
Livraria Lello:	213
Porto Wine Cellars:	214
Church of São Francisco:	214
Dom Luís I Bridge:	215
Serralves Museum:	216
Foz do Douro:	216
Bolhão Market:	217
Day Trip to Guimarães:	218
Porto Cuisine:	218
Final Thoughts:	219
CHAPTER 3: MADEIRA	225
Funchal's Old Town:	226
Madeira Botanical Garden:	227
Monte Palace Tropical Garden:	228
Levadas of Madeira:	228
Cabo Girão:	229
Santana's Traditional Houses:	230
Pico do Arieiro:	231
Day Trip to Porto Santo:	231

- The Basket Toboggan Ride: 232
- Madeira Cuisine: 233
- Final Thoughts: 233

CHAPTER 4: AZORES — 239
- São Miguel Island: 240
- Pico Island: 241
- Faial Island: 242
- Terceira Island: 242
- Flores Island: 243
- Angra do Heroísmo: 244
- Azorean Whaling: 244
- Whale and Dolphin Watching: 245
- The Geothermal Wonders of the Azores: 246
- Azorean Cuisine: 246
- Final Thoughts: 247

CHAPTER 5: ALGARVE — 253
- Lagos: 254
- Benagil Cave: 255
- Faro: 255
- The Ria Formosa: 256
- Sagres and Cape St. Vincent: 257
- Silves: 257
- Algarve's Beaches: 258
- Golfing in Algarve: 259
- Day Trip to Tavira: 259
- Algarve Cuisine: 260
- Final Thoughts: 261

CHAPTER 6: ÉVORA AND ALENTEJO — 267
- Évora Cathedral: 268
- Évora's Roman Temple: 269
- Chapel of Bones: 269
- Monsaraz: 270
- Evoramonte Castle: 270
- Vila Viçosa and its Ducal Palace: 271
- Marvão: 272
- Cante Alentejano: 272
- The Megalithic Monuments of Alentejo: 273

INDEX — 9

- Alentejo Cuisine: 273
- Final Thoughts: 275

Chapter 7: Coimbra — 281
- University of Coimbra: 282
- Joanina Library: 283
- Monastery of Santa Cruz: 284
- Quinta das Lágrimas: 284
- Portugal for Little Ones: 285
- Botanical Garden of Coimbra: 286
- The Old Cathedral of Coimbra: 287
- The New Cathedral of Coimbra: 287
- Exploring the River Mondego: 288
- Coimbra Cuisine: 289
- Final Thoughts: 290

Chapter 8: Braga and Guimarães — 295
- Bom Jesus do Monte: 296
- Braga Cathedral: 297
- Guimarães Castle: 297
- Palace of the Dukes of Braganza: 298
- São Martinho de Tibães Monastery: 299
- Guimarães Historical Center: 299
- Sameiro Sanctuary: 300
- Citânia de Briteiros: 301
- Raio Palace: 301
- Braga and Guimarães Cuisine: 302
- Final Thoughts: 303

Chapter 9: Douro Valley — 309
- Régua: 310
- Douro River Cruise: 310
- Wine Tasting in Douro: 311
- Mateus Palace: 312
- Pinhão and its Train Station: 312
- Vineyard Visits: 313
- Miradouro de São Leonardo de Galafura: 313
- Lamego: 314
- Harvesting Grapes: 314
- Douro Valley Cuisine: 315
- Final Thoughts: 316

Chapter 10: Portuguese Cuisine — 321
- Bacalhau: 322
- Portuguese Pastries: 323
- Seafood in Portugal: 323
- Portuguese Cheese: 324
- Portuguese Wines: 325
- Alentejo Bread: 326
- Portuguese Olive Oil: 326
- Azeitão Cheese: 327
- Portuguese Coffee Culture: 328
- Portuguese Cuisine: 328
- Final Thoughts: 329

Chapter 11: How to Travel Portugal on a Budget — 335
- Timing Your Trip: 336
- Affordable Accommodations in Portugal: 336
- Portuguese Food on a Shoestring: 337
- Free and Affordable Attractions: 338
- Navigating Portugal Affordably: 338
- Thrifty Shopping: 339
- Travel Insurance: 340
- Off-Peak Travel: 340
- Volunteering Opportunities: 341
- Portuguese Budget Cuisine: 341
- Final Thoughts: 343

Chapter 12: 10 Cultural Experiences You Must Try in Portugal — 349
- 1 - Fado Performance: 350
- 2 - Portuguese Cooking Class: 351
- 3 - Traditional Azulejos Workshop: 351
- 4 - Douro Valley Wine Tour: 352
- 5 - Walking Tour of a Historic City: 353
- 6 - Attending a Portuguese Festival: 353
- 7 - A Visit to a Portuguese Market: 354
- 8 - Portuguese Language Class: 354
- 9 - Portugal's Coffee Culture: 355
- 10 - Portuguese Traditional Dance Class: 356
- Final Thoughts: 356

Conclusion — 359

SPAIN
Travel guide

Introduction

Welcome, dear traveler, to your quintessential guide to the enchanting splendors of Spain! An enthralling journey awaits you in this country where past and present collide in a vibrant spectacle of cultures, landscapes, flavors, and rhythms. With this guide, we invite you to embark on an odyssey that delves into the heart and soul of Spain, unearthing the multi-faceted charms that make this country a destination of timeless allure.

Our journey starts by immersing ourselves in the pulsating heart of Spain, the capital city, Madrid, explored in Chapter 1. Witness the royal grandeur of Palacio Real, discover masterpieces at the Prado Museum, and feel the energy of Plaza Mayor. Traverse through the vibrant markets, explore the city's rich history whispered by its streets, and treat your taste buds to the gastronomic delights that are uniquely Spanish.

Chapter 2 transports you to the sun-kissed beaches and architectural wonders of Barcelona. Gaze in awe at the surreal creations of Gaudí, get lost in the Gothic Quarter's narrow lanes, and enjoy the city's buzzing nightlife. Barcelona, with its vibrant culture and dynamic cityscape, is a canvas painting a vivid tale of history, art, and Catalan spirit.

The magnetic allure of Seville is explored in Chapter 3. Feel the passion of flamenco, be enchanted by the Moorish charm of the Alcazar, and experience the fervor of Feria de Abril. Seville's rhythm and allure are sure to cast a spell on you.

In Chapter 4, we navigate through the beauty of Valencia, a city where the futuristic City of Arts and Sciences resides in harmony with the medieval charm of the Old Town. Be captivated by Valencia's blend of old and new, and don't miss the chance to indulge in an authentic Paella Valenciana in its birthplace.

Chapter 5 leads us to the artistic and culinary hub of Bilbao. Home to the iconic Guggenheim Museum and boasting a thriving food scene, this city is the soul of the Basque Country. Bilbao's unique blend of traditional and avant-garde will leave you yearning for more.

In Chapter 6, we journey south to Granada, where the Alhambra's majestic silhouette against the Sierra Nevada will captivate your senses. Granada is a historic gem where every corner tells a story of its Moorish past.

Chapter 7 unveils the spiritual Santiago de Compostela, the culmination of the famous Camino de Santiago pilgrimage. Its stunning cathedral, ancient streets, and spiritual aura make Santiago a city of unique spiritual and cultural significance.

Chapter 8 transports you to the seaside city of San Sebastián, a gastronomic paradise tucked away in Spain's northern Basque Country. From its breathtaking La Concha beach to its renowned pintxos, San Sebastián is a treat for your senses.

Córdoba, in Chapter 9, is a tapestry of history and culture. Explore the mesmerizing Mezquita, wander through the Judería, and experience the vibrancy of the Fiesta de los Patios. Córdoba is a living testament to Spain's diverse cultural history.

Chapter 10 is a culinary journey through the flavors of Spain. From the smoky essence of a well-made paella to the succulent taste of jamón ibérico, and from the sweet delight of churros to the refreshment of sangria, Spanish cuisine is a narrative of its regions, its history, and its people.

Chapter 11 provides essential tips and advice on exploring Spain with a savvy eye on your budget. This practical guide arms you with valuable insights on transportation options, affordable accommodations, cost-effective eateries, and free attractions.

Finally, Chapter 12 immerses you in unique Spanish cultural experiences. Learn how to flamenco dance, participate in a Spanish cooking class, join a local fiesta, or walk a portion of the Camino de Santiago. These experiences will not only create unforgettable memories but also provide an intimate understanding of the passionate Spanish spirit.

This guide is your passport to an unforgettable journey through Spain's kaleidoscope of experiences. As you delve into its diverse landscapes, rich history, vibrant culture, and delicious cuisine, you'll find Spain unveiling its many facets, letting you in on its secrets and traditions. By the end of your journey, you'll carry a piece of Spain within you, a cherished memory that will beckon you to return to this extraordinary land. Let's go – your Spanish adventure awaits!

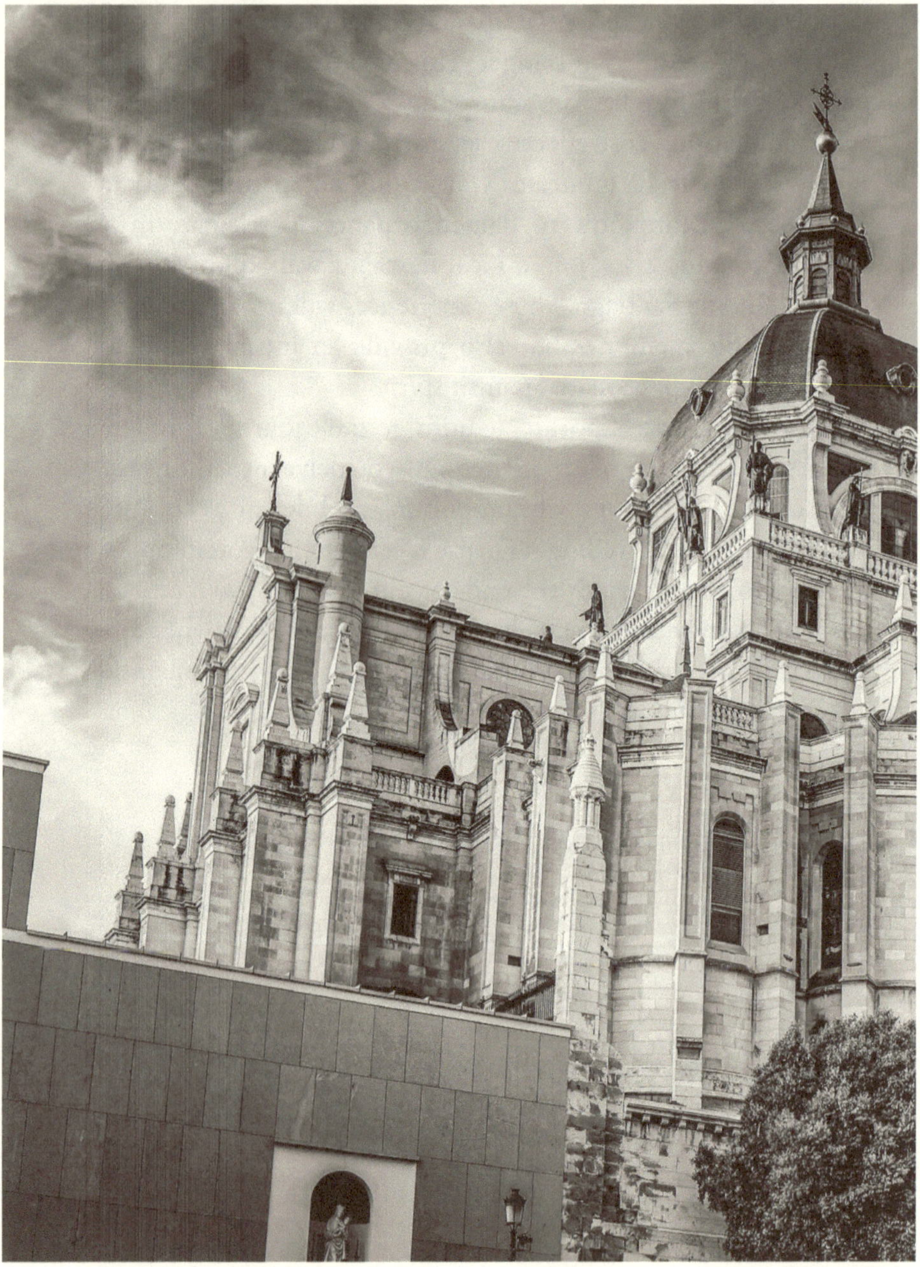

CHAPTER 1: MADRID

CHAPTER 1:
Madrid

Welcome to the magnetic heart of Spain, Madrid! Spain's largest city and capital, Madrid, exudes an irresistible energy that seizes every visitor from the moment they set foot on its streets. A city that never sleeps, Madrid is a vibrant symphony of culture, history, art, gastronomy, and nightlife. A place where every winding alley has a story to tell, and every grand square is a stage set for life's countless dramas to unfold.

As the sun shines brightly on the city, Madrid reveals itself in all its grandeur. Ornate Baroque buildings stand tall alongside sleek modern structures, creating a cityscape that effortlessly blends tradition and modernity. Streets lined with chestnut trees echo with the sound of life, from the clink of coffee cups in sun-drenched terraces to the banter of Madrileños as they go about their day.

The city's cultural richness is unparalleled. Madrid is home to some of the world's greatest museums, such as the Prado, Reina Sofia, and Thyssen-Bornemisza, boasting incredible collections of European art. In the heart of Madrid, art isn't confined to museums; it spills out onto the streets, coloring everything from grand buildings to hidden alleyways with a creative touch. Madrid is also a city of green spaces. The city's parks, like the expansive Retiro Park, are perfect refuges from the urban hustle. These parks are not just places of relaxation, but also bustling hubs of activities, where you can row a boat, see a free concert, or explore a rose garden.

No matter how many times you've been here, Madrid always has something new and unexpected to offer. It might be a hidden tapas bar, a charming boutique, a secret garden, or an impromptu flamenco performance on the streets. That's the beauty of Madrid - it's a city that encourages you to explore and rewards you with delightful surprises at every turn.

And when the sun sets, Madrid truly comes alive. It's a city famous for its late nights, where tapas bars buzz with conversation, theaters hum with anticipation, and nightclubs pulse with the latest beats. From quiet wine bars to lively flamenco shows, Madrid's nightlife is as diverse as it is thrilling.

Whether you're an art enthusiast, a food lover, a history buff, or a partygoer, Madrid offers an experience tailored just for you. As we journey through this captivating city, you'll discover that Madrid is not just Spain's capital; it's a living, breathing entity that celebrates life in all its forms. So, hold on tight as we dive into the energetic heart of Spain, exploring the places, tastes, and experiences that make Madrid an unforgettable destination.

The Prado Museum

Welcome to the crown jewel of Madrid's art scene, the Prado Museum. Stepping into the hallowed halls of the Prado is like embarking on a journey through the annals of European art history. Housed in an imposing Neo-Classical building, the Prado's collection spans over 8,000 paintings, including works from Spanish masters like Velázquez, Goya, and El Greco, along with other renowned artists such as Rubens and Titian.

The Prado isn't just a gallery; it's a timeless testament to human creativity, where every canvas whispers a tale from the past. As you wander through its corridors, you'll come face to face with art pieces that have shaped Western art's narrative. Not to be missed are Velázquez's "Las Meninas", Goya's "The Third of May 1808", and Bosch's "The Garden of Earthly Delights".

Given the museum's vast collection, it's wise to plan your visit ahead of time. Decide which masterpieces you'd like to see, or opt for a guided tour for a more immersive experience. Remember that the museum is free in the evenings from Tuesday to Saturday and all day on Sundays.

Retiro Park

In the heart of Madrid, the Retiro Park serves as the city's green lung, a tranquil oasis amidst the urban hustle. Covering 125 hectares and home to over 15,000 trees, this vast park offers a welcome respite to locals and tourists alike. It's a place where joggers weave their paths through tree-lined trails, families picnic under leafy canopies, and lovers row boats across the tranquil Retiro Pond.

Beyond its natural beauty, the park also boasts architectural gems like the Crystal Palace, a stunning glass and iron structure that hosts contemporary art exhibitions. The Rose Garden, bursting into colors during spring, and the Monument to Alfonso XII, overlooking the grand pond, are other key attractions worth exploring.

Retiro Park is a year-round destination, each season offering a unique charm. However, the park truly comes alive during weekends when locals descend en masse, filling the air with laughter, music, and cheer. Don't forget to check out the book fair held every spring and the free concerts in the summer.

Madrid's Royal Palace

Standing tall on a bluff overlooking the river Manzanares, the Royal Palace of Madrid is an epitome of opulence and a testament to Spain's regal past. It's the largest royal palace in Western Europe by floor area, a stunning representation of Baroque and Classicism architecture.

The palace's sumptuously decorated rooms, with their luxurious furnishings, fine tapestries, and exquisite porcelain, reflect the splendor of the Spanish monarchy. The highlights of the palace include the Throne Room, the Royal Armoury, and the Hall of Mirrors. A visit to the palace isn't complete without stepping into its beautiful gardens, the Campo del Moro and Sabatini Gardens.

Although the palace isn't the official residence of the king, it's used for state ceremonies, so ensure it's open to the public on your visit day. The palace offers free entry during certain hours for EU citizens, and it's advisable to get there early to avoid long queues. Audio guides are available to enrich your exploration of this grand edifice.

Gran Vía

Madrid's Gran Vía is more than a street; it's a bustling microcosm of the city's vibrant spirit. Often referred to as Madrid's Broadway, Gran Vía is the city's entertainment epicenter, its buildings housing theatres, cinemas, and retail stores. Architecturally, Gran Vía is a parade of eclectic styles, with stunning examples of Art Deco, Neo-Mudejar, and Modernist buildings lining its stretch.

Strolling down Gran Vía is like walking through a living tapestry of Madrid's history. Every corner, every building has a story to tell. Highlights include the Telefónica Building, a towering skyscraper from the 1920s, and the Edificio Metrópolis, a stunning French-inspired building crowned with a glistening dome. Whether you're shopping, catching a show, or simply soaking up the atmosphere, Gran Vía pulsates with energy round the clock. Remember that most stores close in the afternoon for siesta and reopen in the evening. And while the street is safe, it's always wise to be mindful of your belongings in crowded areas.

San Miguel Market

In the heart of Madrid's old town, the San Miguel Market stands as a testament to the city's culinary prowess. This early 20th-century iron market is a gastronomic paradise, with over 30 stalls offering a plethora of Spanish delicacies. From fresh produce and seafood to tapas, pastries, and a selection of wines, the market is a feast for the senses.

As you wander through the market, take time to sample some of the best flavors Spain has to offer. Taste the melt-in-your-mouth jamón ibérico, savor the freshness of a seafood paella, or indulge in a glass of chilled cava.

The market is bustling at all hours, but it's particularly vibrant in the evening when locals gather for drinks and tapas. It's advisable to visit with an empty stomach and an open mind, ready to dive into the Spanish culinary scene. Note that the market can get crowded, so patience is key.

Santiago Bernabeu Stadium

No visit to Madrid is complete without a pilgrimage to the Santiago Bernabeu Stadium, the hallowed home ground of Real Madrid. Whether you're a football enthusiast or not, touring this iconic stadium is a mesmerizing experience. With a seating capacity of over 80,000, the stadium is one of the world's most prestigious football grounds.

The Bernabeu tour takes you on a journey through the history of Real Madrid, one of the most successful clubs in football. You'll get to visit the players' tunnel, the bench, the dressing rooms, and even step onto the pitch. The tour also includes a visit to the Trophy Room, a testament to the club's illustrious history.

Tours run daily, and it's advisable to book tickets in advance, especially during the football season. If you're lucky, you might even catch a live game, a spectacle that's sure to give you goosebumps. Remember that the stadium is enormous, so wear comfortable shoes for the tour.

Almudena Cathedral

Facing the Royal Palace, Almudena Cathedral is a symbol of Madrid's spiritual heart and a testament to the city's architectural prowess. Although its construction began in 1879, the cathedral was only completed in 1993, making it one of the newest grand churches in Europe. The fusion of various architectural styles, including Gothic revival on the exterior and Neo-Romanesque in its crypt, reflects the time span across which it was built.

Within the cathedral, your gaze will undoubtedly be drawn upwards, where the vaulted ceilings display a unique blend of traditional and contemporary designs. The stained glass windows and beautifully painted cupola add to the cathedral's serene atmosphere, inviting quiet reflection amidst the city's hustle and bustle.

Don't miss the chance to visit the cathedral's museum where you can delve into Madrid's religious history and ascend to the dome for a panoramic view of Madrid's cityscape. Remember to dress respectfully as this is still an active place of worship.

Madrid Nightlife

When the sun sets, Madrid truly comes to life. Madrid's nightlife, famous throughout Spain, offers a variety of experiences from the pulsating energy of nightclubs to the traditional tapas bars tucked away in the city's narrow streets. Madrid is known for its late-night dining culture, where locals often start their dinner well past 9 PM, followed by a night of revelry.

A trip to Madrid would be incomplete without experiencing a live flamenco show. These passionate performances of dance, music, and song are an integral part of Spanish culture. Venues like Corral de la Morería and Casa Patas offer unforgettable flamenco shows that capture the spirit and fervor of this traditional art form.

Remember that Madrid's nightlife starts late and goes on until the early hours of the morning. Pace yourself, hydrate, and remember that the Madrid metro operates until 1:30 AM, and night buses run all night for your convenience.

Thyssen-Bornemisza Museum

Completing Madrid's Golden Triangle of Art, the Thyssen-Bornemisza Museum is a must-visit for art enthusiasts. The museum's collection is one of the most extensive and diverse in Madrid, comprising more than 1,000 artworks from the 13th to the late 20th century. Here, you can explore everything from medieval art to contemporary pieces, including significant works from the Renaissance, Baroque, and Impressionist periods.

The museum houses works by great masters such as Rubens, Rembrandt, Degas, Renoir, Van Gogh, and Picasso. Notably, it hosts an exceptional collection of American paintings, which is unique in European museums. For modern art lovers, movements such as Pop Art, Expressionism, and European avant-garde are well-represented.

Audioguides are available in various languages and are a great way to deepen your understanding of the artworks. The museum also offers free entry on Monday afternoons, but expect larger crowds during this time. The museum's shop is a great place to pick up art-themed souvenirs.

Day Trip to Toledo

Just a stone's throw away from Madrid, Toledo, the City of Three Cultures, awaits. A UNESCO World Heritage site, Toledo is a splendid blend of Christian, Jewish, and Muslim influences that have left their mark over centuries. Its historic center, perched on a hill above the Tagus River, is a labyrinth of narrow streets, home to an array of monuments spanning various architectural styles.

Take time to visit the imposing Alcázar, a stone fortification at the city's highest point. Walk through the narrow alleys of the Jewish Quarter, with its synagogues and the Sephardic Museum. Visit the cathedral, a masterpiece of Gothic architecture, and take in the serenity of the Mosque of Cristo de la Luz, a symbol of Toledo's multicultural heritage.

Day trips to Toledo can be easily arranged from Madrid, either by bus, train, or organized tours. Make sure to wear comfortable shoes as Toledo's streets can be steep and cobbled. And don't leave without trying the city's famous marzipan!

Madrid Cuisine

Madrid is a gastronomic paradise, where traditional Spanish dishes meld with international influences, resulting in a flavorful fusion that will delight any foodie. Begin your culinary exploration with a visit to one of the city's bustling food markets, such as Mercado de San Miguel or Mercado de San Antón. Here you can sample a smorgasbord of Spanish treats, from tapas and pintxos to fresh seafood and delectable pastries.

Tasting Madrid's signature dishes is a journey in itself. Savor the cocido madrileño, a hearty stew of meats and vegetables that is perfect for Madrid's cooler months. Bite into a bocadillo de calamares, a calamari sandwich that is a staple of Madrid's street food. And, of course, you can't leave without trying the churros con chocolate, a favorite Spanish dessert.

Madrid is also a great place to try Spain's world-famous wines. Whether you prefer the robust reds of Rioja, the crisp whites of Rueda, or the bubbly delights of Cava, Madrid's bars and restaurants offer a wine for every palate.

When dining in Madrid, remember that locals usually have late dinners, often starting around 9 or 10 PM. Tipping is not mandatory in Spain, but leaving a few coins is a good practice in restaurants. Lastly, don't forget to explore Madrid's burgeoning vegan and vegetarian scene, with a growing number of restaurants catering to plant-based diets.

Final Thoughts

Your journey through Madrid only marks the beginning of the richness that Spain has to offer. This metropolis of joy, with its vibrant life, profound history, and diverse culture, is a microcosm of the country. As you wander through its streets, don't forget to stray off the beaten path. Explore neighborhoods like Malasaña, known for its alternative scene, or La Latina, where you can experience Madrid's best Sunday flea market, El Rastro.

While the city's main attractions are a must-visit, Madrid's charm is also found in the everyday life, in the sidewalk cafes, in the warmth of its people, in the rhythm of its nightlife. It's a city that never sleeps yet always dreams, a city that embraces the future without forgetting its past.

Remember to make the most of Madrid's excellent public transportation system. The metro, buses, and suburban trains make it easy to move around the city and its surrounding areas. Also, consider getting the Madrid Tourist Travel Pass for unlimited travel on public transport.

As you leave Madrid, remember that Spain's diversity extends beyond its capital. The fiery passion of Andalusia, the rugged landscapes of Extremadura, the modernist beauty of Catalonia - every region holds its own unique allure. So, as you say adiós to

Madrid, say hola to the rest of Spain. Let your Spanish journey continue to surprise you, to teach you, to inspire you. Madrid is not the end; it's just the beginning. Vamos, let's keep exploring!

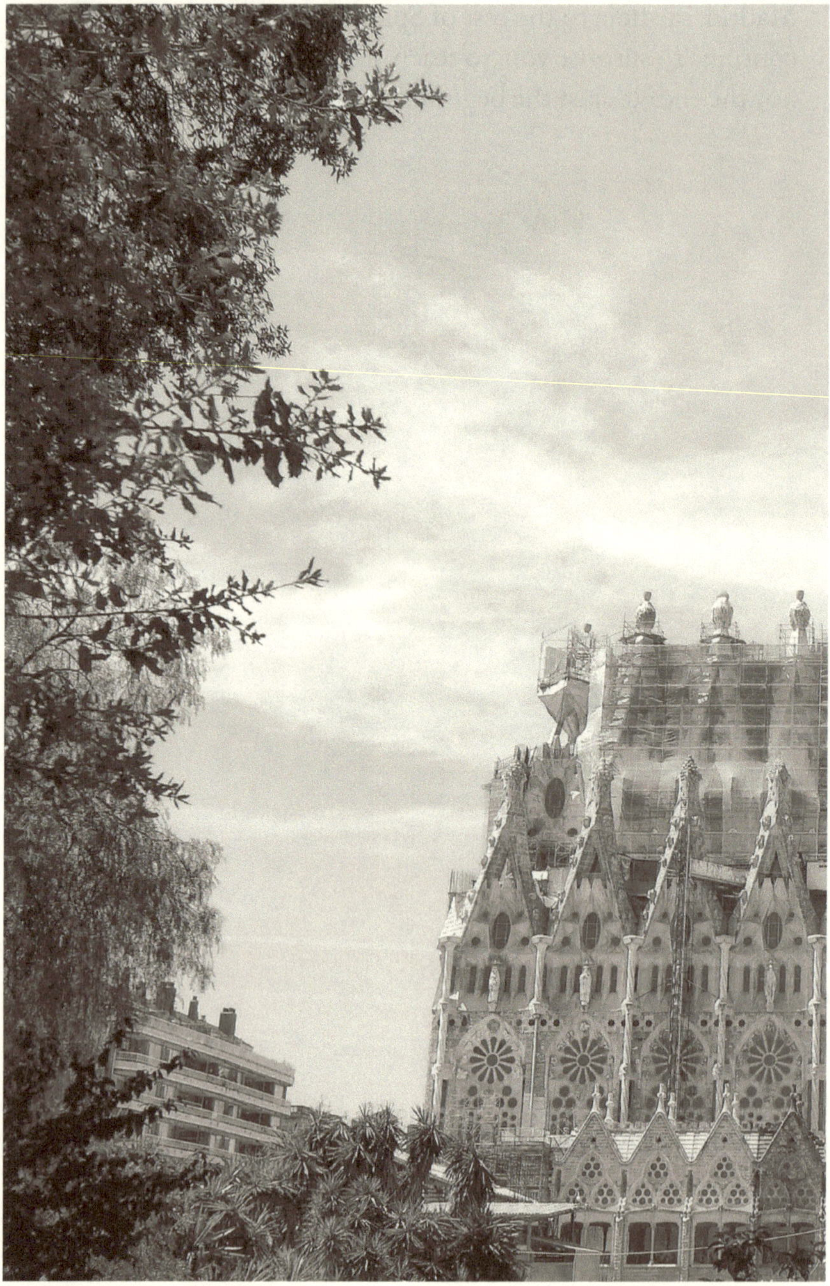

CHAPTER 2: BARCELONA   33

CHAPTER 2:
Barcelona

Nestled between the Mediterranean Sea and the hills of Montjuïc, Barcelona sparkles with a vibrancy and style all its own. Catalonia's proud capital, a city of sun-dappled beaches, awe-inspiring architecture, and vibrant streets, Barcelona beckons with its unique charm and boundless energy. As Spain's second-largest city, it is a metropolis where centuries-old history and innovative design intertwine, creating a tapestry of experiences that captivate every kind of traveler.

Barcelona is perhaps most famous for its association with the celebrated architect Antoni Gaudí, whose masterpieces like the Sagrada Familia and Park Güell, dot the city's landscape. Gaudí's imagination and creativity have left a profound mark on Barcelona, and his distinctive modernist style adds a whimsical touch to the city's skyline. The curved lines, bright colors, and intricate details of his works have become synonymous with Barcelona's identity.

But Gaudí's creations are just the tip of the iceberg. The city's historic Gothic Quarter, or Barri Gòtic, takes you back in time, its labyrinthine alleys telling stories of Roman settlements, medieval splendor, and cultural transformations. Visit the magnificent Barcelona Cathedral, explore the remnants of the ancient Roman city at the History Museum, or simply lose yourself in the quarter's atmospheric cobblestone streets.

Barcelona's past is always within your reach, whispering tales of bygone eras.

Yet, Barcelona is not a city stuck in time. It's a hub of innovation and creativity, reflected in its dynamic food scene, its penchant for avant-garde design, and its thriving arts and music culture. The city's museums pay homage to the likes of Picasso and Miró, while its music festivals attract world-renowned artists. Barcelona's many markets and restaurants offer culinary delights, from traditional Catalan cuisine to global gastronomy, making it a food lover's paradise.

Barcelona is a city of contrasts, where tradition and innovation exist side by side. Its diverse neighborhoods, each with their own personality, offer endless opportunities for exploration. From the trendy beachfront district of Barceloneta to the bohemian Gràcia, the upscale Eixample to the vibrant Raval, Barcelona is a city of a thousand faces.

Above all, Barcelona is a city that knows how to live. Whether it's strolling along the sun-kissed beaches, relaxing in a terrace café on Las Ramblas, tasting tapas in a bustling market, dancing the night away in a club, or simply sitting in a quiet square watching the world go by, there's always a way to enjoy life in Barcelona. So let's start this journey, dive into the soul of Catalonia, and discover what makes Barcelona such an enchanting city.

Sagrada Familia

Imposing, intricate, and incomparable, the Sagrada Familia stands as a testament to Antoni Gaudí's visionary genius. Begun in 1882, this architectural marvel remains unfinished to this day, yet it's one of the most iconic landmarks of Barcelona. This colossal basilica, a fusion of Gothic and curvilinear Art Nouveau forms, presents a breathtaking panorama of towers, facades, and interior spaces richly adorned with religious symbolism.

Inside, the Sagrada Familia is a symphony of light and color. The forest-like columns reach up to the star-studded ceiling, while the spectacular stained-glass windows imbue the basilica with a magical glow. The Nativity Facade tells the story of Jesus' birth, life, and teachings, the Passion Facade portrays his suffering and death, and the Glory Facade, still under construction, will represent the path to God.

Buying tickets online in advance is highly recommended to avoid long queues. An audioguide is available, which gives insightful details into Gaudí's vision and the basilica's complex symbolism. Remember to dress respectfully, as the Sagrada Familia is a consecrated place of worship. Climbing one of the towers offers panoramic views of Barcelona, but requires a separate ticket.

Park Güell

Another of Gaudí's masterpieces, Park Güell, is a public park system composed of gardens and architectonic elements perched on Carmel Hill. Originally intended as an exclusive housing estate, the project was unsuccessful, but the resulting park is a UNESCO World Heritage Site that draws millions of visitors each year. This enchanting park is a fusion of natural landscapes and architectural innovations, all infused with Gaudí's unique style.

As you wander through the park, you'll encounter whimsical structures like the dragon-styled mosaic salamander "El Drac", the undulating ceramic tile bench, and the gingerbread-like gatehouses. The elevated square offers panoramic views over Barcelona, and the columned hall beneath, designed to be a market, is an architectural marvel.

The Monumental Zone, which houses most of Gaudí's creations, requires a ticket. However, the surrounding gardens and areas are freely accessible. Tickets for the Monumental Zone often sell out during peak tourist season, so it's advisable to book online in advance. The park is quite hilly, so wear comfortable shoes and bring water, especially in summer.

Gothic Quarter

Stepping into Barcelona's Gothic Quarter is like stepping into a time machine, where narrow, winding streets lead you through centuries of history. This is the oldest part of the city, where remnants of Roman walls stand beside medieval monuments. It's a place where every corner, square, and alleyway has a story to tell, making it a must-visit for history enthusiasts.

The heart of the Gothic Quarter is the magnificent Barcelona Cathedral, a stunning example of Gothic architecture. Nearby, the remnants of the Roman Temple of Augustus and the ancient Jewish Quarter, or "El Call", speak of Barcelona's diverse historical layers. Plaça del Rei, a medieval public square, is said to be where Columbus was received after his voyage to America.

Walking tours are an excellent way to explore the Gothic Quarter, as local guides can provide insight into the area's rich history. It's worth noting that while the area is generally safe, it's known for pickpockets, so keep an eye on your belongings. Numerous small shops, cafes, and restaurants line the streets, offering ample opportunities for rest and refreshment.

Barcelona's Beaches

Barcelona's location on Spain's northeastern coast ensures a vibrant beach scene, a delightful balance between urban life and seaside relaxation. The city's coastline stretches over 4.5 kilometers and is divided into several distinct beaches, each offering its unique atmosphere and attractions. Whether you're a sun worshiper, an avid swimmer, or simply enjoy beachside cafes, Barcelona's beaches are a paradise.

The most popular is Barceloneta Beach, known for its golden sand, lively atmosphere, and excellent seafood restaurants. Further north, Nova Icaria Beach is more peaceful and family-friendly, while Mar Bella Beach is known for its water sports facilities and a separate nudist area. Bogatell Beach, popular among locals, offers a quiet respite from the crowded city.

Visiting early in the morning or late afternoon can help avoid the peak crowds, especially during summer. Beach facilities are well-maintained, including showers, restrooms, and beach bars, or 'chiringuitos.' Be aware of your belongings, as beaches can attract opportunistic thieves. Also, remember that while Barcelona's beaches are beautiful, they are also urban beaches – for pristine, natural beaches, consider a day trip along the Costa Brava.

La Rambla

La Rambla, a bustling tree-lined boulevard stretching from Plaça de Catalunya to the waterfront, is the pulsating heart of Barcelona. This vibrant pedestrian street, divided into several sections, is a hive of activity day and night, brimming with shops, cafes, flower stalls, street artists, and performers. It's a place where locals and tourists converge, making it an essential part of the Barcelona experience.

Key attractions along La Rambla include the grand Liceu Theatre, one of Europe's leading opera houses, and the colorful Mercat de la Boqueria, a food market where you can sample a wide range of Spanish delicacies. Towards the southern end, the Maritime Museum and the Columbus Monument mark the historic gateway to the Mediterranean.

While La Rambla is a must-visit, it can be crowded and is known for overpriced restaurants and tourist traps. Keep an eye on your belongings, as pickpockets may operate in the area. Consider exploring the side streets and alleys branching off La Rambla, which lead into the Gothic Quarter and the trendy Raval neighborhood.

Picasso Museum

Dedicated to the life and works of Pablo Picasso, the Picasso Museum in Barcelona is an essential destination for art enthusiasts. Located in the hip El Born district, the museum is housed in five adjoining medieval palaces, an aesthetic match to the artistic treasures within. With over 4,000 works, it boasts one of the most extensive collections of Picasso's artworks, tracing his artistic journey from the early years to his final works.

Highlights include the Blue Period paintings, the iconic Las Meninas series, and numerous sketches and ceramics that reveal Picasso's creative process. While Picasso's later, more famous works are not well represented, the museum offers a deep understanding of his formative years and his strong connection with Barcelona.

It's recommended to book tickets online in advance to avoid queues. The museum offers free entry on Thursday afternoons and the first Sunday of every month, but these times can be busy. An audio guide is available, offering in-depth commentary on Picasso's artworks and life. Also, don't miss the temporary exhibitions, which often feature works by Picasso's contemporaries.

Casa Batlló

In Barcelona's elegant Eixample district, Casa Batlló is a shining example of Antoni Gaudí's distinctive architectural style. This UNESCO World Heritage site, often dubbed the 'House of Bones' for its skeletal facade, is an explosion of colors, shapes, and imagination. Its design, filled with symbolism and inspired by nature, is a testament to Gaudí's genius.

The building's interior is as impressive as its facade. From the whimsical staircases to the aquatic-themed rooms, each detail is meticulously crafted. The roof terrace, shaped like the back of a dragon, offers panoramic views of the city. The building's transformation from a conventional house into an artistic masterpiece speaks volumes about Gaudí's vision.

When planning a visit, consider buying tickets online in advance to avoid queues. The 'Gold Priority' ticket offers a more exclusive experience, including a vintage photo souvenir. The guided tour, available with an audioguide, is highly recommended to fully appreciate Gaudí's creative process and the symbolism within Casa Batlló.

Barcelona Nightlife

Barcelona, often called 'the city that never sleeps,' offers a nightlife as diverse and vibrant as the city itself. Whether you're seeking trendy bars, live music venues, flamenco shows, or world-class nightclubs, Barcelona caters to every taste. The city's nightlife is not just about partying; it's a way of life, reflected in the locals' penchant for late-night dinners and gatherings.

Areas like the Gothic Quarter and El Born are packed with intimate tapas bars and traditional bodegas. Gracia, a bohemian neighborhood, is known for its live music venues and artisanal breweries. For a glamorous night out, head to the waterfront clubs in Port Olimpic. Flamenco lovers should not miss Tablao Cordobes in La Rambla, renowned for its authentic performances.

Remember, nightlife in Barcelona starts late and goes on until the early morning hours. Be prepared for late dinners (often after 9 PM) and even later clubbing. Dress code varies depending on the venue, but generally, Barcelonians dress stylishly for a night out. Always keep an eye on your belongings, especially in crowded places.

Day Trip to Montserrat

Just an hour's train ride from Barcelona, Montserrat is a serene mountain retreat, home to a Benedictine monastery and a revered statue of the Black Madonna, Catalonia's patron saint. This spiritual and cultural hub, nestled amidst rugged mountain peaks, offers a refreshing escape from the city bustle. Montserrat's unique setting and religious significance attract pilgrims and tourists alike.

Take a funicular or hike up the mountain to reach the monastery. Here, you can visit the basilica, see the Black Madonna, and enjoy the soul-stirring performance of the famed Montserrat Boys' Choir. The mountain's peak, accessible via a funicular, provides breathtaking views of the surrounding landscape.

Getting to Montserrat is straightforward, with regular trains from Barcelona's Plaça d'Espanya station. Once there, the rack railway or cable car can transport you to the monastery. To avoid crowds, aim to visit on weekdays and arrive early in the morning. Besides the monastery, Montserrat Natural Park offers excellent hiking trails, ranging from easy to challenging, rewarding you with stunning panoramic vistas.

Camp Nou

As the home of FC Barcelona, one of the world's most successful football clubs, Camp Nou is more than just a stadium. It's a pilgrimage site for football fans, boasting a rich history and an electrifying atmosphere. With a seating capacity of nearly 100,000, it's the largest stadium in Europe, echoing with chants, cheers, and the spirit of competition during match days.

The Camp Nou Experience, a tour of the stadium and its museum, is a must for football enthusiasts. The tour includes access to the players' tunnel, the pitch, the press room, and the commentary boxes. The museum showcases a fascinating collection of trophies, memorabilia, and interactive exhibits about the club's history.

Whether you're an FC Barcelona fan or not, experiencing a live match at Camp Nou can be thrilling. If this isn't possible, the stadium tour and museum visit are available all year round. Book your tickets online in advance to secure your spot. Don't forget to visit the FC Barcelona store for souvenirs and football merchandise.

Barcelona Cuisine

A gastronomic hub, Barcelona presents a culinary mosaic where traditional Catalan cooking meets innovative gourmet trends. The city's food scene is as diverse and colorful as its culture, featuring an array of seafood, locally grown produce, and regional wines. Barcelona's culinary landscape ranges from quaint tapas bars and market stalls to Michelin-starred establishments.

Seafood is an integral part of Barcelona's cuisine. Feast on dishes like paella, a flavorful rice dish with seafood, and fideuà, a similar dish made with noodles. Tapas, small plates meant for sharing, can be found all over the city. Popular tapas include patatas bravas (spicy potatoes), gambas al ajillo (garlic shrimp), and pimientos de padrón (fried green peppers).

For dessert, don't miss out on trying crema catalana, Catalonia's version of crème brûlée. Wine enthusiasts will appreciate Barcelona's proximity to several prominent wine regions, including Penedès and Priorat. For a local drink, try vermut, a fortified wine often served as an aperitif.

Culinary experiences in Barcelona extend beyond dining. Visit La Boqueria Market on La Rambla to experience the city's vibrant food culture. Join a cooking class or a food tour to learn more about Barcelona's gastronomy. Remember, dining in Barcelona is a leisurely experience, so take your time to savor the food and enjoy the convivial atmosphere.

Final Thoughts

Barcelona, an enchanting city where creativity blossoms, is full of surprises at every corner. With its stunning architecture, vibrant arts scene, and mouth-watering cuisine, the city promises an unforgettable experience for all who visit. As we conclude this chapter, let's touch upon some final tips and hidden gems to ensure your Barcelona trip is truly remarkable.

The city's excellent public transport makes getting around easy and convenient. The T10 ticket offers ten rides on buses, trams, and metro and is a cost-effective option for travelers. Barcelona is also a bike-friendly city, with numerous bike rental services and designated cycle paths.

Venture beyond the touristy areas and explore the lesser-known neighborhoods like Poblenou, known for its industrial heritage, arts scene, and the Rambla de Poblenou, a quieter alternative to La Rambla. For a unique shopping experience, visit the Encants Flea Market, one of the oldest markets in Europe, where you can find everything from antiques to second-hand goods.

While Barcelona's major sights are truly worth visiting, don't forget to take the time to simply wander around, soak up the atmosphere, and enjoy the city's rhythm. From the lively festivals and cultural events to tranquil parks and beautiful sunsets at the beach, there's much to love about Barcelona.

As we say goodbye to Barcelona and look forward to the next chapters of our Spanish journey, remember that travel is more than just visiting places. It's about immersing ourselves in the local culture, connecting with people, and creating memories that last a lifetime. So, here's to Barcelona, and here's to the adventures that await in Spain!

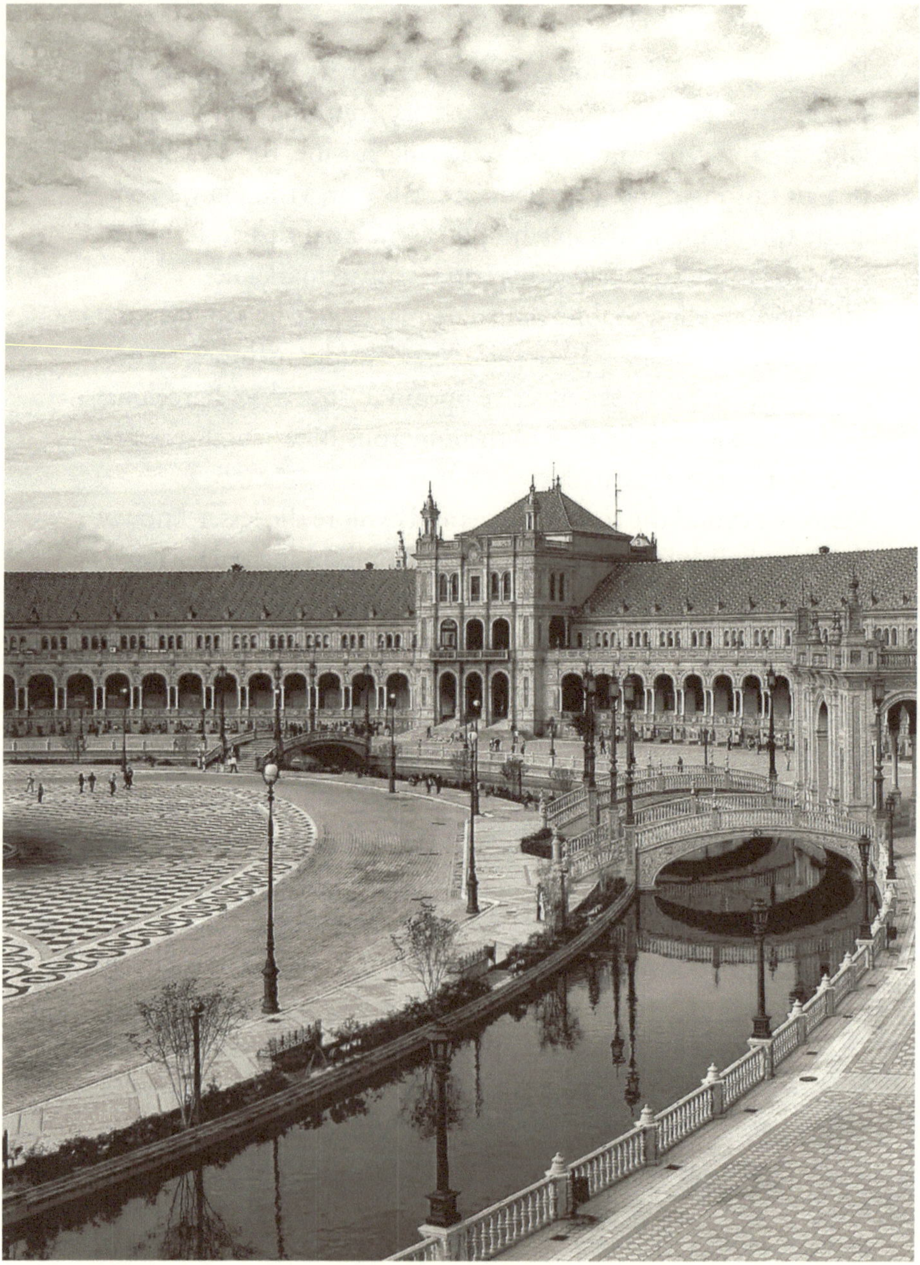

CHAPTER 3: SEVILLE

CHAPTER 3:
Seville

The charm of Spain's Andalusian region is encapsulated by its vibrant capital, Seville, a city that marries the grandeur of a rich historical past with the irresistible allure of flamenco, fiestas, and a zestful food culture. Unfolding at the banks of the Guadalquivir River, Seville is a testament to Spain's complex history, adorned by architectural gems from the Moorish, Gothic, and Renaissance eras. Wrapped in the radiance of the sun and veiled in the aroma of blooming orange trees, Seville is a sensory delight.

Seville's storied past is a tale of civilizations, each of which left indelible imprints on its landscape and character. The Moors, who ruled here for over 500 years, constructed magnificent palaces and fortresses that today serve as picturesque reminders of a bygone era. The Christians, too, contributed immensely, creating awe-inspiring cathedrals and plazas. This intricate dance between Moorish and Christian cultures has created a city that feels like an open-air museum, full of tales waiting to be discovered.

Seville's soulful energy is magnified by the captivating rhythm of flamenco, a musical tradition originating from the Andalusian region. This deeply emotional dance form echoes in the city's ancient walls, infusing life into its cobblestone streets. From flamenco tablaos (venues) in the traditional Triana district to impromptu street performances, the passion of flamenco permeates Seville's atmosphere, creating a bond that connects locals and visitors alike.

Beyond its historical treasures and cultural richness, Seville also surprises with its flair for the avant-garde. It's a city where the cutting-edge architecture of structures like Metropol Parasol seamlessly merges with the ancient landmarks, projecting a cityscape that's as varied as it's intriguing. Seville isn't trapped in its past; it uses its history as a stepping stone towards a progressive future.

Of course, a journey through Seville isn't complete without indulging in its delectable cuisine. The city is a gastronomic paradise, where traditional Andalusian flavors meld with innovative culinary techniques. Whether it's savoring tapas at a bustling local market or dining at a chic rooftop restaurant overlooking the city, every meal in Seville is an event to be celebrated. Unraveling the charm of Seville means surrendering to its rhythm — basking in its sunshine, strolling through its historic quarters, swaying to the rhythm of flamenco, and savoring its culinary delights. As we delve into the marvels of Seville in this chapter, prepare to be enchanted by the splendors that this Andalusian gem has to offer. So, let's embark on this journey, for Seville awaits!

The Alcázar

Standing regally in the heart of Seville, the Alcázar is a palatial fortress and a shining example of Mudejar architecture, a unique style that blends Moorish and Christian design principles. The UNESCO World Heritage Site, whose foundations date back to the 10th century, is an intriguing labyrinth of ornate rooms, tranquil courtyards, and verdant gardens. As you navigate through the complex, the intricate tilework, arched doorways, and elegant stucco work reveal a fascinating blend of cultures.

In the Alcázar, every corner tells a story of Seville's multi-layered past. The Patio de las Doncellas, with its reflective water features, and the Salón de Embajadores, or Hall of Ambassadors, with its spectacular domed ceiling, are especially memorable. Outside, the lush gardens, dotted with fountains, pools, and pavilions, offer a serene retreat from the city's bustle.

When visiting, it's worth taking an audio guide or a guided tour to fully understand the history and significance of this incredible complex. Be sure to book your tickets online in advance, as the Alcázar is a popular attraction, and lines can be long. Also, remember to take time to soak in the peaceful atmosphere of the gardens.

Seville Cathedral and Giralda

The Seville Cathedral, or Cathedral of Saint Mary of the See, is not only the largest Gothic cathedral in the world but also an architectural marvel steeped in history. This colossal structure impresses with its soaring ceilings, intricate stone carvings, and priceless artworks. Perhaps the most iconic feature of the cathedral is La Giralda, a former minaret turned bell tower, which provides stunning panoramic views of the city.

Inside the cathedral, the vast nave, the ornate altarpiece, and the tomb of Christopher Columbus are not to be missed. Climbing La Giralda, an experience made easier by the absence of stairs in favor of a ramp, rewards you with breathtaking views of Seville's rooftops and beyond.

Remember to dress modestly when visiting the Seville Cathedral, as it is an active place of worship. An audio guide is available and recommended to appreciate the historical and artistic details of the cathedral fully. Plan your visit early in the day or late in the afternoon to avoid crowds, and don't forget your camera to capture the remarkable architectural features.

Plaza de España

Designed for the Ibero-American Exposition of 1929, Plaza de España is a striking semi-circular complex combining Renaissance and Moorish styles. The plaza, with its ornate bridges over a canal, beautifully tiled alcoves, and a towering central fountain, is a feast for the eyes. It's surrounded by Maria Luisa Park, providing a lush backdrop to this architectural spectacle. Each alcove at the plaza represents a different province of Spain, adorned with colorful tilework depicting historical scenes. These alcoves make for great photo opportunities. The canal offers boat rentals, and the building houses some government offices and a museum.

Visiting the Plaza de España is free, and it's a great place to relax, enjoy a picnic, or take a leisurely boat ride on the canal. It can be particularly enchanting in the evening when the buildings are illuminated. Don't miss the opportunity to wander around Maria Luisa Park while you're in the area.

Triana District

Triana, located on the west bank of the Guadalquivir River, is a vibrant neighborhood with a unique identity. Known as the cradle of flamenco, it's a place where music, dance, and tradition thrive in every corner. Triana's past as a potter's quarter is still visible in the colorful ceramic tiles adorning its streets and buildings, adding a distinctive touch to the district.

A stroll through Triana's atmospheric streets reveals charming squares, lively markets, and historic churches. A visit to the Casa de la Memoria or the Flamenco Dance Museum offers a deep insight into the passionate world of flamenco, with exhibits and live performances. Don't miss the Mercado de Triana, a bustling food market, where you can sample local delicacies.

When in Triana, make sure to catch a live flamenco show for an authentic Andalusian experience. Enjoy a meal at one of the traditional tapas bars, and take a walk along Calle Betis for a picturesque view of the Seville skyline. Remember, Triana is best explored on foot, so wear comfortable shoes.

Metropol Parasol

In stark contrast to Seville's historic landmarks stands Metropol Parasol, a contemporary structure that has become a symbol of the city's modern face. Known locally as "Las Setas" (The Mushrooms) due to its distinctive shape, this wooden structure is one of the world's largest and offers panoramic views of the city from its walkways.

Beneath the parasol, you'll find the Antiquarium, a museum displaying Roman and Moorish artifacts discovered during the construction of the site. The structure itself houses a market, several bars and restaurants, and an elevated plaza for events.

Visit Metropol Parasol during the day to explore the Antiquarium and enjoy a meal in the market. However, don't miss the opportunity to ascend to the walkway at sunset. The golden light falling on the city offers an unforgettable view. There is a small fee to access the walkway, but it includes a drink at the rooftop bar.

María Luisa Park

María Luisa Park is Seville's principal green space, offering a tranquil escape from the urban hustle. This expansive park, designed in a mix of Moorish and English garden styles, is a haven of shady avenues, picturesque plazas, and vibrant flower beds. From playful fountains to exotic birds, it's a place full of delightful surprises.

The park houses several landmarks, including the grand Plaza de España, the charming Plaza de América, and the Museum of Popular Arts and Traditions. Whether you're enjoying a leisurely stroll, a romantic boat ride on the park's small canal, or a picnic under the trees, María Luisa Park is a refreshing retreat.

María Luisa Park is always open and free to enter, making it a great place for an early morning jog or a late-night walk. Renting a rowboat in the Plaza de España's canal can be a fun activity, and don't miss the opportunity to admire the beautiful tile work in the plazas. The park is also a perfect place for bird-watching, with many peacocks and ducks calling it home.

Seville Bullring

The Real Maestranza de Caballería de Sevilla, known simply as the Seville Bullring, is one of the most important and historic bullrings in Spain. This colossal circular structure, with its Baroque façade and impressive arena, is more than just a venue for bullfighting; it's a testament to a deeply-rooted tradition that remains a part of Spanish culture.

Inside, the Bullfighting Museum offers a compelling exploration of the history and evolution of bullfighting, showcasing a collection of costumes, photographs, and paintings. A guided tour of the arena and the stables provides an insightful look at the complexities of this controversial sport.

When planning a visit to the Seville Bullring, consider the cultural significance of bullfighting in Spain. While it may not appeal to everyone, the architectural grandeur and historical importance of the venue are undeniable. Guided tours are offered daily and provide a comprehensive overview of the site. If you choose to attend a bullfight, ensure you understand the nature of the event and its associated traditions.

Day Trip to Jerez

Less than an hour's drive from Seville, Jerez de la Frontera offers a delightful excursion. This charming city is renowned for its horse culture, flamenco music, and sherry wine production, representing the quintessence of Andalusian tradition.

Jerez is home to the Royal Andalusian School of Equestrian Art, a prestigious institution where you can watch spectacular horse shows. Also worth visiting is the Alcazar of Jerez, a Moorish fortress with beautiful gardens and a camera obscura. As for flamenco, several peñas (clubs) offer intimate performances, offering an authentic local experience.

When visiting Jerez, a tasting tour of a sherry bodega is a must, as this city is the birthplace of this famous fortified wine. Try to time your visit with a horse show at the Equestrian School, and enjoy an evening of flamenco for a truly Andalusian day out. Public transport between Seville and Jerez is frequent and convenient, but consider renting a car if you wish to explore the surrounding wine country.

Flamenco Show

Flamenco, a vibrant blend of song, dance, and guitar, is the heartbeat of Andalusian culture. This passionate and powerful art form, recognized as an Intangible Cultural Heritage by UNESCO, can be experienced in Seville's numerous tablaos (flamenco venues). A flamenco show, with its raw emotion and rhythmic intensity, is an experience that touches the soul.

Seville's flamenco scene is diverse, with performances ranging from intimate shows in small bars to larger productions in dedicated tablaos. Some venues also offer a dinner option, allowing you to savor local cuisine as you enjoy the performance. Among the popular spots are Casa de la Guitarra, Los Gallos, and El Palacio Andaluz.

When choosing a flamenco show, look for one that emphasizes authenticity over spectacle. Smaller venues often provide a more intimate and genuine experience. Although there are shows available throughout the day, a late-night performance is usually more atmospheric. Remember, flamenco is not just a show, but a profound expression of Andalusian identity – a window into the soul of Spain's southern region.

Torre del Oro

The Torre del Oro (Golden Tower), a dodecagonal military watchtower, stands majestically on the bank of the Guadalquivir River, its golden reflection shimmering in the water. Built in the early 13th century during the Almohad dynasty, the tower has served various functions over the centuries, from a defensive structure to a prison and even a safe for precious metals, hence its name.

Today, the Torre del Oro houses a small maritime museum that showcases Seville's rich naval history, featuring maps, compasses, models of old ships, and historical documents. The rooftop of the tower offers panoramic views over the Guadalquivir River and the cityscape, a sight particularly enchanting at sunset.

Visiting the Torre del Oro is a great way to delve into the maritime history of Seville. The views from the top are well worth the climb, especially on clear days. Try to plan your visit for late afternoon to enjoy a beautiful sunset from the rooftop. The entrance to the tower is free on Mondays, but it can get quite crowded.

Seville Cuisine

Seville's culinary scene is a glorious fusion of traditional Andalusian flavors and innovative gastronomic techniques. From the bustling food markets to the rustic tapas bars and gourmet restaurants, every corner of the city promises a culinary delight that is as colorful and vibrant as Seville itself.

Tapas, small savory dishes often enjoyed with a glass of local wine, are at the heart of Sevillian cuisine. Favorites include patatas bravas (spicy potatoes), espinacas con garbanzos (spinach with chickpeas), salmorejo (a cold tomato and bread soup), and montadito de pringá (a small sandwich filled with slow-cooked meat).

For a truly local experience, visit a neighborhood food market such as the Mercado de Triana or Mercado de Feria. Here, you can explore a variety of fresh produce, seafood, and local specialties. Don't miss out on tasting a glass of sherry or manzanilla, fortified wines native to the Andalusian region.

While in Seville, venture into a traditional tapas bar, where you can immerse yourself in the local dining culture. Be adventurous and try a variety of dishes. For seafood lovers, fried calamari, gambas al ajillo (garlic shrimp), and boquerones en vinagre (anchovies in vinegar) are must-try tapas. Pair your meal with a glass of local wine or a refreshing tinto de verano, a popular summer drink made with red wine and soda.

Final Thoughts

Seville, with its vibrant culture, magnificent architecture, and warm, inviting people, is a city that enchants and inspires. Each corner of this Andalusian gem reveals a new surprise, a new story, a new melody that lingers in the heart long after the journey ends.

When planning your visit, remember to take time to wander through the narrow, winding streets of the city's old quarters, such as the Santa Cruz or Arenal district, where the authentic charm of Seville truly shines. The city's numerous churches, like the Church of El Salvador or the Basilica of La Macarena, are also worth visiting for their artistic and historical significance.

Keep in mind that Seville, like much of Spain, operates on a different schedule than most European cities. Many shops close in the afternoon for siesta, and dinner often doesn't start until 9 p.m. or later. Embrace this relaxed pace and take the opportunity to enjoy a leisurely afternoon stroll or a relaxing break at a café.

Don't forget to venture outside the city center. The nearby town of Carmona offers a glimpse into a more rural Andalusian life, and the ancient city of Itálica, with its well-preserved Roman ruins, is just a short trip away.

As you prepare to say adiós to Seville, the memories of vibrant flamenco performances, sun-drenched plazas, fragrant orange trees, and mouth-watering tapas will no doubt fill your heart with longing for your next visit. Seville is not just a destination; it is a feeling, a celebration of life's simple pleasures, a melody that calls you back time and again.

So, hasta luego, Seville. We will dance again soon in the shadow of the Giralda, under the Andalusian sun.

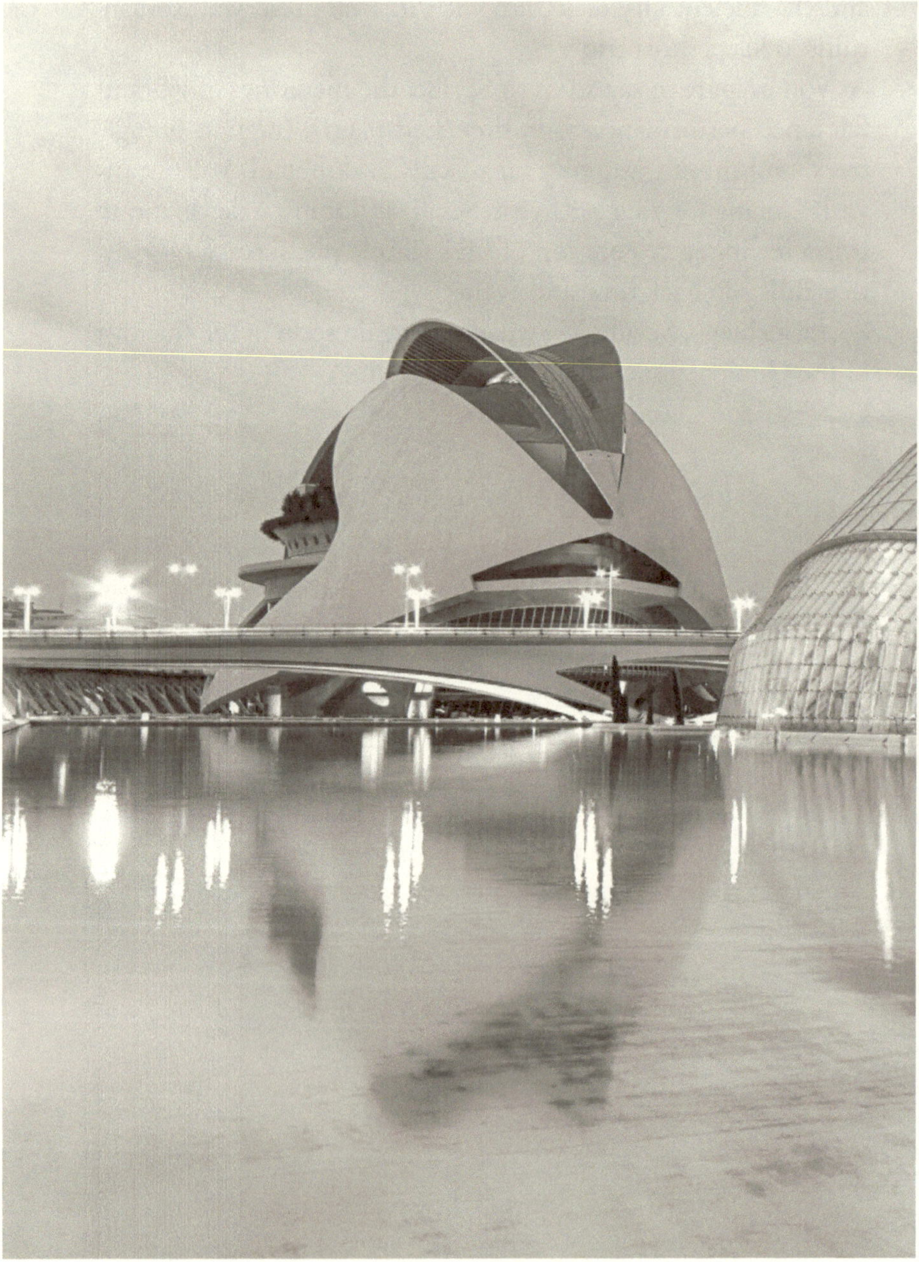

CHAPTER 4: VALENCIA

CHAPTER 4:
Valencia

Valencia, Spain's third-largest city, nestled on the country's eastern coastline, is a captivating fusion of ancient traditions and contemporary creativity. The birthplace of the famous paella, Valencia, seamlessly blends a rich cultural heritage with ground-breaking architecture and a vibrant gastronomic scene. It's a city where you can walk through the narrow, medieval streets of the Barrio del Carmen one moment and marvel at futuristic buildings in the City of Arts and Sciences the next. This dynamic juxtaposition is what makes Valencia a truly unique destination, offering diverse experiences to its visitors.

Valencia's rich history is palpable throughout the city. Its origins date back to 138 BC, when it was founded as a Roman colony. The legacy of the various civilizations that have called Valencia home – Romans, Visigoths, Moors, and Christians – is reflected in its rich architectural tapestry. From the impressive Valencia Cathedral, which houses the Holy Grail, to the Silk Exchange, a masterpiece of Gothic civil architecture, the city's monuments and buildings tell fascinating tales of a storied past.

But Valencia is not just about its historical legacy. It is a city that has embraced innovation and modernity with open arms. The City of Arts and Sciences, a futuristic complex of museums, theaters, and other cultural venues, is a testament to Valencia's commitment to cutting-edge architecture and design. The city's transformed riverbed, now a magnificent park that snakes through the urban landscape, reflects its innovative approach to urban planning.

The soul of Valencia, however, lies in its vibrant traditions and festivals. The Fallas Festival, a unique celebration filled with monumental sculptures, fireworks, and parades, is a spectacle that fills the city with energy and color each March. Equally captivating is the city's culinary culture. Valencia is the birthplace of paella, Spain's most famous dish, and exploring its food markets and tapas bars is a gastronomic adventure.

Beyond the city limits, the natural beauty of the Valencian community beckons. The Albufera Natural Park, home to the largest lake in Spain and a haven for diverse bird species, is a must-visit for nature lovers. Likewise, the beautiful beaches of the Costa Blanca and charming towns like Altea are just a short trip away.

Whether it's the allure of historical treasures, the excitement of contemporary architecture, the joy of lively festivals, the temptation of gastronomic delights, or the call of nature, Valencia has something to enchant everyone. So, let's embark on this journey to discover Valencia, where the old coexists with the new in a beautiful symphony.

City of Arts and Sciences

The City of Arts and Sciences, or Ciutat de les Arts i les Ciències, is a dazzling cultural complex that embodies Valencia's innovative spirit. The brainchild of renowned architect Santiago Calatrava, it's a collection of futuristic buildings that seem more like sculptures than edifices, spread over an area equivalent to 40 football fields. The complex includes the Hemisfèric (an IMAX cinema and digital planetarium), the Príncipe Felipe Science Museum, and the Palau de les Arts Reina Sofia (an opera house and performing arts center), among other attractions.

As you explore the site, you'll be fascinated by the fluidity of Calatrava's designs, which draw inspiration from natural forms such as the human eye and the skeleton of a whale. The structures, surrounded by turquoise pools of water, offer an arresting spectacle, especially when illuminated at night. Whether you're keen on opera, interested in science, or simply a fan of extraordinary architecture, the City of Arts and Sciences offers a unique cultural experience.

Consider purchasing a combined ticket if you plan to visit more than one venue. Evenings offer an enchanting atmosphere, with the buildings lit up against the night sky. And don't forget to capture some photographs; the complex is one of the most photographed sites in Valencia.

Valencia Cathedral

Standing proudly in the heart of Valencia, the Valencia Cathedral is a testament to the city's rich architectural heritage. Built between the 13th and 15th centuries, the cathedral showcases a harmonious blend of styles, from Romanesque and Gothic to Baroque. The cathedral's most remarkable treasure is the Santo Cáliz, believed by many to be the Holy Grail.

The Cathedral's interior is equally captivating, with its beautiful frescoes, stained glass windows, and intricate carvings. The octagonal bell tower, El Miguelete, offers panoramic views over the city for those willing to climb its 207 steps. Don't miss the stunning golden Basilica of the Virgin located next to the cathedral, home to the revered image of the Virgin Mary.

To fully appreciate the Cathedral's historical and religious significance, consider hiring an audio guide or joining a guided tour. Remember to dress respectfully when visiting. Climbing the Miguelete Tower is a must for the stunning views it offers, but be prepared for a steep ascent.

Central Market

Valencia's Central Market, or Mercado Central, is a food lover's paradise. Housed in a stunning Modernist building adorned with ceramic tiles, glass, and iron, the market is one of the largest in Europe. Here, over 900 stalls display an array of fresh produce, from fruits, vegetables, and meats to cheeses, spices, and an impressive array of seafood.

As you wander through the bustling aisles, you'll be drawn in by the vibrant colors and enticing aromas. It's the perfect place to sample local products like jamón ibérico, Valencian oranges, or horchata, a traditional drink made from tigernuts. For a more in-depth experience, look for a cooking class that includes a tour of the market.

The market is open from Monday to Saturday, and it's best to arrive early to avoid crowds and to find the freshest produce. Don't forget to check out the market's Art Nouveau architecture, especially the beautiful stained glass and mosaics. And remember, it's not just about buying; engaging with the friendly vendors is part of the experience.

Turia Gardens

Turia Gardens is an urban oasis that stretches for about nine kilometers across Valencia. The park, set in the former riverbed of the Turia River, is the perfect place to escape the city's hustle and bustle. Here, locals and tourists alike enjoy cycling, running, or simply relaxing under the shade of lush trees. The park also houses several cultural and recreational attractions, including the City of Arts and Sciences and the Gulliver Park, a playground based on the tale of Gulliver's Travels.

The gardens are a testament to creative urban planning. They feature beautifully landscaped sections with palm trees, fragrant orange groves, and rose gardens. Sculptures, fountains, and bridges add to the park's charm. The park is also home to a multitude of bird species, making it a haven for birdwatchers.

Turia Gardens are open all day and night, providing a safe and enjoyable place for a leisurely walk or bike ride at any time. Bike rentals are available at various points along the park. Don't forget to visit the Palau de la Música, a concert hall located in the gardens with a beautiful glass dome.

La Lonja de la Seda

The Lonja de la Seda, or Silk Exchange, is one of the most iconic monuments in Valencia and a UNESCO World Heritage site. Built in the late 15th century, the Lonja is a symbol of Valencia's golden age when it was a major center for silk trade. With its soaring Gothic arches and intricate stone carvings, the building is an outstanding example of secular Gothic architecture.

Inside, the main attraction is the Sala de Contratación, or Contract Hall, with its forest of twisted columns stretching towards the ribbed vaulted ceiling. Upstairs, you can visit the Consulado del Mar, where a stunning wooden ceiling showcases Renaissance art. The Lonja's Patio de los Naranjos, a courtyard filled with orange trees, offers a serene spot to soak up the atmosphere. The Lonja de la Seda is open daily, and entrance is free on Sundays. An audio guide is available for those wishing to delve into the history of the Silk Exchange. Don't forget to admire the facade's carvings, which include a variety of curious and grotesque figures.

Bioparc Valencia

Bioparc Valencia represents a new concept in zoo design, where visitors can observe animals in as close to their natural habitats as possible, without visible barriers. Located at the western end of Turia Gardens, the park spreads over 10 hectares and recreates the landscapes of Africa, from the Savannah to Madagascar. The park is home to a wide array of species, including gorillas, leopards, rhinos, giraffes, and lemurs, many of them participating in European conservation programs. Thanks to the zoo-immersion concept, you can watch these animals up close, separated only by streams, ponds, or rocks. The park also offers daily feeding talks, where you can learn more about the animals from the keepers.

Plan at least half a day to fully enjoy the Bioparc experience. The park is less crowded on weekdays or early in the morning, which is also a good time to observe animals as they're most active. Remember to wear comfortable shoes, as there's a lot of walking involved.

The Albufera Natural Park

Albufera Natural Park, located just south of Valencia, is a paradise for nature lovers. Covering over 21,000 hectares, the park is home to the Albufera Lagoon, one of the largest and most important wetland areas in the Iberian Peninsula. Here, you can observe an abundance of bird species, making it a popular spot for birdwatching, especially during migration periods.

Visitors can enjoy a boat trip on the lagoon, walk along the trails, or visit the traditional fishing villages scattered around the park. The rice fields surrounding the lagoon create a distinctive landscape, especially during the growing season when the fields are flooded, creating a mirror effect with the sky.

Consider hiring a local guide to help spot and identify the many bird species that inhabit the park. Boat trips on the lagoon are a highlight and offer a unique perspective of the park. Also, don't miss out on trying a traditional Valencian paella, which gets its unique flavor from the rice grown in the fields of Albufera.

Day Trip to Altea

Nestled between the sea and mountains, Altea is a charming town that's perfect for a day trip from Valencia. Known for its whitewashed old town, blue-domed church, and beautiful sea views, Altea is often referred to as the crown jewel of Costa Blanca. Wander through the narrow, cobbled streets, admire the Mediterranean architecture, and take in the panoramic views from the Plaza de la Iglesia.

The town also boasts a thriving art scene, with numerous galleries and craft shops. The seafront promenade is lined with restaurants and cafes, making it the perfect place to unwind and enjoy local cuisine, with the Mediterranean Sea as your backdrop. Travel to Altea by train for a scenic journey along the coast. The old town is hilly, so wear comfortable shoes. Also, remember to check the schedule for the last train back to Valencia, as it can change depending on the season.

Fallas Museum

The Fallas Museum offers a glimpse into Valencia's most famous and extravagant festival, Las Fallas. Held annually in March, the festival sees the city filled with enormous, intricate sculptures ("fallas") that are eventually set ablaze. The museum houses a collection of "ninots" (figurines) that were saved from the flames, offering a fascinating look at the artistry and satire involved in their creation.

The displays, organized chronologically, allow visitors to trace the evolution of Fallas art over the decades. Besides the ninots, the museum also provides information about the festival's history, traditions, and the painstaking process of building the fallas. The Fallas Museum is a must-visit for anyone interested in Valencia's unique cultural heritage. Be sure to take advantage of the audio guides available, as they provide valuable context and anecdotes about the displays. Visit during Fallas season for the most immersive experience, but be prepared for larger crowds.

Valencia's Silk Exchange

The Silk Exchange, or "La Lonja de la Seda", is a magnificent example of late Gothic architecture. Built between 1482 and 1548, it was the center of Valencia's silk trade, which contrib-

uted significantly to the city's prosperity during the 15th and 16th centuries. Today, it stands as a symbol of the city's rich history and has been declared a UNESCO World Heritage Site.
Visitors can explore the grand Trading Hall, with its stunning spiral columns, the orange-tree-filled Patio, and the Consulate of the Sea, which once resolved maritime and trade disputes. The building's intricate stone carvings, reminiscent of medieval craftsmanship, are also a sight to behold.
A visit to La Lonja de la Seda is like stepping back in time. The detailed audioguide, available in multiple languages, provides interesting historical context. Try to visit in the morning or late afternoon when the sunlight beautifully illuminates the Trading Hall's column forest.

Valencia Cuisine

Valencia is the birthplace of Spain's most famous dish, paella. Valencian cuisine emphasizes fresh, local ingredients, and it's hard to get more authentic than a traditional Valencian paella. Unlike other variations, the original recipe includes rabbit, chicken, green beans, and butter beans, all cooked in a shallow pan over a wood fire.
Beyond paella, Valencia offers a diverse culinary scene. Other regional dishes to try include "fideuà" (a noodle-based dish similar to paella), "arroso al forn" (oven-baked rice), and "horchata" (a sweet drink made from tiger nuts) paired with "fartons" (elongated sugar-glazed pastries). Valencia's Central Market, one of the largest in Europe, is the perfect place to discover the region's fresh produce and gourmet products.
If you're a foodie with a sweet tooth, Valencia will not disappoint you. The city's pastry shops offer an array of traditional sweets,

including "turron" (a type of nougat), "buñuelos" (deep-fried dough balls often eaten during the Fallas Festival), and "pasteles de boniato" (sweet potato pastries). Sampling these local treats is a must when in Valencia.

For those interested in diving deeper into Valencia's culinary culture, consider signing up for a cooking class. This is an excellent opportunity to learn how to prepare traditional dishes like paella under the guidance of local chefs. Not only will you gain a deeper appreciation for the region's cuisine, but you'll also acquire a new set of culinary skills to take home with you.

When in Valencia, eating paella by the sea is a must-do. Remember that traditional Valencian paella is usually served at lunchtime, and it's common for restaurants to require orders for a minimum of two people. Also, the local custom is to eat paella straight from the pan!

Final Thoughts

Valencia is a city that expertly balances the past with the future. From the futuristic City of Arts and Sciences to the historic Silk Exchange, it offers an intriguing blend of sights that cater to a wide range of interests. Take a leisurely stroll in the extensive Turia Gardens, relax on the city's beautiful beaches, or immerse yourself in the local culture by visiting the bustling Central Market and the Fallas Museum.

Although Valencia may not be as internationally famous as Madrid or Barcelona, it offers an authentic Spanish experience. The city has a unique rhythm of life, from its leisurely afternoon "siestas" to its vibrant nightlife. Its traditions, such as the Fallas Festival and the ubiquitous paella, provide visitors with an intimate glimpse into the Valencian way of life.

In addition to the highlights covered in this chapter, the city offers numerous other attractions. The Oceanogràfic, part of the City of Arts and Sciences complex, is Europe's largest aquarium and home to over 500 different species. For art lovers, the Valencian Institute of Modern Art hosts an excellent collection of 20th-century Spanish art. History enthusiasts shouldn't miss the Torres de Quart and Torres de Serranos, two impressive Gothic city gates that once formed part of Valencia's city wall. Ultimately, Valencia is a city that invites exploration and rewards curiosity. Its mix of history, culture, cuisine, and innovative design makes it a must-visit destination for any travel enthusiast. From its sun-soaked beaches to its ancient winding streets, Valencia offers a myriad of experiences just waiting to be discovered. No matter how long you stay, you'll leave with a piece of this magical city in your heart and a desire to return to uncover more of its secrets. Valencia truly is a hidden gem, representing the best of Spain and all its captivating allure.

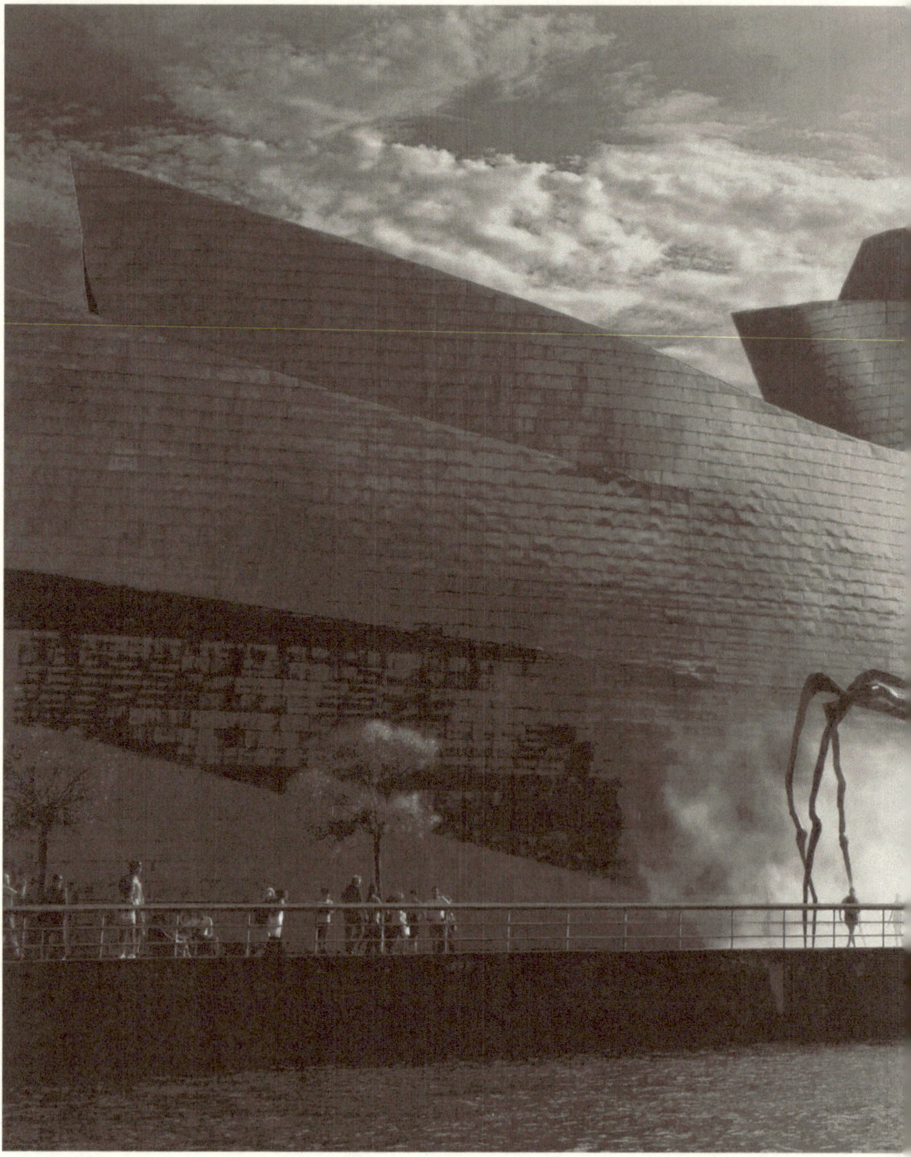

CHAPTER 5: BILBAO 75

CHAPTER 5:
Bilbao

Nestled in the heart of Spain's Basque Country, the city of Bilbao offers a rich blend of old-world charm, cutting-edge architecture, and a lively cultural scene. Once a major industrial centre, Bilbao has evolved over the years into an exciting, modern city known for its innovative spirit and vibrant atmosphere.

Visitors to Bilbao are met with a dazzling array of experiences. As you wander through the city, you'll find yourself immersed in its remarkable transformation. From the historical Casco Viejo (Old Town) with its narrow, winding streets and picturesque plazas, to the ultramodern Guggenheim Museum, which has become a symbol of the city's regeneration, there's a delightful surprise around every corner.

One of Bilbao's defining features is its commitment to art and culture. The Guggenheim Museum, with its bold, futuristic design and impressive contemporary art collection, is a testament to this. However, art in Bilbao is not confined to the walls of its galleries. Public art installations and creative architectural designs can be found throughout the city, turning a casual stroll into an open-air museum tour.

However, there's more to Bilbao than its arts scene. The city is also a foodie's paradise, renowned for its culinary tradition. From pintxos bars serving up bite-sized Basque delights to Michelin-starred restaurants offering gastronomic experiences, the city's food culture is as diverse and dynamic as its architecture.

Bilbao's location, surrounded by green rolling hills and close to the sea, provides a beautiful backdrop to the cityscape. It also offers plenty of opportunities for outdoor activities, from leisurely walks along the Nervión river to adventurous hikes in the nearby mountains. For a refreshing escape from the city, consider a day trip to the stunning Gaztelugatxe island, just a short drive away.

Embracing both tradition and innovation, Bilbao represents the best of the Basque Country. With its rich history, dynamic arts scene, delectable cuisine, and friendly locals, the city provides an unforgettable travel experience. This guide will take you on a journey through Bilbao's must-see attractions, its hidden gems, and the tastes and sounds that give the city its unique character. Welcome to Bilbao, the revitalised city of the Basque Country.

Guggenheim Museum

The Guggenheim Museum is a must-visit for any art and architecture lover. Designed by renowned architect Frank Gehry, its shimmering, curved exterior, covered in titanium plates, is a sight to behold and has become an icon of modern architecture. The museum stands as a symbol of Bilbao's transformation from an industrial port city to a hub of contemporary art and culture.

Inside, the Guggenheim Museum houses an extensive collection of contemporary art, featuring works from international artists such as Jeff Koons and Anish Kapoor. The museum's permanent collection is complimented by a rotating series of temporary exhibitions, which further enrich the artistic offering.

The museum itself, with its soaring atrium and interconnecting spaces, offers an immersive and exploratory experience.

Visitors are encouraged to explore the exterior spaces of the museum as well, which hosts several installations, including Jeff Koons' famous "Puppy", a towering terrier covered in flowering plants. The Guggenheim offers free entrance on select dates and times, and it's recommended to book your tickets in advance, particularly during peak seasons.

Casco Viejo

The Casco Viejo, also known as the "Seven Streets," is the historical heart of Bilbao. Its labyrinth of narrow streets, filled with beautifully preserved traditional Basque architecture, offers a striking contrast to the modern structures of the new city. Casco Viejo is rich in history, character, and local life, making it a captivating area to explore.

Here, you'll find the city's original cathedral, Santiago Cathedral, and numerous other historical landmarks. The streets are teeming with a variety of shops, from local artisan boutiques to more well-known Spanish brands. Casco Viejo is also home to the bustling Ribera Market, one of the largest covered markets in Europe.

The evenings bring a vibrant atmosphere to the quarter, as the streets fill with locals enjoying pintxos (small snacks) and drinks in the many bars and restaurants. For a local experience, join the evening pintxos crawl or take part in a traditional Basque cider tasting.

Bilbao Fine Arts Museum

Offering a balance to the contemporary art at the Guggenheim, the Bilbao Fine Arts Museum showcases a collection spanning from the Middle Ages to the present. Its collection, considered one of the finest in Spain, comprises over 10,000 works including paintings, sculptures, drawings, and applied arts.

The museum features works by significant Spanish artists such as El Greco, Zurbarán, Goya, and Sorolla, as well as notable Basque artists. Also, it hosts a collection of international art, with pieces from artists like Van Dyck, Gauguin, and Bacon.

The museum is located next to the Doña Casilda Iturrizar Park, making it a perfect stop during a leisurely walk. Free guided tours are offered in both Spanish and English, providing a deeper understanding of the artworks. Every Wednesday, the museum offers free admission, making it a great opportunity for budget-conscious travelers. However, the museum is often less crowded during regular weekdays.

Artxanda Funicular

A trip to Bilbao wouldn't be complete without a visit to the scenic viewpoint of Artxanda. Accessible via a charming century-old funicular railway, the summit of Mount Artxanda offers breathtaking panoramic views of Bilbao and its surrounding areas.

Once at the top, aside from the views, visitors can explore walking trails, gardens, and recreational areas. There are also several restaurants and a picnic area, making it an ideal spot for a leisurely lunch while enjoying the scenery. The viewpoint is especially popular at sunset, when the cityscape of Bilbao is bathed in a warm, golden glow.

The funicular station is just a short walk from the city center, making it an easily accessible excursion. It's recommended to purchase round-trip tickets in advance to avoid queues. Also, don't forget to bring a camera to capture the stunning views.

San Mamés Stadium

San Mamés Stadium, dubbed "The Cathedral" by locals, is more than just a sports venue; it's the beating heart of Bilbao's football culture. Home to Athletic Bilbao, one of Spain's oldest football clubs, the stadium holds a significant place in the city's identity and social life.

The stadium, with its impressive modern design, offers a capacity of over 53,000 seats and is known for its electrifying atmosphere during matches. Even if you're not a football fan, taking a guided tour of the stadium and its museum provides fascinating insights into the club's history and Basque football culture.

Tours are usually available on non-match days and include access to the pitch, changing rooms, and the press room. Tickets can be purchased in advance online or at the stadium. If your visit coincides with a match day, experiencing a game with the passionate local fans is an unforgettable experience.

Day Trip to Gaztelugatxe

Just a short drive from Bilbao, Gaztelugatxe is a natural wonder that captures the rugged beauty of the Basque Country's coastline. This small island, topped by a hermitage dedicated to John the Baptist, is connected to the mainland by a winding stone bridge and 241-step staircase.

Once at the top, visitors are rewarded with stunning views of the Cantabrian Sea and the surrounding cliffs. The site has gained international fame as a filming location for the television series "Game of Thrones", where it was featured as the fortress of Dragonstone.

Gaztelugatxe can be reached by car or public transport from Bilbao. It's recommended to wear comfortable shoes for the hike and to visit early in the morning or late in the afternoon to avoid crowds. After the climb, ringing the bell of the hermitage three times and making a wish is a local tradition not to be missed.

Plaza Nueva

Plaza Nueva, or New Square, is a quintessential meeting point in the heart of Bilbao's old town, Casco Viejo. This 19th-century Neoclassical square, framed by uniform arcaded buildings, is filled with shops, cafés, and restaurants, where locals and tourists alike come to enjoy pintxos and Basque sidra (cider).

Throughout the week, Plaza Nueva is a hub of activity, hosting a weekly Sunday market where collectors come to hunt for stamps, coins, and other curiosities. During local festivals, the square is often at the heart of the celebrations, brimming with music, traditional dances, and theatrical performances.

Venture to the plaza in the late afternoon or evening when it's buzzing with life. Many of the surrounding bars offer pintxo-pote, a local tradition of pairing a pintxo (a small snack) with a drink, usually on specific days of the week. It's a great way to sample local flavors and immerse yourself in the local culture.

Bilbao Riverside Walk

One of the best ways to appreciate Bilbao is by taking a leisurely walk along the banks of the Nervión River. This scenic route, stretching from the Old Town to the Guggenheim Museum, allows you to enjoy a mix of Bilbao's historic charm and modern architecture, all while taking in the lively riverfront atmosphere. Along the way, you'll pass by iconic landmarks such as the Arriaga Theatre, the City Hall, and the Bilbao Ribera Market, the largest covered market in Europe. You'll also have a chance to admire some of the city's impressive bridges, including the Zubizuri, a modern footbridge designed by architect Santiago Calatrava.

The riverside walk can be enjoyed at any time of the day, but is particularly atmospheric in the evening, when many of the buildings and bridges are beautifully illuminated. Keep in mind that the path is also bike-friendly, so consider renting a bicycle for a quicker tour of the area.

Azkuna Zentroa

Azkuna Zentroa, formerly known as Alhóndiga Bilbao, is a multi-purpose venue that perfectly embodies the innovative spirit of the city. Originally built as a wine warehouse in the early 20th century, the building was transformed into a vibrant cultural and leisure center by the renowned French designer Philippe Starck.

Today, Azkuna Zentroa offers a variety of spaces including a media library, exhibition halls, a fitness center, and a rooftop swimming pool with a transparent floor that allows visitors below to watch swimmers overhead. Its interior is remarkable for its 43 uniquely designed columns, each representing different architectural styles and civilizations.

The center hosts a wide range of activities, from art exhibitions and film screenings to workshops and fitness classes. Check their event calendar in advance to see what's on. Don't miss the opportunity to visit the rooftop, where you can enjoy a swim with a unique view or relax at the café while admiring the cityscape.

Bilbao's Bridges

Bilbao's urban landscape is characterized by the presence of numerous bridges that cross the Nervión River, connecting different parts of the city. These bridges are not just functional structures; they are landmarks that each carry a piece of Bilbao's history and architectural identity.

Among the most emblematic is the Zubizuri, or "White Bridge". Designed by the world-renowned architect Santiago Calatrava, the bridge is known for its distinctive arching design and glass-tiled walkway. Equally noteworthy is the La Salve Bridge, an older construction that gained a new look with a red gate addition, courtesy of French artist Daniel Buren, to celebrate the 10th anniversary of the Guggenheim Museum.

Other significant bridges include the Arenal Bridge, a beautifully preserved 19th-century iron bridge that connects the Old Town with the Ensanche district, and the Deusto Bridge, an elegant bascule bridge that has stood since the 1930s. For a unique experience, visitors can also cross the Vizcaya Bridge, the world's oldest transporter bridge and a UNESCO World Heritage Site, via its gondola or the high-level walkway.

Bilbao Cuisine

The gastronomy of Bilbao is a celebration of the region's bounty and the Basque culinary tradition. At the heart of this are the pintxos, Basque Country's version of tapas, but often more intricate and innovative. These small bites are usually served atop a slice of bread, and range from traditional combinations such as cod and peppers to avant-garde creations that wouldn't be out of place in a gourmet restaurant.

Exploring the city's pintxos bars is an essential part of the Bilbao experience. Many establishments line the streets of the Casco Viejo and the Ensanche district, offering counters laden with an array of colourful pintxos. Tradition dictates that you stand at the bar while enjoying your pintxo, accompanied by a glass of txakoli, a slightly sparkling white wine typical of the region.

Beyond pintxos, Bilbao also offers high-end dining options with several Michelin-starred restaurants. Notable mentions include Azurmendi, where chef Eneko Atxa serves innovative dishes in an eco-friendly greenhouse, and Mina, which prides itself on its seasonally changing tasting menus. Another culinary highlight in Bilbao is the Mercado de la Ribera, a vibrant market where you can buy fresh local produce or enjoy cooked meals at the food stalls.

Bilbao's gastronomy also extends to its confectionery. Pastries like 'canutillos de Bilbao' filled with custard, and 'Bilbainitos', small cakes topped with nuts and glazed with apricot jam, are some local favourites you can find in the city's pastelerías. Remember, the secret to fully enjoying the culinary scene in Bilbao is to eat as the locals do: go 'pintxo-pote', hopping from bar to bar, tasting different dishes along the way.

Final Thoughts

Bilbao's transformation from a gritty industrial hub to a vibrant city of art, culture, and gastronomy is nothing short of remarkable. This metamorphosis is not only evident in the city's physical landscape, but also in the spirit of its people who are proud of their Basque heritage while embracing the new.

For visitors seeking more cultural insights, the Basque Museum provides an in-depth look at the Basque people's history and culture. Similarly, the Maritime Museum is an excellent place to understand the city's close relationship with the Nervión River and its maritime past.

While the city's revitalised centre and the Guggenheim often take centre stage, don't miss the chance to explore Bilbao's diverse neighbourhoods. From the bohemian vibe of the Bilbao la Vieja to the traditional ambiance of the Deusto district, each area offers a different perspective of Bilbao.

Bilbao also serves as an excellent base for exploring the Basque Country. Coastal cities like San Sebastián, known for its beautiful beaches and gastronomic scene, and smaller fishing towns like Lekeitio and Bermeo, are just a short drive away. Nearby, the UNESCO Biosphere Reserve of Urdaibai offers beautiful natural scenery and excellent bird watching opportunities.

As a visitor, embrace the Bilbao lifestyle. Take leisurely strolls along the riverside promenade, delve into the lively food scene, appreciate the architecture, and immerse yourself in the city's art and culture. Remember, Bilbao is more than just a city; it's an experience, a testament to resilience and reinvention, a place where tradition and innovation coexist harmoniously, a true industrial phoenix that has risen with even greater splendour. Make your own journey here, and let Bilbao leave an indelible mark in your traveller's heart.

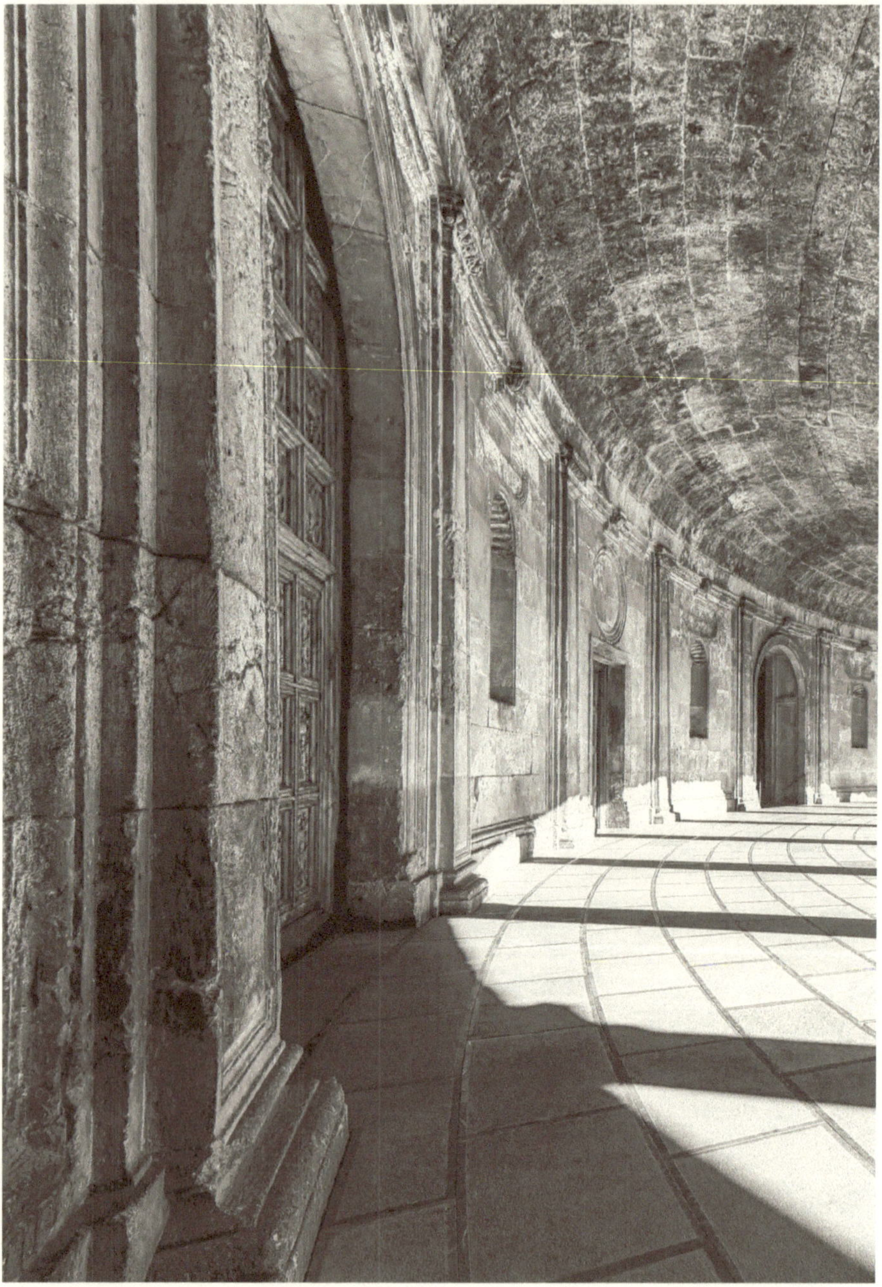

CHAPTER 6: GRANADA 89

CHAPTER 6:
Granada
....

Nestled at the foot of the Sierra Nevada Mountains, in the autonomous region of Andalusia, lies Granada, a city that effortlessly weaves together threads of different cultures into a stunning tapestry. Home to the magnificent Alhambra Palace and the historic Arab quarter of Albayzín, Granada is a city where Moorish influence still echoes strong, complemented by a rich Christian heritage and a lively, contemporary spirit.

This city tells a tale of convergence, where two prominent cultures of history – Islam and Christianity – met and left their indelible marks. Centuries of coexistence have created an environment where intricate Islamic artisanship blends seamlessly with grandiose Christian architecture, creating a distinctive architectural landscape that holds the power to fascinate and inspire.

But Granada is more than just a visual treat; it's a city to be experienced with all senses. The aroma of exotic spices wafting from the Arab market, the distant strumming of a Spanish guitar that guides you through the narrow, winding alleyways of Albayzín, the chorus of birds that accompany a peaceful stroll through the Generalife gardens, or the taste of a traditional tapa enjoyed in a lively bar — these are the moments that define the Granada experience.

A significant part of Granada's charm also lies in its geographical diversity. From the snow-capped peaks of Sierra Nevada, where adventure seekers can indulge in winter sports, to the sunny Mediterranean beaches of Costa Tropical just an hour's drive away, Granada offers an array of natural landscapes that are as diverse as its cultural heritage.

And then, there is the city's vibrant modern life. With a large student population, Granada is always brimming with energy. Cafés, taverns, and tapas bars line the city streets, and the sound of flamenco rhythm regularly fills the night air. Street art, particularly in the district of Realejo, adds a touch of contemporary vibrancy to the city's historic backdrop.

A trip to Granada is like stepping into a beautifully written historical novel. Each monument, each street, and each square has a story to tell — tales of sultans and queens, of poets and artists, of conquests and reconquests. Yet, despite its deep connection to the past, Granada remains firmly rooted in the present. It's a city where history and modernity engage in a constant dance, creating an ambiance that is uniquely Granadan.

As you plan your journey to this enchanting Andalusian city, prepare to be captivated by its historical treasures, its natural beauty, its vibrant culture, and its warm, hospitable people. Granada is more than a destination; it's an experience that lingers in your memory long after your visit. So come and uncover the many facets of this Andalusian gem, and let the magic of Granada weave its spell on you.

The Alhambra

The Alhambra, often considered the crown jewel of Granada, is an impressive testament to the city's Moorish legacy. This majestic hilltop fortress and palace complex, whose name translates to "The Red One" due to its reddish walls, dates back to the 9th century. However, it was the Nasrid Dynasty in the 13th and 14th centuries that gave the Alhambra its most distinguished features: intricate geometric patterns, arabesques, and calligraphic inscriptions that embellish walls, ceilings, and arches, reflecting the pinnacle of Islamic art and architecture.

The complex includes the Nasrid Palaces, the Alcazaba fortress, and the Generalife gardens. Each part of the Alhambra reveals its own history and grandeur, with ornate courtyards like the Court of the Lions, panoramic viewpoints such as the Tower of the Princesses, and lush gardens radiating tranquillity.

Booking your tickets well in advance is highly recommended due to the Alhambra's popularity. Audioguides are available to enrich your visit with historical and architectural details. The view of the Alhambra illuminated at night, seen from the Mirador de San Nicolas in the Albayzín district, is a sight not to be missed.

Albayzín

Albayzín, Granada's old Arab quarter, is an enchanting maze of narrow winding streets, whitewashed houses, hidden squares, and stunning views. Recognized as a UNESCO World Heritage site, it's an area where Granada's Moorish past feels vividly alive. As you stroll along the cobblestone lanes, the scent of jasmine fills the air, and the sound of trickling water from hidden fountains completes the idyllic setting.

The district's highlight is the Mirador de San Nicolas, a viewpoint that offers a breathtaking panorama of the Alhambra against the backdrop of the Sierra Nevada mountains. Also, visit the historic El Bañuelo, an excellently preserved Arab bathhouse, and the ancient mosque that now serves as the Church of San Salvador.

Keep in mind that the streets of Albayzín are steep and can be a bit challenging to navigate. However, taking your time to explore, maybe stopping for a Moroccan tea or visiting one of the many artisanal shops, is part of the charm of this historic quarter.

Sacromonte

Perched above the city, adjacent to Albayzín, the Sacromonte district is known as the heartland of Granada's Roma (Gypsy) community and is famed for its unique cave dwellings and flamenco tradition. The caves, dug into the hillside, were initially inhabited by the Romani people in the 15th century and have since become synonymous with the district's identity.

Sacromonte is also recognized as the birthplace of the Zambra style of flamenco, an emotive dance filled with passionate rhythms and movements. Watching a live Zambra performance in one of the neighborhood's caves, like those in Cueva de La Rocío or Cueva del Sacromonte, is an unforgettable experience that perfectly encapsulates the district's rich cultural heritage.

Additionally, the Sacromonte Abbey offers stunning city views and houses important religious artifacts. Walking tours are an excellent way to explore and understand the district's history and cultural significance. Keep in mind that the area's terrain is hilly, so wear comfortable shoes and take your time to enjoy the views and atmosphere.

Granada Cathedral

A masterpiece of Spanish Renaissance architecture, the Granada Cathedral, also known as the Cathedral of the Incarnation, is a symbol of Christian influence in Granada. Constructed on the site of the city's main mosque after the Christian Reconquista, the cathedral took nearly two centuries to complete, resulting in an intriguing mix of architectural styles.

The grand façade of the cathedral will catch your eye, but it's the interior that truly mesmerizes. Vast, elegant, and filled with light, the cathedral's main chapel showcases an impressive collection of artwork, while the numerous side chapels each tell their own unique story. Notably, the cathedral houses a magnificent 18th-century organ, known for its historical significance and musical quality.

Guided tours are available to provide a deeper understanding of the cathedral's history and architectural details. Don't miss the opportunity to climb to the top of the cathedral for a panoramic view of the city. As the cathedral is a popular attraction, consider visiting early in the day to avoid crowds.

Royal Chapel of Granada

Adjacent to the Granada Cathedral, you'll find the Royal Chapel of Granada, a mausoleum that holds significant historical importance. It's here where Catholic Monarchs Ferdinand and Isabella, the rulers responsible for the Reconquista that ended Moorish rule in Spain, are laid to rest.

The chapel is an exemplary piece of Gothic architecture, with its stunning vaulted ceiling and detailed stained-glass windows. The main attraction, however, is the marble tombs of the

Catholic Monarchs and their successors, which are beautifully sculpted and surrounded by intricate ironwork. Also, don't miss the small museum within the chapel that exhibits a collection of royal artefacts, including Queen Isabella's personal art collection and Ferdinand's sword.

Remember to dress respectfully when visiting this active place of worship. Guided tours are available and highly recommended to fully appreciate the historical and cultural significance of the Royal Chapel.

Day Trip to Sierra Nevada

For those seeking a respite from the city's cultural landmarks, a day trip to the Sierra Nevada offers a different kind of spectacle. This mountain range, whose name means "Snowy Range" in Spanish, is home to Spain's highest peak, Mulhacén, and provides a stunning backdrop to the city of Granada.

During the winter, the Sierra Nevada becomes a popular skiing destination, with a variety of slopes suitable for both beginners and experienced skiers. In the summer months, the mountains transform into a haven for hikers, with trails that offer breathtaking views over Andalusia. You can also visit the Sierra Nevada National Park, a biodiversity hotspot that hosts numerous endemic species.

To reach the Sierra Nevada, you can opt for public transportation, car hire, or organized tours. For skiing or hiking, it's essential to check the weather conditions beforehand and prepare accordingly. And no matter the season, don't forget to bring a camera to capture the unforgettable vistas that the Sierra Nevada provides.

Generalife

Located adjacent to the Alhambra, the Generalife serves as a tranquil oasis away from the city bustle. This picturesque estate was the leisure place of the Nasrid kings of Granada, providing a cool respite from the Andalusian heat. Comprising lush gardens, ornamental fountains, and elegant pavilions, the Generalife offers a serene escape where nature and architecture blend harmoniously.

The key attractions include the Patio de la Acequia, a long pool flanked by flower beds, fountains, and myrtle hedges, and the Patio de la Sultana, known for its ancient cypress tree linked to a romantic legend. Each corner of Generalife is imbued with a sense of tranquility, enhanced by the ambient sound of trickling water.

To avoid the crowds, consider visiting early in the morning or late in the afternoon. Your Alhambra ticket will include access to the Generalife, but remember to adhere to your allocated time slot.

Granada's Street Art

While Granada's history is etched into its ancient buildings, the city's vibrant street art scene offers a modern contrast. Much of this work is concentrated in the Realejo and Albayzín districts, where walls, shutters, and underpasses have become canvases for local and international artists.

Granada's most famous street artist is Raúl Ruiz, known as 'El Niño de las Pinturas'. His thought-provoking murals, often featuring children and elderly people coupled with poetic phrases, have become emblematic of the city's street art scene. Each piece is a statement, reflecting on society, philosophy, or local culture. You can explore Granada's street art on your own, or join a guided street art tour to gain deeper insights into the artists and their work. Either way, keep your camera at the ready, as these striking artworks make for excellent photo opportunities.

Hammam Al Ándalus

Step into Hammam Al Ándalus, and you'll be transported back in time to the days of Al-Andalus. This traditional Arab bath, situated at the foot of the Alhambra, provides a unique opportunity to immerse yourself in Andalusian history while indulging in a soothing spa experience.

The Hammam is a labyrinth of vaulted rooms, each filled with pools of varying temperatures. The ritual involves moving between these pools, from the warm bath to the hot bath, then cooling off in the cold bath, before finally resting in the relaxation room. There's also the option to receive a traditional kessa massage, which will leave your skin feeling incredibly smooth.

Booking in advance is highly recommended as the Hammam can fill up quickly. Remember to bring your bathing suit, and prepare for a truly relaxing experience that blends history, culture, and wellness.

Carrera del Darro

Lined with historic buildings, rustic cafes, and views of the Alhambra, Carrera del Darro is considered Granada's most romantic street. Winding along the Darro River, this cobblestone path is as charming as it is historic. The street dates back to the Arab era and serves as a silent witness to the city's rich past.

As you stroll down Carrera del Darro, make sure to take in the sights of El Bañuelo, the city's best-preserved Arab baths, and the Archaeological Museum housed in a 16th-century palace. The numerous bridges crossing the river, such as the picturesque Puente del Cadí, offer postcard-worthy views of the Alhambra perched on the hillside.

Visiting during early morning or late evening allows you to see the Alhambra bathed in the golden glow of sunrise or sunset, a truly unforgettable sight. Remember to wear comfortable shoes as the cobblestones can be tricky to navigate.

Granada Cuisine

Granada's culinary scene is a delectable blend of cultures, reflecting its Moorish past and Spanish identity. The city is famed for its tapas culture; it's one of the few places in Spain where tapas are served free with every drink order. Each bar tends to have its specialty, offering a chance to embark on a gastronomic journey with each visit.

One of the must-try dishes is 'habas con jamón' (broad beans with ham), a classic Granadian dish symbolizing the blend of Muslim and Christian influences. For those with a sweet tooth, 'Piononos', small cakes named after Pope Pius IX and soaked in syrup and topped with cream, are a local treat originating from the nearby town of Santa Fe.

Beyond the city center, the Albayzín district is perfect for tasting Moroccan influenced cuisine, while the Sacromonte neighborhood is known for its cave restaurants, serving up hearty 'Zambra' style dishes, often accompanied by a flamenco show.

Granada is also known for its locally produced wines, especially from the Contraviesa-Alpujarra region. These high-altitude vineyards produce exceptional vintages that perfectly accompany the local cuisine.

Foodies should consider a guided tapas tour for a curated experience or simply follow their instincts and appetites. Either way, dining in Granada is an adventure of flavors, with each bite capturing a piece of the city's diverse culinary heritage.

Final Thoughts

With its stunning landscapes, rich history, and unique cultural blend, Granada is more than just a travel destination; it's a sensory experience that seizes your heart and soul. This city, where Moorish and Christian cultures have intertwined for centuries, offers a compelling narrative of coexistence and evolution, told through its streets, buildings, and food.

Exploring Granada beyond the main sights yields many rewards. Visit the 'Carmenes' of the Albayzín, traditional Andalusian houses with secret gardens that offer tranquility and a glimpse into local life. For panoramic views of the city, climb up to the San Miguel Alto viewpoint, and watch as the sunset paints the Alhambra in shades of gold.

Attend a 'Zambra' Flamenco show in the Sacromonte caves for an unforgettable night of passion and artistry. Shop for traditional crafts in Alcaicería, the old silk market, where you can find unique souvenirs such as Fajalauza ceramics and Granada-style taracea woodwork.

Don't forget to slow down and simply absorb the city's unique atmosphere. Take time to wander, sip coffee in charming plazas, and engage in 'la sobremesa', the Spanish tradition of relaxing and chatting after a meal. Enjoy the unexpected moments - a sudden view of the Alhambra, the fragrance of jasmine on a quiet street, the sound of a guitar echoing in the evening air. These are the heartbeats of Granada, a city that echoes with the past but pulses vibrantly in the present.

From the majestic Alhambra to the narrow alleyways of Albayzín, from the lively tapas bars to the tranquil tea houses, Granada enchants at every turn. As you prepare to depart, you'll find that a piece of your heart remains, forever entwined with the spirit of this timeless city. In Granada, the tale of two cultures continues, and it's one that you'll be eager to return and read again and again.

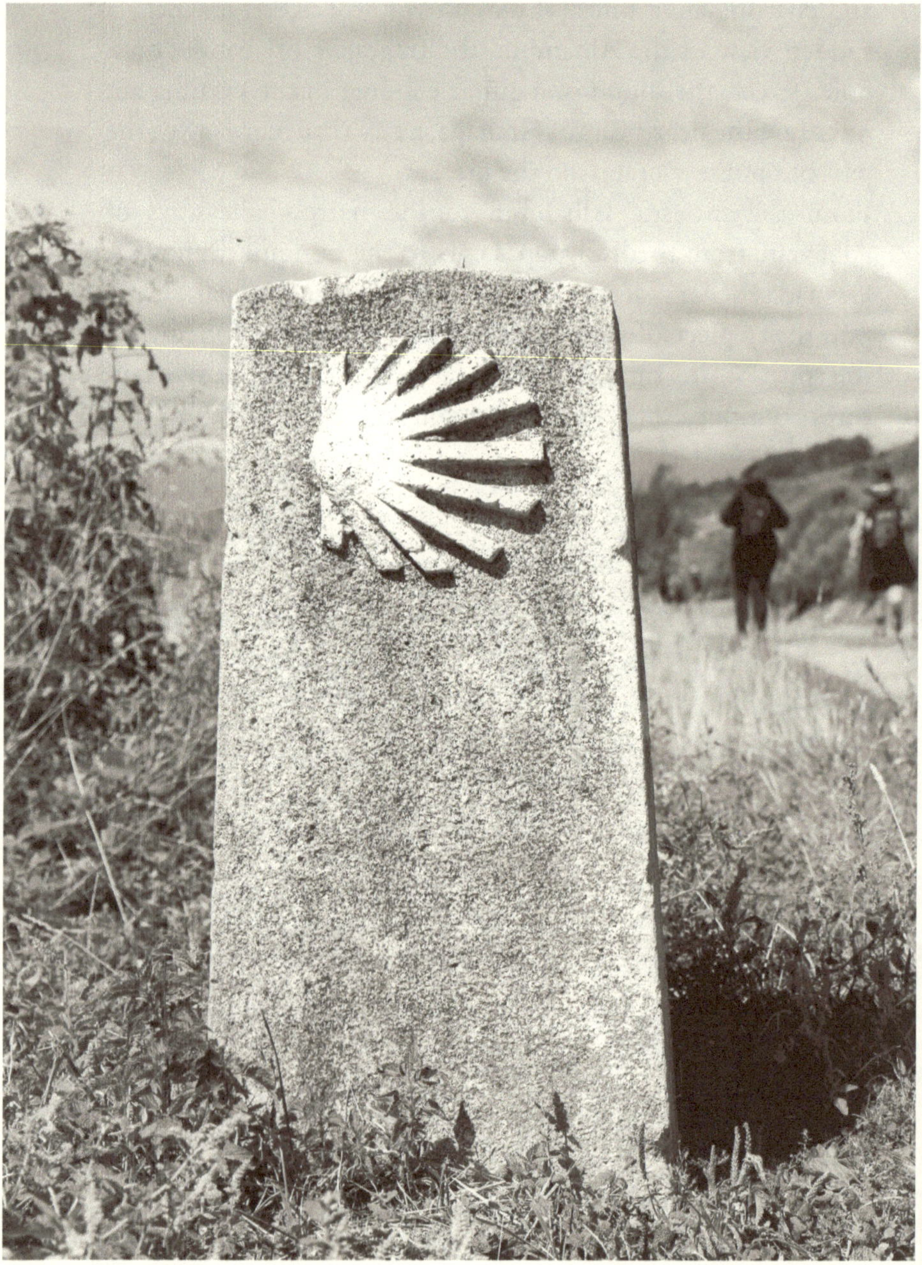

CHAPTER 7: SANTIAGO DE COMPOSTELA 103

CHAPTER 7:
Santiago de Compostela

Nestled in the verdant region of Galicia, in Spain's northwest corner, lies Santiago de Compostela - a city that brims with profound historical, cultural, and spiritual significance. For centuries, it has served as the hallowed conclusion to the legendary Camino de Santiago, a vast network of ancient pilgrimage paths that crisscross Europe, culminating at the city's imposing cathedral. Yet, to understand Santiago de Compostela is to acknowledge that its allure extends far beyond its status as a revered pilgrimage site. This is a city of contrasts, where cobbled, centuries-old passageways harmoniously coexist with a pulsating, contemporary spirit, mirroring its dual identity as both a UNESCO World Heritage site and a bustling university town. Santiago de Compostela's old town, with its stone-clad streets and grand plazas, invites visitors into a captivating chronicle of time. Its architectural tableau is a testament to the city's rich past, displaying a visual symphony of Romanesque, Gothic, and Baroque styles, with the awe-inspiring Santiago Cathedral towering as the city's spiritual and architectural cornerstone. Every corner, every stone of this well-preserved old town whispers tales - tales of weary yet determined pilgrims, tales of scholarly pursuits in venerable institutions, tales of traditional Galician life, and tales of an effervescent modern cultural scene that refuses to be overshadowed by the city's storied past.

Venture beyond its historical heart, and Santiago de Compostela continues to enchant. The city's bustling food markets, like the beloved Mercado de Abastos, are gastronomic playgrounds, teeming with fresh produce from the Galician countryside and the Atlantic Ocean that laps its coasts. Santiago's tapas bars, dotted throughout the city, are social and culinary hubs, where locals and visitors alike congregate over plates of pulpo a feira (octopus) and glasses of Albariño.

For those seeking tranquillity, the city's numerous parks and green spaces offer respite from urban exploration. The Alameda Park, in particular, with its ancient trees and sweeping views of the old town, is a favorite amongst locals for leisurely strolls and quiet contemplation. Additionally, Santiago de Compostela's location provides easy access to the ruggedly beautiful Galician coast, with destinations like the dramatic Cape Finisterre, known as the "End of the World" in Roman times, just a short trip away.

Yet, perhaps the most striking aspect of Santiago de Compostela is its intangible yet palpable essence. It's found in the clinking of the botafumeiro, the cathedral's famous incense burner, in the camaraderie shared over a communal meal in a local tavern, in the quiet, early morning hours as the city still slumbers, and in the jubilant smiles of pilgrims who have completed their arduous journey. This essence, a blend of enduring tradition and dynamic modernity, is the city's true magic.

As we embark on this journey through Santiago de Compostela, we invite you to discover the city that has captured the hearts of pilgrims and travelers for over a thousand years. From its spiritual roots to its vibrant contemporary culture, Santiago de Compostela offers a wealth of unforgettable experiences that reward every journey, whether it's a pilgrimage of faith, a quest for cultural insights, or simply a desire to explore one of Spain's most captivating destinations.

Santiago Cathedral

Nestled within Santiago de Compostela's enchanting old town, the Santiago Cathedral stands as a beacon of the city's profound spiritual significance. The cathedral's imposing edifice, a grand architectural fusion of Romanesque, Gothic, and Baroque styles, provides a visual feast. However, it is within the cathedral's ancient walls that the real magic resides.

Walking into the cathedral is akin to stepping into a world filled with grandeur, history, and a palpable sense of the divine. Visitors are immediately greeted by the Pórtico de la Gloria, the cathedral's famous entryway. The ornately sculpted arch, completed in the 12th century, depicts scenes from the Bible, offering a glimpse into the rich religious narratives of the time.

Beyond the grand entryway, the cathedral's interior continues to mesmerize. The Main Chapel, adorned with a grand altarpiece, is a masterpiece of Spanish Baroque style, while the soaring vaults and intricate stained-glass windows imbue the cathedral with a celestial glow. However, the most sought-after destination for many is the crypt, home to the shrine of St. James, whose remains are believed to rest here, drawing pilgrims from around the world to venerate the apostle.

Don't forget to embrace the tradition of hugging the statue of St. James, located behind the main altar, a symbolic act of gratitude upon completing the pilgrimage. Before you leave, also be sure to witness the spectacle of the botafumeiro, the cathedral's giant incense burner. Swung by eight men, the botafumeiro fills the cathedral with a fragrant haze, a sight that, once witnessed, is not easily forgotten.

The cathedral is an active place of worship, so be sure to respect religious services. Also, note that the botafumeiro is not swung during all services, so check the schedule in advance if you wish to experience this unique event.

The Legendary Camino de Santiago

The Camino de Santiago, or the Way of St. James, is more than just a long-distance trail. It is a journey that transcends geographical and cultural borders, uniting pilgrims from every corner of the globe in a common quest for spiritual enlightenment. For over a thousand years, these paths have served as a conduit, guiding the faithful towards the hallowed grounds of the Santiago Cathedral.

The Camino is not a singular path but rather a web of routes that extend across Europe, all leading to Santiago de Compostela. The most popular of these is the Camino Francés, which stretches some 800 kilometers from Saint-Jean-Pied-de-Port in France to Santiago. Walking this route is a challenging endeavor, with pilgrims traversing diverse landscapes, from the rugged Pyrenees mountains to the vineyards of La Rioja, to the verdant hills of Galicia.

Regardless of the chosen path, the Camino experience is as much about the journey as it is the destination. Along the way, pilgrims encounter historical landmarks, serene countryside, and vibrant cities. Even more importantly, they forge bonds with fellow travelers, sharing stories, meals, and mutual encouragement.

If you plan to walk the Camino, ensure you're adequately prepared. This includes having the right gear, such as comfortable walking shoes, as well as training beforehand. Also, remember to collect stamps on your 'pilgrim's passport' along the way, as you'll need this to receive your Compostela certificate upon reaching Santiago.

City of Culture of Galicia

Stepping into the City of Culture of Galicia, visitors find themselves transported into an awe-inspiring amalgamation of art, technology, and knowledge. Located on Mount Gaiás, this avant-garde architectural complex is a testament to Galicia's investment in preserving its cultural heritage while embracing the future.

Designed by renowned architect Peter Eisenman, the City of Culture is a true architectural marvel. Its design, an intricate maze of winding pathways and undulating roofs, draws inspiration from the medieval streets of Santiago de Compostela. Covering a vast area, the complex houses several key buildings including the Museum of Galicia, the Library of Galicia, and the Galician Archive.

Each visit to the City of Culture offers a unique experience. From exploring Galician history at the museum to admiring panoramic views from the rooftop terraces, there's much to see and do. Art and technology enthusiasts will appreciate the regular exhibitions and workshops that promote innovation and creativity. Wear comfortable shoes as the area is extensive and involves some uphill walking. There is an on-site café where you can take a break and enjoy the impressive views of Santiago.

Mercado de Abastos

After the Santiago Cathedral, the Mercado de Abastos holds the title as the second most visited site in Santiago de Compostela. Bustling with activity, this vibrant market is the heartbeat of the city's culinary scene. Here, locals and visitors alike come to sample and purchase the region's fresh produce.

Housed within a series of granite buildings, the market boasts over 300 stalls selling a variety of goods. From the catch of the day to farm-fresh vegetables, local cheese, and Galician wine, the Mercado de Abastos is a haven for food lovers. The air is filled with the tantalizing aromas of fresh herbs, spices, and baked goods, stimulating the senses.

Perhaps the market's most unique feature is its 'Sea to Market' service. Customers can purchase seafood directly from the coast via video call, and the fresh catch is delivered to the market within hours. For an authentic taste of Galician life, a visit to the Mercado de Abastos is a must. Arrive early in the morning for the best selection. Don't miss the opportunity to try pulpo a la gallega (octopus Galician style), a local delicacy.

Alameda Park

The Alameda Park, located near the old town, is a verdant oasis offering a respite from Santiago's bustling streets. This beautifully manicured park has been a favourite among locals for centuries, serving as a tranquil space for relaxation, recreation, and social gatherings.

As you stroll along its leafy promenades, you'll discover a variety of flora, charming fountains, and sculptures, including the iconic 'Two Marias' statue. From the park, you can also enjoy stunning views of the Santiago Cathedral, particularly from the Paseo de la Herradura, a popular viewpoint.

Whether you're keen on a leisurely walk, a picnic, or simply people-watching, Alameda Park provides the perfect setting. Its tranquillity, combined with its accessibility, make it a cherished part of Santiago's urban landscape. Don't forget to pack a picnic and a book. The park's benches and lawns provide perfect spots for a leisurely lunch and a relaxing afternoon.

Day Trip to Cape Finisterre

Venturing out of Santiago de Compostela for a day trip to Cape Finisterre promises an experience like no other. Hailed as the 'End of the World' by the Romans, this striking cape juts out into the vast Atlantic Ocean, offering a setting of remarkable solitude and profound depth.

The journey to Cape Finisterre navigates through the idyllic Galician countryside, abundant with quaint hamlets and the region's signature undulating landscapes. Upon reaching the cape, one is met with unending views of the expansive ocean, a sight that's particularly spellbinding during sunset.

The lighthouse perched on the cliff adds to the dramatic scenery, standing as a beacon at the edge of the known world. Remember to bring along some warm clothing, as the cape can get windy, regardless of the season. Also, if time permits, pay a visit to the nearby town of Finisterre, known for its seafood cuisine.

The Old Quarter

Immersing oneself in the Old Quarter of Santiago de Compostela is akin to stepping back in time. This historic heart of the city, marked by narrow, winding alleys, atmospheric plazas, and venerable buildings, hums with the echoes of yesteryears.

Recognised as a UNESCO World Heritage Site, the Old Quarter serves as an open-air museum, laying out Santiago's rich cultural and historical narrative. Each square within the quarter emanates a unique allure, inviting exploration and discovery.

Walking is undoubtedly the best way to experience the Old Quarter. Be sure to explore the numerous hidden courtyards, shops selling local crafts, and traditional tapas bars. And don't miss the chance to attend the Pilgrim's Mass at the Cathedral if it coincides with your visit.

The University

The University of Santiago de Compostela, one of the oldest and most prestigious universities in Spain, stands as a monument to the city's long-standing scholarly tradition. Its sprawling campus is an amalgamation of stately historic buildings and modern facilities, reflecting the institute's seamless blend of tradition and innovation.

As you walk through its corridors and courtyards, you are treading the same path as countless scholars and intellectuals who have contributed significantly to various fields over the centuries. The university's library, in particular, is a treasure trove of knowledge, housing an impressive collection of books and manuscripts.

Visitors are welcome to tour the university grounds and buildings. Try to plan your visit during one of the many cultural events or academic conferences that the university hosts. These events often provide intriguing insights into Spain's academic culture and offer a chance to interact with the students and faculty.

The Way of St. James

The Camino de Santiago, or the Way of St. James, is not just a route leading to the Santiago de Compostela Cathedral, it is a transformative journey etched with personal discoveries, camaraderie, and spiritual growth. A tradition stretching back to the Middle Ages, this pilgrimage remains a vital part of the city's identity.

The experience of walking the Camino is as varied as the pilgrims themselves, with paths winding through mountains, plains, and villages, each providing a unique perspective on the Spanish landscape. Completing the pilgrimage, whether for religious, personal, or cultural reasons, often instills a sense of accomplishment and reflection.

For those considering embarking on the Camino, it's important to prepare both physically and mentally. Be sure to pack light, bring comfortable shoes, and have a clear understanding of the route you intend to follow. And remember, the Camino is as much about the journey as it is about the destination.

Hostal dos Reis Católicos

When it comes to unique accommodations, the Hostal dos Reis Católicos takes the crown. Situated in the Praza do Obradoiro, opposite the Santiago de Compostela Cathedral, this five-star hotel holds the distinction of being the oldest hotel in the world. Originally constructed in 1499 as a hospital to tend to the weary pilgrims journeying along the Camino de Santiago, it has now been transformed into a luxurious hotel that still retains its historical charm. The facade of the building is an exquisite example of Plateresque style, and the four courtyards within provide a peaceful retreat.

Staying at the Hostal dos Reis Católicos is like stepping back in time, with each room boasting its own unique features. While booking a room here might be a bit of a splurge, even if you're not staying overnight, consider dining at their restaurant for a taste of Galician cuisine in an atmospheric setting.

Santiago Cuisine

An integral part of Santiago's charm lies in its gastronomy. The city offers a palette of flavors that reflect the region's agricultural wealth and coastal bounty, combined with time-honored culinary traditions. When it comes to food in Santiago, you are in for a feast of Galician cuisine.

Seafood is a standout feature of Galician cuisine, with dishes like Pulpo a la Gallega (octopus with paprika and olive oil), and shellfish prepared in various ways. Meat lovers can delight in the hearty Galician stew (Caldo Gallego) and the famed Ternera Gallega, a top-quality local beef.

Empanadas Gallegas, savory pies with various fillings, are also a popular local staple. For dessert, Santiago is famous for its Tarta de Santiago, an almond cake typically adorned with the cross of Saint James. This sweet treat is the perfect accompaniment to a cup of coffee in one of the city's cozy cafes.

Tapas bars and restaurants are plentiful in the Old Quarter, offering a lively dining scene. Tasting your way through the city is a delightful experience in itself. However, for those interested in a more hands-on approach, consider joining a cooking class or a food tour to delve deeper into the local cuisine.

It is also worth noting that Galicia is a renowned wine-producing region. While in Santiago, don't miss the chance to sample local wines, particularly the Albariño, a white wine known for its aromatic, fresh character. For a more immersive experience, consider visiting one of the many vineyards in the region.

In Santiago, every meal has the potential to turn into a culinary journey, celebrating the region's abundant produce and the Galicians' passion for food. Whether it's enjoying tapas with new-found friends or savoring a leisurely meal in a fine dining restaurant, Santiago's gastronomy is sure to leave a lasting impression.

Final Thoughts

In Santiago de Compostela, every stone tells a story, every street leads to a discovery, and every journey, regardless of its starting point, seems to find its conclusion. This ancient city, nestled in the green heart of Galicia, is a symbol of perseverance, spirituality, and the constant dialogue between the past and the present.

Wandering the streets of Santiago's old town is like stepping back in time. Its centuries-old buildings, each more captivating than the last, coexist harmoniously with lively bars, boutique shops, and modern cultural institutions. Every corner of this UNESCO World Heritage site offers an opportunity to delve deeper into the rich tapestry of Galician history and culture.

Beyond the city's historical and religious landmarks, Santiago de Compostela also offers a range of modern amenities and experiences. The Auditorio de Galicia, located in the Vista Alegre Park, regularly hosts concerts and other cultural events. For shopping enthusiasts, the area around the Rua do Franco offers a blend of local and international shops, along with several unique Galician crafts boutiques.

For nature enthusiasts, Santiago's numerous parks and green spaces provide a welcome respite from the hustle and bustle of city life. The Park of San Domingos de Bonaval, located on a hillside, offers great views over the city and houses the Museum of the Galician People. Similarly, a walk along the Sar River offers a quieter, more natural perspective of Santiago.

Whether you're here to embark on the spiritual journey of the Camino de Santiago, explore the depth of Galician culture, or simply enjoy the city's unique blend of history and modernity, Santiago de Compostela offers an experience like no other. Its compelling blend of the sacred and the secular, the ancient and the contemporary, the cultural and the natural, ensures that there is something for every traveler.

To truly capture the essence of Santiago, take the time to sit in one of its plazas, sip on a glass of Albariño, and watch as pilgrims of all walks of life conclude their journey. This simple yet profound experience encapsulates what Santiago de Compostela is all about: a city where journeys end, memories begin, and the spirit of the Camino lives on.

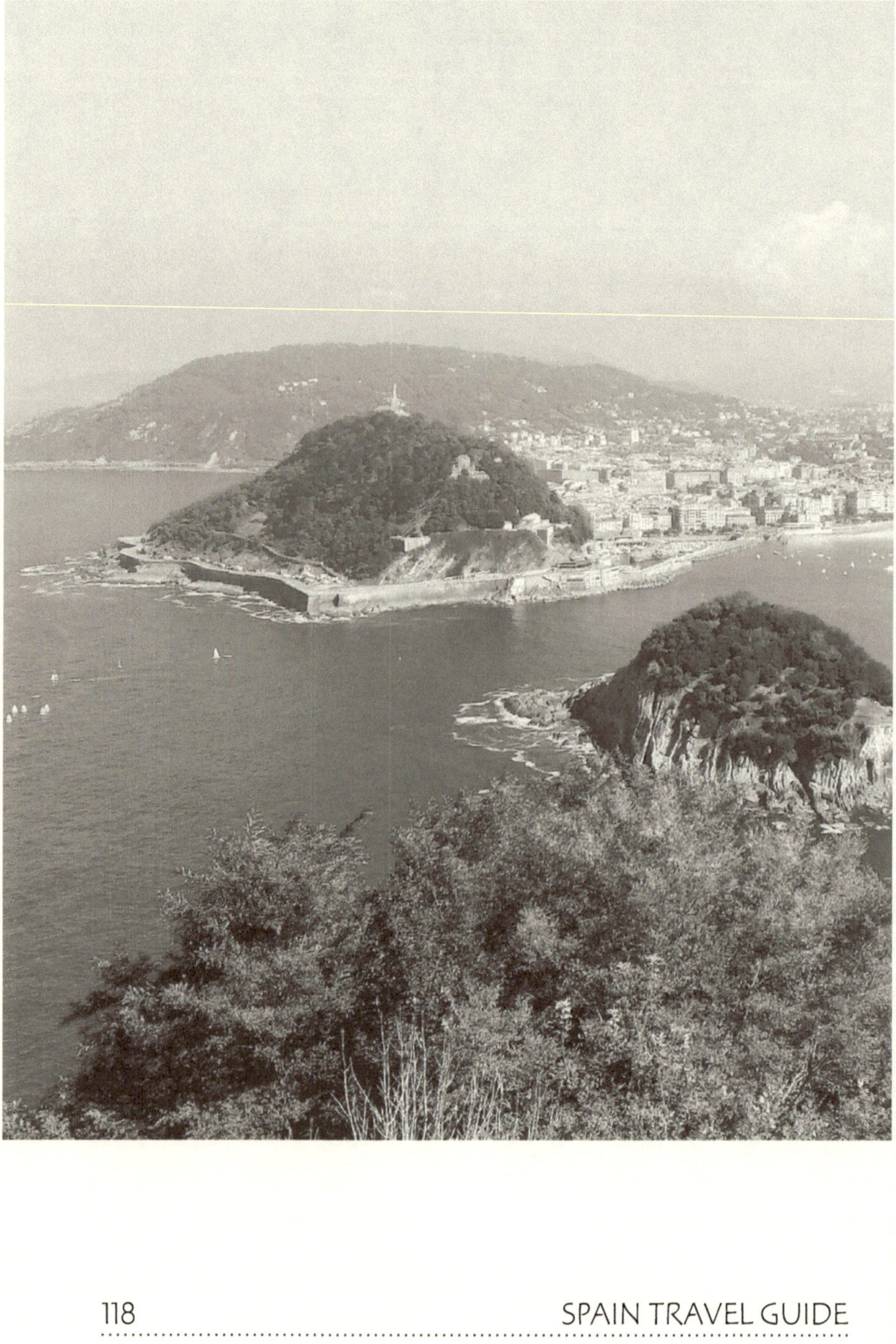

CHAPTER 8: SAN SEBASTIÁN

CHAPTER 8:
San Sebastián

San Sebastián, or Donostia as it's known in the Basque language, is the embodiment of sophistication and charm. Nestled on the northern coast of Spain, this elegant seaside city harmoniously combines natural beauty with cultural dynamism, making it a captivating destination for travelers worldwide. With its stunning Belle Époque architecture, pristine sandy beaches, and world-class culinary scene, San Sebastián is undoubtedly the pearl of the Basque Country.

One of the city's most captivating features is its stunning natural setting. Framed by the crystal-clear waters of the Bay of Biscay and encircled by lush, rolling hills, San Sebastián's scenery is a feast for the eyes. The city is perfectly situated for exploring the broader Basque region, with its dramatic landscapes, ancient traditions, and unique language.

At the heart of San Sebastián lies its Old Town, or Parte Vieja, a bustling hub teeming with narrow alleys, centuries-old buildings, and a plethora of pintxos bars serving up the region's delicious cuisine. Here, history reverberates through the walls, from the imposing Baroque facade of the Basilica of Saint Mary of the Chorus to the quaint charm of Constitution Square.

Yet, San Sebastián is not a city that rests on its historical laurels. It has also positioned itself as a modern cultural capital. Whether you're exploring the cutting-edge exhibitions at

Tabakalera Contemporary Culture Centre, catching a film at the prestigious San Sebastián International Film Festival, or simply strolling through the vibrant streets soaking in the atmosphere, the city pulsates with cultural energy.

Despite all its natural and cultural wealth, what truly sets San Sebastián apart is its status as a gastronomic powerhouse. With more Michelin stars per capita than almost anywhere else in the world, it's a veritable paradise for food lovers. But whether you're dining in a high-end restaurant or enjoying pintxos at a local bar, the emphasis is always on quality, local produce, and the celebration of Basque culinary traditions.

In summary, San Sebastián is a city that effortlessly captures the imagination. Its blend of natural beauty, historic charm, cultural vitality, and culinary prowess makes it a must-visit destination. Whether you're a nature lover, history buff, culture vulture, or foodie, San Sebastián has something special to offer you. Now, let's delve deeper into what makes this Basque gem truly shine.

La Concha Beach

Often cited as one of the world's most beautiful urban beaches, La Concha Beach is an iconic part of San Sebastián. Its name, meaning "The Shell" in Spanish, perfectly describes its crescent-shaped coastline, framing the azure waters of the Bay of Biscay. Lined with white sand and punctuated by the scenic Santa Clara Island in the bay's center, the beach offers postcard-worthy views at every turn.

La Concha is perfect for a range of beach activities, from sunbathing and swimming to paddleboarding and kayaking. The beach is known for its calm, clear waters, thanks to the protective presence of the Santa Clara Island and the two montes—

Monte Igueldo and Monte Urgull—that flank it. The picturesque promenade running alongside the beach is perfect for leisurely strolls, with several cafes and ice cream parlors en route. When planning your visit to La Concha Beach, keep in mind that it can get quite crowded during the summer months, especially in August. Arriving early in the day can help you secure a good spot. Also, don't forget to explore the charming gardens of Miramar Palace located nearby, offering an elevated view of the beach.

Old Town

San Sebastián's Old Town, or Parte Vieja, is a maze of narrow, winding streets, packed with historic buildings, vibrant pintxos bars, and specialty shops. This compact neighborhood is the city's beating heart, where the past meets the present in a dynamic fusion of history, culture, and gastronomy.

The Old Town is home to some of the city's most iconic landmarks, including the robust San Vicente Church, considered the oldest in the city, and the Constitution Square, previously a bullfighting arena. The square's balconies still bear numbers from the time when spectators would rent them for viewing the bullfights.

Exploring the Old Town is best done on foot, meandering through its pedestrian-friendly streets and taking in the atmosphere. Be sure to try the renowned pintxos—small snacks traditionally skewered to a slice of bread—in the many bars that line the streets. For a different perspective of the area, consider joining a guided tour, which will offer insights into the rich history and culinary traditions of the Old Town.

Monte Igueldo

Monte Igueldo offers the most breathtaking panoramic views of San Sebastián. Rising majestically at the western end of La Concha Bay, this hill serves as a fantastic viewpoint, overlooking the city's charming urban layout, the sparkling bay, and the surrounding verdant hills.

At the top of Monte Igueldo, you'll find an old-fashioned amusement park with vintage rides and attractions that have been enchanting visitors for over a century. However, the real draw is the hill's vantage point, from where you can capture spectacular photos, especially at sunrise or sunset.

To reach the top of Monte Igueldo, you can take the charming old funicular railway, which has been in operation since 1912. The journey itself is a delightful experience, offering increasingly impressive views as you ascend. Remember to pack a picnic to enjoy at the summit, and, of course, don't forget your camera to capture the unforgettable vistas.

San Sebastián International Film Festival

Every September, San Sebastián transforms into a bustling film capital as it hosts the prestigious San Sebastián International Film Festival. Established in 1953, this event is one of the most important film festivals in the world, alongside Cannes, Venice, and Berlin, and has become a significant platform for showcasing Basque, Spanish, and Latin American films.

The festival brings together a constellation of stars and industry professionals who gather for the celebration of cinema. From premieres and screenings to workshops and parties, the festival is a vibrant affair, illuminating the city with its glitz and glamour.

If you're planning to attend the San Sebastián International Film Festival, it's recommended to book your tickets and accommodations in advance as the city becomes particularly busy during this period. Additionally, take the opportunity to explore the iconic venues of the festival, such as the Kursaal Congress Centre and Auditorium and the Victoria Eugenia Theatre, both architectural masterpieces in their own right.

San Telmo Museum

The San Telmo Museum serves as a treasure trove of Basque culture and history. Housed in a 16th-century Dominican convent, with a modern extension that seamlessly merges the old with the new, this museum provides a comprehensive overview of the Basque Country's rich heritage.

Inside, you'll find a vast collection that spans prehistory to the present, featuring artifacts, artworks, and multimedia displays. The museum's exhibitions offer fascinating insights into the Basque people's traditions, language, and way of life, as well as the region's natural history.

When visiting the San Telmo Museum, take your time to explore the exhibitions thoroughly. The museum offers audio guides and has plenty of explanatory panels, most of which are translated into English. Also, don't miss the chance to appreciate the building itself, especially the contemporary wing designed by the architects Nieto Sobejano, which is a masterpiece of modern architecture.

Day Trip to Pasaia

A short drive or a scenic boat ride east of San Sebastián will take you to Pasaia, a charming coastal town steeped in maritime tradition. Nestled in a narrow fjord-like bay, Pasaia is composed of four districts, each with its unique character. Donibane and San Pedro, located on opposite sides of the bay, are particularly worth visiting.

The town is known for its well-preserved historic architecture, vibrant fishing port, and the Albaola Sea Factory, where visitors can watch the construction of historical ships using traditional methods. Literary enthusiasts will also enjoy visiting the house-museum of the French author Victor Hugo, who was enchanted by Pasaia during his visit in 1843.

A day trip to Pasaia offers a wonderful opportunity to immerse yourself in authentic Basque maritime culture. Remember to try the town's excellent seafood, particularly the txipirones (squid) and bacalao a la pasaitarra (cod in a local sauce). For an unforgettable experience, consider the boat ride back to San Sebastián at sunset when the views of the coastline are especially enchanting.

La Bretxa Market

The vibrant La Bretxa Market offers a tantalizing window into the culinary world of San Sebastián and the Basque Country. Located in the Old Town, the market is housed in a historic building that combines 19th-century architecture with modern additions.

Stroll through the bustling aisles and you'll encounter a plethora of fresh, locally-sourced produce: from colourful vegetables and ripe fruits to a range of meats and the freshest seafood. You can also find artisan cheeses, olives, spices, and a range of local delicacies. Upstairs, there are shops selling clothes and household goods.

Visiting La Bretxa Market is an experience, and taking the time to explore its offerings will provide you with a vivid understanding of Basque gastronomy. To get the best produce, try to arrive in the morning when the market is busiest. And don't forget to pick up some local delicacies to enjoy later or as unique edible souvenirs from your visit.

Peine del Viento

The Peine del Viento, or the Wind Comb, is one of San Sebastián's most iconic landmarks. Located at the foot of Monte Igueldo, this remarkable sculpture is the work of Basque artist Eduardo Chillida and architect Luis Peña Ganchegui. It comprises three iron sculptures, firmly anchored to the rocks, braving the relentless waves and wind.

The artistic creation, with its dramatic play of nature and art, embodies the spirit of the Basque Country. The sculptures also serve as vents for an underground network of tunnels, which, when hit by the waves, create a unique symphony of sounds and a spectacle of water sprays.

Visiting the Peine del Viento at different times of day offers varying experiences; however, the dramatic view of the sculpture against the sunset is particularly memorable. There are also several cafes and restaurants nearby where you can enjoy a meal or a coffee while admiring the scenic views.

Miramar Palace

Perched atop a hill overlooking La Concha Bay, Miramar Palace is a symbol of the city's history and grandeur. The palace was designed in the late 19th century by the English architect Selden Wornum for the Spanish royal family, reflecting an English country house style that stands out among the predominantly Basque architecture of the city.

Surrounded by lush gardens, the palace offers breathtaking views of the city and the bay. Today, the building is owned by the city council and used for various cultural events, while the gardens are open to the public.

During your visit to the Miramar Palace, make sure to stroll around the beautiful gardens and enjoy the panoramic views. The palace is also located near the start of the scenic walk to the Peine del Viento, so consider combining the two visits. Also, the palace is most easily accessible by foot or bike, as parking can be challenging in the area.

Tabakalera

Situated in a restored former tobacco factory, Tabakalera is a hub for contemporary culture in San Sebastián. Today, this vast space is devoted to creation, training, and research into contemporary art across multiple disciplines - from visual arts and film to dance and performance arts.

The Tabakalera is more than just an art centre; it's a dynamic space that invites the public to interact with art and artists. It features exhibition halls, workshops, performance spaces, and a cinema specializing in independent films. There's also a library, a restaurant, and a café within the premises.

When you visit Tabakalera, take time to explore the rotating exhibitions, attend a performance or film screening, or even participate in a workshop. Check their website in advance to see what's on. And don't forget to visit the rooftop terrace, which offers panoramic views over San Sebastián.

San Sebastián Cuisine

Food in San Sebastián is not just a matter of sustenance, but a way of life. The city is renowned worldwide for its gastronomy, boasting more Michelin stars per square metre than any other city, save Kyoto, Japan. But the culinary culture here extends well beyond the upscale dining rooms of Michelin-starred restaurants.

The city's Old Town, known as Parte Vieja, is brimming with pintxos bars, serving up the Basque version of tapas. These bite-sized delights range from traditional offerings like anchovies and olives to miniature culinary masterpieces that showcase the creativity of local chefs. Pintxos bar hopping is a beloved local tradition and an experience not to be missed.

Seafood is a pillar of San Sebastián's cuisine, thanks to the city's coastal location. Local favourites include hake cheek, baby squid, and cod, typically cooked simply to let the quality of the ingredients shine through. Don't miss out on trying the famous Basque cheesecake, a creamy and caramelized delight that has gained global fame.

Another essential food experience in San Sebastián is dining at a txoko, or gastronomic society. These private clubs are places where members come together to cook, eat, and socialize. Some txokos open their doors to tourists for a truly local dining experience.

A visit to San Sebastián would not be complete without exploring the city's food markets. Here, you'll find the fresh, high-quality ingredients that form the basis of Basque cuisine. La Bretxa and San Martín markets are two of the most popular, offering a range of local produce, meat, and seafood.

In San Sebastián, food is a celebration of the city's culture, heritage, and the bounty of its surrounding land and sea. Whether you're savoring a pintxo at a bustling bar, indulging in a Michelin-starred meal, or picking up fresh produce at a market, you're participating in a culinary tradition that's at the heart of life in this Basque city.

Final Thoughts

As your journey through San Sebastián comes to a close, you'll likely find yourself captivated by the city's charming mix of natural beauty, cultural richness, and unparalleled gastronomic scene. The city's inherent sophistication extends beyond its refined architecture and high-end dining; it can be found in the rhythm of life along its sandy beaches, in its buzzing pintxos bars, and even in the quiet elegance of its tree-lined streets.

There is much more to explore in San Sebastián than could be encapsulated in this guide. From the aquarium that offers a glimpse into the marine life of the Bay of Biscay, to the numerous festivals like Jazzaldia, the city's international jazz festival, and Semana Grande, a week-long celebration filled with music, fireworks and traditional Basque sports.

Active travellers might enjoy surfing at Zurriola Beach, known for its excellent waves, or kayaking in the Bay of La Concha. Alternatively, consider cycling along the network of bike lanes that crisscross the city, offering an eco-friendly way to explore at your own pace.

When in San Sebastián, be sure to take the time to simply stroll along its streets, take in the architecture, and immerse yourself in its atmosphere. The charm of San Sebastián is as much in its everyday moments as it is in its landmarks. Visit the local markets, stop for a café con leche in a sun-drenched plaza, or simply watch the world go by from a bench on the promenade.

While this guide provides an overview of what San Sebastián has to offer, the true magic of the city lies in the unique experiences you'll stumble upon during your visit. So embrace the Basque way of life, indulge in the gastronomic delights, and let the spirit of San Sebastián captivate you.

San Sebastián is not just a destination, but a feeling – one that's sure to leave a lasting impression long after you've returned home. So here's to the memories you're about to create and the enchanting allure of San Sebastián – the sophisticated seaside city that's waiting to welcome you.

SPAIN TRAVEL GUIDE

CHAPTER 9: CÓRDOBA 133

CHAPTER 9:
Córdoba

Lying in the heart of Andalusia, Córdoba is a city that has seen the rise and fall of empires. A UNESCO World Heritage city, Córdoba is a captivating blend of cultures, a testament to its rich history as a centre of Roman, Moorish, and Christian civilizations. As you walk its narrow, winding streets, you'll feel the echoes of its past, reflected in the harmony of its architectural treasures and the spirit of its people.

Once the capital of the Islamic Emirate and then Caliphate in the Iberian Peninsula, Córdoba was a beacon of learning and culture, boasting an unprecedented mix of libraries, universities, and medical schools. This intellectual fervour has left its mark on the city, which, today, is an inspiring blend of the past and the present.

At the heart of Córdoba lies the Mezquita, an architectural marvel that encapsulates the city's cultural syncretism. Once a mosque, now a cathedral, the Mezquita is a tangible embodiment of Córdoba's layered history. But this is just one of many gems you'll find in Córdoba; the city is replete with historic landmarks, from the royal fortress of Alcázar de los Reyes Cristianos to the ruins of the Umayyad city of Medina Azahara.

Yet Córdoba is more than its monuments. It is a living city, pulsating with energy and colour. Each May, the city erupts in a riot of colours during the Festival de los Patios, when residents open their private courtyards, adorned with vibrant flowers, to the public. These courtyards, or patios, are another symbol of Córdoba's distinct culture, offering a unique blend of Arabic and Andalusian traditions.

Córdoba's charm extends beyond the city itself. Just a short trip away lies the Sierra de Hornachuelos, a natural park that offers a refreshing escape from the urban landscape. Here, you can explore lush Mediterranean forests, spot local wildlife, and even visit some of the charming rural villages nestled within the park.

A visit to Córdoba is a journey through history, a chance to experience the melting pot of cultures that have shaped its identity. Whether you're exploring its ancient landmarks, wandering through its picturesque patios, or indulging in the local cuisine, Córdoba promises an unforgettable journey into the heart of Andalusian culture.

The Mezquita

Stepping into the Mezquita of Córdoba is like traversing the history of Andalusian architecture in a single visit. Originally built as a Visigothic church in the 6th century, it was converted into a mosque following the Islamic conquest, and then transformed again into a Catholic cathedral in the 13th century. Its architectural style reflects this historical timeline, resulting in a unique fusion of Gothic, Islamic, and Renaissance elements.

The heart of the Mezquita is its expansive prayer hall, filled with a forest of red and white arches that create an optical illusion of infinite space. The mihrab, or prayer niche, is an intricately decorated masterpiece of Islamic art, contrasted by the towering Renaissance altarpiece that now dominates the centre of the building. Walking through this architectural marvel, one can't help but feel a sense of awe at the interplay of cultures.

To get the most out of your visit to the Mezquita, consider hiring a guide or downloading an audio guide, which can provide in-depth information about its history and architecture. The site can get crowded, especially during the peak tourist season, so aim for an early morning or late afternoon visit. Don't forget to take a moment to sit and absorb the unique atmosphere of this remarkable place.

Alcázar de los Reyes Cristianos

Córdoba's Alcázar de los Reyes Cristianos, or Castle of the Christian Monarchs, is a regal edifice that bears witness to some of the most pivotal moments in Spain's history. Built in the 14th century by Alfonso XI, it served as the primary residence of Ferdinand and Isabella, and it was here that they met with Christopher Columbus before his famous voyage to the New World. The Alcázar's austere military exterior belies the beauty that awaits within. Its stunning gardens, filled with ponds, fountains, and lush vegetation, provide a tranquil retreat from the city's hustle and bustle. The fortress itself houses a collection of Roman mosaics and sarcophagi, as well as the haunting Royal Baths, illuminated by star-shaped skylights.

When visiting the Alcázar, be sure to climb to the top of the towers for a panoramic view of Córdoba, with the Mezquita and the Guadalquivir River creating a picture-perfect backdrop. Try to time your visit to enjoy the gardens at sunset when they take on a magical glow.

Medina Azahara

Located on the outskirts of Córdoba, the ruins of Medina Azahara offer a glimpse into the opulence of the Umayyad Caliphate. Built in the 10th century by Caliph Abd ar-Rahman III, this once-magnificent city was a symbol of power and wealth, with its name meaning "The Shining City."

Today, the remains of the palaces, mosques, and administrative buildings are a poignant reminder of the city's former grandeur. Despite the ravages of time, you can still marvel at the detailed carvings, ornate arches, and intricate tilework that adorn the surviving structures. The site's museum provides valuable context and houses artifacts recovered during excavations.

A visit to Medina Azahara requires some planning. It's located about 8 km outside of Córdoba, and public transportation options are limited. It's best to visit with a tour or by car. The site is vast, so wear comfortable shoes, bring plenty of water, and allow enough time to explore. The panoramic views of Córdoba from the site are well worth the trip.

The Roman Bridge

Spanning the Guadalquivir River, the Roman Bridge of Córdoba is one of the city's most iconic landmarks. Originally constructed in the 1st century BC, it has been rebuilt and refurbished multiple times over the centuries, but it still retains its Roman foundation and historical charm. The 16 arches that support the bridge offer an impressive vista and have become a symbol of the city.

Strolling across the Roman Bridge is like taking a walk through time. You'll be treading the same path that Roman soldiers,

Moorish caliphs, and Christian monarchs once used. At the southern end of the bridge, you'll find the Calahorra Tower, a fortified gate that now houses a museum dedicated to Andalusian history.

The bridge offers stunning views of the Mezquita and the Alcázar, particularly during sunrise or sunset. Consider walking the bridge at different times of the day to experience the changing light and atmosphere. The bridge is pedestrianized, so take your time, soak in the sights, and perhaps pause for a photo or two.

The Courtyards

Córdoba's courtyards, or "patios," are an integral part of the city's cultural identity and a delightful spectacle for visitors. These private spaces are lovingly adorned with a profusion of colourful flowers and plants, creating a cool and fragrant haven amidst the city's narrow streets and whitewashed houses. The tradition of decorating patios dates back to Roman and Moorish times and is a unique aspect of Cordoban life.

The courtyards are particularly enchanting during the annual Festival de los Patios, held in May, when residents compete for the title of the most beautiful patio. During this time, many private homes open their doors to allow the public to admire their stunning floral displays.

If you're visiting outside of the festival period, several patios are open year-round. The Palacio de Viana, for example, boasts 12 magnificent courtyards. Do remember to respect the privacy of residents if you're peeking into private patios. It's also worth noting that the vibrancy and variety of the flowers can depend on the time of year.

Day Trip to the Sierra de Hornachuelos

For those craving a break from the city's architectural wonders, a day trip to the Sierra de Hornachuelos Natural Park provides a refreshing change of scenery. Located around an hour's drive from Córdoba, this expansive park is one of the largest protected areas in Andalusia, with landscapes ranging from lush forests and tranquil lakes to rugged cliffs and rolling meadows. The park is home to an impressive array of wildlife, including deer, wild boars, and a variety of bird species, making it a haven for nature lovers. There are numerous trails to explore, catering to hikers of all levels, as well as picnic spots and recreational areas for those who prefer a more leisurely pace.

To reach the Sierra de Hornachuelos, you'll need to rent a car or join a tour, as public transport options are limited. Make sure to pack water, snacks, and a map of the park, as some areas can be quite remote. And, of course, don't forget your camera to capture the park's serene beauty.

The Jewish Quarter

The Jewish Quarter, or "Judería," is one of Córdoba's most fascinating districts. This labyrinth of narrow, winding streets and flower-filled courtyards is steeped in history and offers an intimate glimpse into Córdoba's multicultural past. The quarter dates back to the Middle Ages when it was the center of Jewish life in the city.

Key points of interest within the Jewish Quarter include the ancient Synagogue, one of the few surviving examples in Spain, and the Sephardic House, a museum dedicated to preserving the legacy of the Sephardic Jews. Strolling around, you'll also find delightful artisan shops, traditional taverns, and small plazas.

While exploring, keep an eye out for the statue of Maimonides, a revered Jewish philosopher born in Córdoba. His teachings continue to inspire scholars worldwide. The Jewish Quarter is best explored on foot, allowing you to fully appreciate its unique atmosphere. It's easy to get lost, but that's part of the charm—every corner reveals a new surprise.

Córdoba Synagogue

Córdoba's Synagogue, located in the heart of the Jewish Quarter, stands as a poignant reminder of the city's Sephardic heritage. Built in 1315, it's one of only three medieval synagogues remaining in Spain. While it's small in size, the building's historical and cultural significance is vast.

Inside, visitors can admire the intricate Mudejar plasterwork that adorns its walls, inscribed with Hebrew psalms and floral motifs. Although no longer used for worship, the synagogue's aura of tranquility and reflection remains palpable.

Visiting the synagogue is a sobering experience, providing a deeper understanding of Córdoba's multicultural history. It's a popular tourist attraction, so try to visit early in the day to avoid the largest crowds. Please remember to respect the sanctity of the space during your visit.

Calahorra Tower

Standing guard at the southern end of the Roman Bridge, the Calahorra Tower is one of Córdoba's most distinctive landmarks. Built by the Moors and later reinforced by Christian monarchs, it has served as a defensive structure, a prison, and even a girls' school throughout its long history.

Today, the Calahorra Tower houses the Museum of Al-Andalus Life, which showcases the rich cultural heritage of the region during the period of Muslim rule. Its exhibits cover a range of topics, from science and philosophy to art and daily life, offering a comprehensive insight into this influential era.

The tower's rooftop offers unparalleled views of the Roman Bridge and the Mezquita, making it a must-visit spot for photography enthusiasts. Consider timing your visit for sunset when the view is at its most magical. Be aware that there are many steps to reach the top, but the panoramic vistas are well worth the effort.

The Flower Street

Calleja de las Flores, or the Flower Street, is one of Córdoba's most picturesque spots. Tucked away in the historic center, this narrow, cobblestone alley is a feast for the eyes with its white-washed walls adorned with vibrant flowers in blue pots, echoing Andalusian tradition.

The end of the alley opens up to a small square with a fountain, from where you get a stunning view of the Mezquita's bell tower framed by a cascade of colorful blooms. The sight is particularly beautiful in spring, when the flowers are in full bloom.

Visit early in the morning or late afternoon to avoid the crowds and capture the best photographs. Also, don't forget to explore the surrounding area, which is full of charming shops, cafes, and other hidden alleys just waiting to be discovered.

Córdoba Cuisine

Córdoba's cuisine is a rich tapestry that mirrors its multicultural heritage. With influences from Roman, Arab, and Christian traditions, the local fare offers a gastronomic journey through time. Whether it's the traditional taverns, contemporary eateries, or bustling food markets, the city is a food lover's paradise, offering something to satisfy every palate.

Start with "salmorejo", a thicker, more robust cousin of gazpacho. This creamy, chilled tomato soup, topped with diced Spanish ham and hard-boiled eggs, is a classic Córdoba dish and the perfect antidote to the city's summer heat. Another quintessential local dish is "flamenquín", deep-fried pork or ham rolls that are a staple in the local tapas scene.

For the main course, indulge in "rabobull", a slow-cooked oxtail stew that's deeply comforting and incredibly flavorful. Alternatively, sample the "berenjenas con miel", or aubergines with honey, a delightful balance of savory and sweet that is sure to surprise your palate. Vegetarian and vegan visitors will also find plenty to enjoy, as many restaurants now offer plant-based versions of traditional dishes.

Sweet lovers, be prepared for a treat. Córdoba's dessert offerings, largely influenced by the city's Sephardic Jewish history, are exceptional. The "pastel cordobés", a puff pastry filled with sweet pumpkin jam, is a must-try. Other popular choices include "alfajores", a honey and almond sweet, and "pestiños", deep-fried pastries soaked in honey.

And then, of course, there is the region's excellent wine. Córdoba is part of the Montilla-Moriles denomination, known for its production of "fino", a dry, crisp white wine perfect for pairing with tapas. There are many bodegas (wine bars) where you can sample the local wines and sherries.

Eating in Córdoba is not just about the food, it's a cultural experience. It's about the joy of sharing a meal, the art of conversation, and the tradition of hospitality that is inherent in the Cordobese way of life. So take your time, savour each bite, and let the flavours of Córdoba take you on a journey of discovery.

Final Thoughts

As your journey through Córdoba comes to an end, you'll carry with you memories of a city that has seamlessly blended its Roman, Moorish, and Christian roots into a vibrant and harmonious present. Its cultural richness, architectural splendor, and culinary delights leave a lasting impression on all who visit. While the grandeur of the Mezquita, the beauty of the Alcázar, and the charm of the Flower Street represent the city's historical face, Córdoba also offers a modern, vibrant side. For a change of pace, explore the contemporary district around Tendillas Square, where you can shop for the latest Spanish fashions or enjoy a meal at a trendy rooftop restaurant with stunning views over the city.

Don't forget to visit the traditional craft workshops dotted around the city. These artisanal havens offer a range of beautiful, locally made products from ceramics and textiles to silverware and leather goods. These items make for perfect souvenirs, encapsulating the spirit and craftsmanship of Córdoba.

If you're visiting in May, do try to catch the Festival of the Patios. This unique cultural event, which sees the city's private courtyards turned into public art spaces, beautifully encapsulates the spirit of Córdoba. These floral displays, full of colour and aroma, are a delight for the senses and a testament to the city's enduring love for beauty.

Moreover, the city's position in the heart of Andalusia makes it an excellent base for exploring the region's natural beauty. From Córdoba, it's easy to take day trips to the Sierra de Hornachuelos Natural Park, the vineyards of Montilla-Moriles, or the historical towns of Écija and Priego de Córdoba.

Lastly, remember to embrace the laid-back rhythm of Córdoba. This is a city that invites you to wander through its cobbled streets, pause to listen to the strains of a flamenco guitar, and to enjoy a leisurely meal in a sun-dappled courtyard. Córdoba isn't just a city to be seen, but to be experienced. Take the time to breathe in its history, savour its flavours, and soak in its vibrant culture.

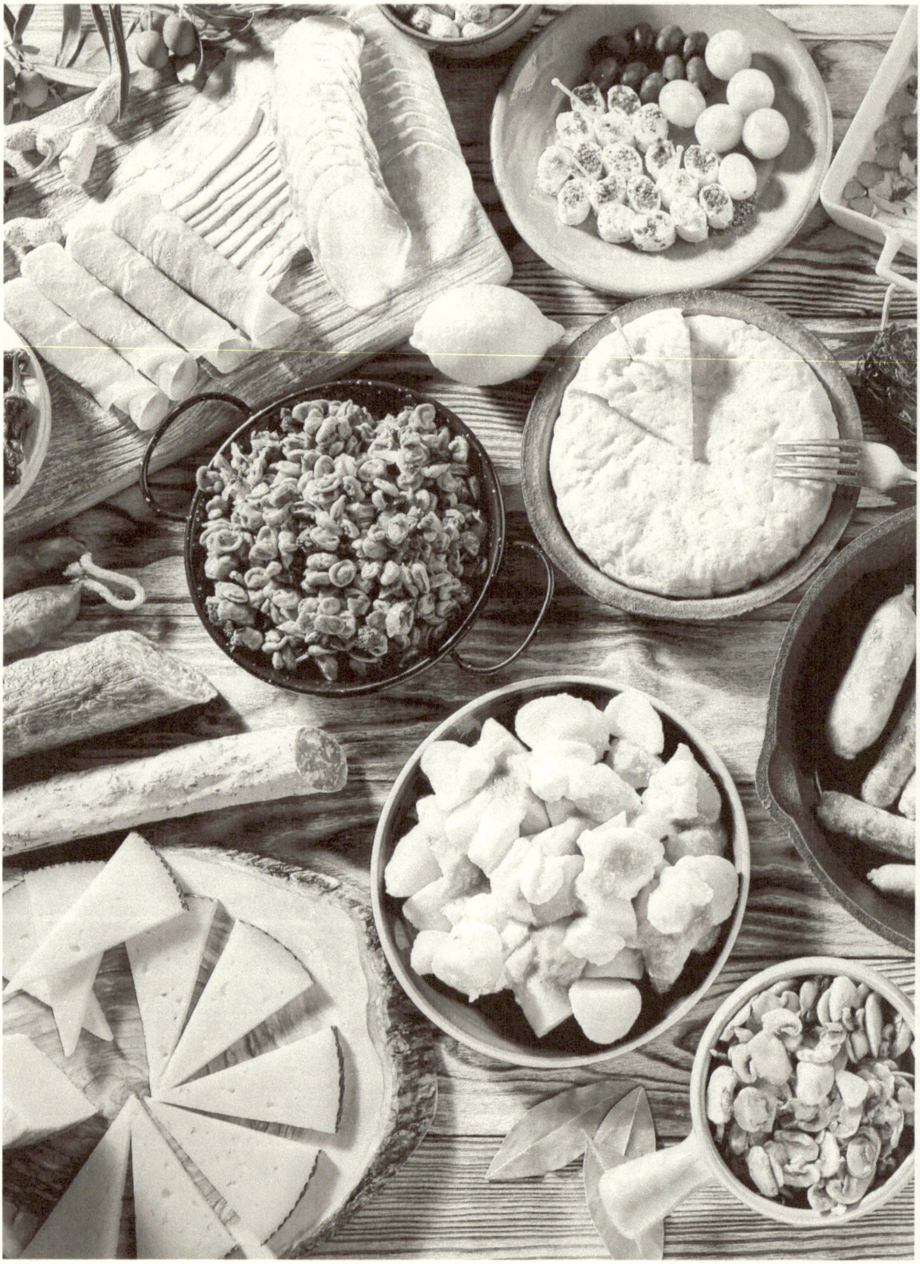

CHAPTER 10: SPANISH CUISINE 147

CHAPTER 10:
Spanish Cuisine

To understand Spain is to understand its food. Every bite into the country's rich and diverse culinary offerings is a glimpse into its history, culture, and spirit. From the sizzling paellas of Valencia to the hearty cocidos of Madrid, from the smoky paprika-laced chorizo of Extremadura to the fresh seafood of Galicia, Spanish cuisine is as diverse as the country's landscapes. Each region, with its unique geography and history, has contributed distinct flavours to the national palate. The lush green hills of the north have given us hearty stews and superb cheeses, while the sun-bathed southern regions are famed for their gazpachos and fried fish. The central plains, with their rich soils, provide grains, vegetables, and pulses, forming the backbone of many Spanish dishes.

Yet, there are common threads that bind these culinary traditions together. The love for fresh, locally-sourced ingredients, the mastery over simple yet bold flavours, the joy of communal eating, and an unwavering commitment to preserving age-old cooking traditions. These are the hallmarks of Spanish cuisine.

Spain's relationship with food goes beyond the kitchen. It's woven into the fabric of daily life. It's seen in the lively chatter around tapas bars, the quiet satisfaction of a well-made home-cooked meal, the yearly festivities revolving around food harvests, and the cherished tradition of the mid-afternoon siesta following a hearty lunch.

But Spanish cuisine is not stuck in the past. It is constantly evolving, with a new generation of chefs reimagining traditional dishes in exciting ways and integrating international flavours into their repertoire. This duality of the old and the new, the traditional and the innovative, adds another layer of complexity to the Spanish culinary scene.

Embarking on a culinary journey through Spain is a gastronomic adventure like no other. It's not just about discovering new flavours and dishes, but also about understanding a way of life. So sit back, tuck in your napkin, and prepare to savor the flavourful diversity of Spanish cuisine.

The Tapas Culture

Tapas, the small plates of food accompanied by a drink, are an integral part of Spanish culture. This tradition began in the Andalusian taverns as a simple slice of bread or meat placed over the glass to keep the flies out, hence the name 'tapa', which means lid. Over time, these edible covers evolved into a culinary tradition in their own right, showcasing a vast array of Spanish flavours.

Today, tapas are served in bars and restaurants throughout the country, and each region has its specialities. From olives, almonds, and chorizo in the south, to seafood, cheeses, and pinchos in the north, the variety of tapas is mind-boggling. They are not just food, but a social activity, a reason to get together and share moments.

For a genuine tapas experience, head to a local "tapería" or "cervecería" in any Spanish city or town. Many locals suggest "tapeo" or a "tapas crawl" - moving from bar to bar, trying out different tapas at each stop. Remember, the essence of tapas is not just about what you eat, but also about the lively company and conversation that comes with it.

Seafood

Given its extensive coastline and history of maritime exploration, it's no surprise that seafood holds a significant place in Spanish cuisine. From the cold Atlantic waters to the warmer Mediterranean Sea, each region contributes a variety of seafood to the Spanish table. Mussels, shrimp, octopus, sardines, and the prized bluefin tuna are just a few examples of the country's seafood bounty.

Paella, the famous rice dish from Valencia, often features a mix of seafood, such as prawns, mussels, and squid. In Galicia, a region known for its exceptional seafood, dishes like "pulpo a la gallega" (octopus with paprika) and "empanada de mariscos" (seafood pie) are popular.

For the freshest seafood experience, visit the coastal towns and cities where you can often eat seafood caught on the same day. You can also check out the seafood markets in major cities. For instance, Madrid's Mercado de Maravillas has a stunning range of seafood, despite the city's inland location. In Barcelona, the famous La Boqueria market offers a vibrant seafood selection amidst its bustling stalls.

Olive Oil

Olive oil is more than just a cooking ingredient in Spain—it's a way of life. Spain is the world's largest producer of olive oil, and the golden liquid is a staple in Spanish kitchens, used in everything from frying and baking to salad dressings and even desserts.

The country boasts several olive oil-producing regions, with Andalusia being the largest. Its Jaén province alone produces more olive oil than any other region in the world. Other notable areas include Catalonia, known for its Arbequina olives, and Extremadura, famed for its robust, peppery oils.

For olive oil enthusiasts, a visit to an olive oil mill or "almazara" offers a fascinating glimpse into the production process. Many mills also offer tastings, where you can learn to appreciate the various flavours and aromas of different oils. You can find these mills scattered across the olive-growing regions. Many Spanish supermarkets also have an impressive selection of local olive oils. Remember, when buying olive oil, look for "virgen extra" on the label, the highest quality category.

Traditional Dishes

Spanish cuisine is as diverse as its landscapes, and each region boasts its unique dishes steeped in tradition. In Valencia, Paella, a saffron-infused rice dish usually cooked with rabbit, chicken, and green beans, is a must-try. Equally famous is Andalusia's Gazpacho, a cold tomato-based soup perfect for hot summer days.

In the landlocked region of Castilla y León, you'll find Cocido Maragato, a hearty meat and chickpea stew, turned upside down, with meat served first. Madrid's winter staple, Cocido Madrileño, is another comforting chickpea-based stew with vegetables, meats, and sausages. Further north, in the Basque Country, the traditional dish is Bacalao a la Vizcaína, salt cod in a red pepper sauce.

One way to explore Spain's diverse food culture is to try these regional dishes in their places of origin. However, if traveling is not an option, many local restaurants throughout the country offer regional specialties. Furthermore, cooking classes are an enjoyable way to learn about these traditional dishes. Many cities offer culinary workshops where you can learn the secrets of Spanish cuisine and bring home a piece of this rich culinary tradition.

Spanish Wines

Spain is one of the world's leading wine producers, renowned for its diversity of wine styles and grape varieties. From the full-bodied reds of Rioja to the unique fortified wines of Jerez, Spanish wines offer something for every palate.

Rioja, Spain's most recognized wine region, produces excellent Tempranillo-based red wines known for their ageing potential. In contrast, Jerez de la Frontera in Andalusia is famous for Sherry, a unique fortified wine with styles ranging from the bone-dry Fino to the sweet Pedro Ximénez.

Whether you are a casual wine drinker or a serious oenophile, visiting a local "bodega" or wine cellar can be a memorable experience. Many wineries offer guided tours and tastings, giving visitors the opportunity to learn about the wine-making process and taste the finished product. Alternatively, wine shops and bars in most cities have a broad selection of Spanish wines. Don't hesitate to ask for recommendations—the Spanish are passionate about their wines and often happy to share their knowledge.

Spanish Cheeses

Cheese in Spain is deeply regional, with each area producing its own distinct varieties. Manchego, the most famous Spanish cheese, is a sheep's milk cheese from La Mancha. It's known for its firm texture and a flavor that ranges from mild to sharp depending on its ageing.

Other notable Spanish cheeses include Cabrales, a blue cheese from Asturias aged in natural caves, and Mahón, a cow's milk cheese from Menorca that can be enjoyed young or aged. In the Basque Country and Navarre, the slightly smoked Idiazábal made from sheep's milk is a traditional favourite.

Cheese shops and local markets are the best places to explore the diversity of Spanish cheeses. These venues often provide tastings, allowing you to discover your favourite. Also, consider visiting a local cheese festival, like the National Cheese Festival in Trujillo, Extremadura, where you can try a wide array of Spanish cheeses in one place. Lastly, when enjoying Spanish cheese, remember it pairs excellently with Spanish wines, creating a perfect gastronomic union.

Spanish Desserts

Spanish cuisine is known not only for its savory dishes but also for its delightful desserts. The national favorite is arguably Churros con Chocolate, a fried dough pastry served with a thick, rich dipping chocolate, often enjoyed for breakfast or a late-night snack. In Catalunya, the signature dessert is Crema Catalana, a creamy custard topped with a layer of hard caramel, similar to the French crème brûlée.

Further south, in Andalusia, you'll find Piononos, small sweet pastries typical of the province of Granada. Named after Pope Pius IX, these delicious cakes are traditionally caramelized on the outside, creamy on the inside, and often served with a dusting of powdered sugar on top.

To truly appreciate the array of Spanish desserts, visit local bakeries or 'pastelerías' where these sweet delicacies are freshly made. You can also sample a variety of these treats in most traditional Spanish restaurants. Alternatively, for those interested in honing their culinary skills, consider taking a cooking class specializing in Spanish desserts. It's a fun, engaging way to learn about the country's sweet traditions.

Spain's Food Markets

Spain's food markets are more than just places to shop; they're vibrant, bustling hubs where locals and tourists alike can experience the rich tapestry of Spanish cuisine. From the world-renowned Mercado de la Boqueria in Barcelona to the Mercado Central in Valencia, these markets offer an abundance of fresh produce, local specialties, and culinary delights.

Stalls brim with colorful fruits and vegetables, freshly caught seafood, artisan cheeses, and an array of cured meats, including the prized Jamón Ibérico. Many markets also feature tapas bars and food stalls, where you can enjoy freshly prepared meals made from ingredients sourced directly from the market.

Visiting a local food market is a must when traveling in Spain. It's a chance to see where the locals shop, learn about regional produce, and perhaps sample some culinary treats. Remember to respect local customs, such as waiting your turn and taking small amounts if you're sampling. And don't forget to bring a shopping bag - you never know what delicious goodies you might want to take with you!

Vegetarian and Vegan Options

While Spain is often associated with meat and seafood dishes, the country's culinary landscape has expanded over the years to cater to vegetarian and vegan diets. Many traditional Spanish dishes are plant-based, like Gazpacho and Pisto, a sort of Spanish ratatouille. Tapas bars often offer vegetarian options such as Pimientos de Padrón (fried green peppers) or Patatas Bravas (spicy potatoes).

Increasingly, cities like Madrid, Barcelona, and Valencia are witnessing a rise in vegetarian and vegan eateries, ranging from casual cafés to gourmet restaurants. In addition, many regular restaurants now offer vegetarian and vegan alternatives on their menus.

When dining out, don't hesitate to ask the staff for vegetarian or vegan options—they are usually accommodating and can recommend suitable dishes. For those looking to prepare their own meals, health food stores and local markets offer a variety of plant-based ingredients. Ultimately, even as a vegetarian or vegan, you can enjoy the gastronomic richness that Spain has to offer.

Sustainable Food Practices

In recent years, Spain has been undergoing a transformation in its approach to food production and consumption. More and more, sustainability and eco-consciousness are becoming integral to the country's culinary landscape. This shift is most noticeable in the surge of organic farming, with Spain leading Europe in organic vineyards and olive groves.

Spain's traditional practices, such as seasonality and the emphasis on local ingredients, align perfectly with sustainable food practices. The trend of "zero kilometer" dining, which promotes using locally sourced ingredients to reduce food miles, is gaining popularity in restaurants across the country.

When traveling in Spain, look for restaurants and markets that highlight local, seasonal, and organic products. Opting for such establishments not only supports local communities but also allows you to taste food at its freshest and most flavorful. You'll also find a growing number of organic stores and farmers markets, which are worth visiting to appreciate the variety and quality of Spanish produce.

Final Thoughts

Reflecting on the cuisine of Spain, it's evident that the country is not just a destination for the palate but also a journey into centuries-old traditions, the richness of diverse cultures, and a growing consciousness towards sustainability. The culinary experience is so integral to the Spanish lifestyle that to truly understand the country, one must dive headfirst into its food and drink.

The city of Seville, not previously mentioned in this chapter, is renowned for its vibrant food scene. The Triana Market, located in the heart of Seville's traditional Triana neighborhood, offers an array of Andalusian specialities. Also, remember to try the city's famous orange wine, a sweet and aromatic accompaniment to any meal.

Spanish cuisine, however, extends beyond the boundaries of mainland Spain. The Canary Islands, for instance, offer a unique culinary identity with dishes like "papas arrugadas" (wrinkled potatoes) served with mojo sauce, while the Balearic Islands are known for "sobrasada", a type of cured sausage.

Remember to be adventurous with your food choices. Whether it's sampling "morcilla" (blood sausage) in Burgos, trying the anchovies in Cantabria, or savoring the delectable Basque pintxos, each region offers something distinct and memorable. A trip to Spain, for the food lover, is like an interactive, open-air museum where you can taste history, culture, and the vibrant soul of Spain. So venture forth, armed with a curious palate and an adventurous spirit, to savour Spain's diverse and rich culinary landscape. Spain is truly a food lover's paradise.

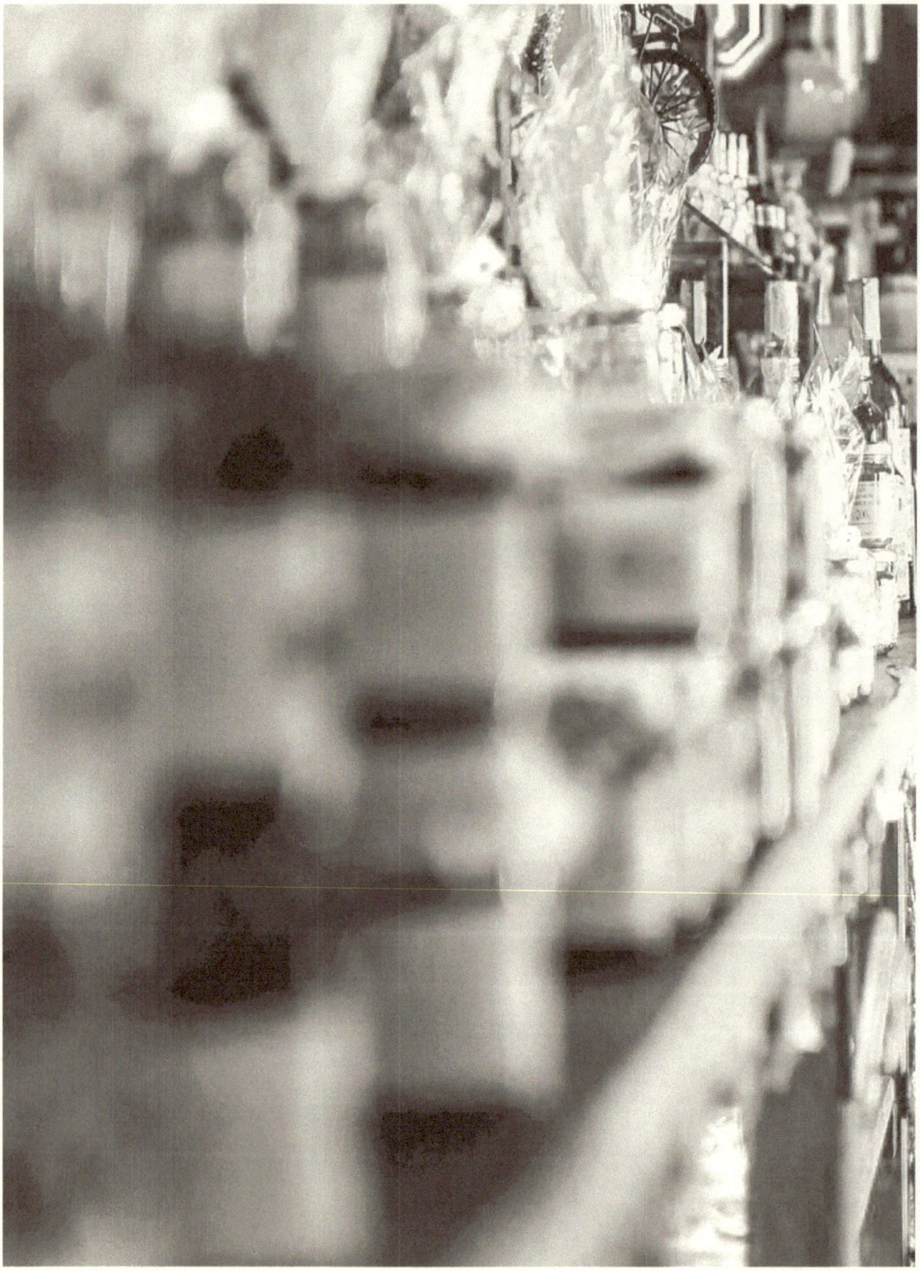

CHAPTER 11: HOW TO TRAVEL ON A BUDGET   161

CHAPTER 11:
How to Travel Spain on a Budget

Spain, a country brimming with world-renowned landmarks, captivating cultures, and delicious cuisine, doesn't have to be an expensive destination. With a bit of planning and some savvy choices, you can enjoy the Spanish charm without exhausting your wallet. From budget-friendly accommodations to affordable dining options, Spain offers numerous ways to explore the country on a budget.

Being conscious about your travel expenses doesn't mean skimping on experiences. Many of Spain's attractions can be explored inexpensively or even for free. Moreover, travelling on a budget often brings you closer to local life, as you explore traditional markets, eat where locals eat, and use public transportation.

The following sections provide practical tips and suggestions to help you plan your Spanish adventure on a budget. From finding affordable accommodation to savouring cheap local eats, these strategies will ensure your journey through Spain is economical yet still rich with experiences.

Budget Accommodation

Spain offers a wide range of budget-friendly accommodation options, which can significantly reduce your travel expenses. Hostels are an excellent choice for budget travellers. Not only do they offer inexpensive dormitory-style rooms, but they also often include amenities like communal kitchens where you can prepare meals, helping you save further on food costs.

Another economical accommodation option in Spain are "pensiones" or guest houses, which provide basic facilities at a reasonable price. They are often family-run and offer a more intimate and local experience compared to larger hotels.

For those who prefer more privacy, consider booking an apartment or a room through online platforms like Airbnb. This is especially cost-effective for longer stays or if you're travelling in a group. Always check the reviews and the location before booking to ensure it meets your needs and expectations.

Eating on a Budget

One of the joys of travelling in Spain is the country's delectable cuisine. Thankfully, enjoying Spanish food doesn't have to be expensive. Tapas bars are a perfect example of how you can eat well on a budget. In many places, especially in the southern region of Andalusia, a free tapa is still served with each drink you order.

Spain's food markets are another excellent option for cheap eats. Here you can sample a variety of local products without spending a lot. Some markets, like Madrid's Mercado de San Miguel or Barcelona's La Boqueria, even have bars and stalls serving prepared meals at a reasonable price.

Another tip to eat cheaply in Spain is to take advantage of the "menu del dia" or menu of the day. This is a set lunch, usually including a starter, main course, dessert, and a drink, often for under 15 euros. It's widely available in restaurants across the country, particularly on weekdays.

Public Transport

Spain's public transportation system is efficient, reliable, and can be a cost-effective way to navigate the country. In cities like Madrid, Barcelona, Valencia, and Seville, buses, trams, and metros form a comprehensive network that can take you just about anywhere you need to go. Many cities offer transport cards that provide unlimited travel for a specific time period, typically 24 hours, 48 hours, or a week, which can save money if you plan to use public transport frequently.

For intercity travel, Spain's long-distance bus network is extensive and often cheaper than trains or flights. Companies like ALSA operate routes across the country. If you prefer trains, consider booking in advance or travelling at less popular times to secure the best fares. Spain's high-speed AVE trains are more expensive, but regional trains offer a budget-friendly alternative. Cycling is another affordable way to get around, particularly in bike-friendly cities like Barcelona or Seville. Many cities have bike-sharing schemes, and rentals are typically reasonably priced. Just remember to wear a helmet and follow local traffic rules.

Free Attractions

Exploring Spain's rich cultural heritage doesn't have to cost a fortune. Many cities offer free or discounted entry to museums and monuments at certain times. For example, the Prado Museum in Madrid and the Picasso Museum in Barcelona both offer free entry during certain hours. It's worth checking the official websites of attractions for up-to-date information on admission fees and "free entry" hours.

Walking tours are a great way to see the city highlights without spending a lot. There are free walking tours available in many Spanish cities - these are typically tip-based, so you can pay what you feel the tour was worth.

Moreover, don't overlook the many free experiences Spain has to offer: strolling through the historic Barrio Gótico in Barcelona, exploring the vibrant street art in Madrid's Malasaña district, or watching a sunset from the beach in Costa del Sol. Sometimes, the best things in life really are free.

Budget Shopping

Spain offers various options for those looking to shop on a budget. Street markets are a great place to start. From clothing and accessories to vintage goods and antiques, you can find a wide variety of items at a bargain price. El Rastro in Madrid and Els Encants in Barcelona are among the country's most famous markets.

For affordable fashion, look no further than Spanish high-street brands like Zara, Mango, and Bershka. They often have sales, particularly during the summer and after Christmas, when you can score high-quality clothes and accessories at a discount.

Also, keep in mind that many cities in Spain have "Mercadillos" or weekly street markets where locals shop for fresh produce, clothes, and household items at lower prices. It's a fantastic way to blend in with the locals while hunting for deals. Lastly, remember that bargaining is generally acceptable at markets, so don't be afraid to negotiate the price!

Cheap Flight and Train Tips

In Spain, flying or taking a train can be a cost-effective mode of transport, particularly if you're traveling long distances or across the country. For flights, budget airlines such as Ryanair and Vueling offer competitive prices, especially if you can be flexible with your travel dates and book in advance. Keep an eye out for promotions and deals, and consider signing up for airlines' newsletters for exclusive offers.

For train travel, Renfe, the Spanish national train company, provides high-speed AVE trains connecting major cities like Madrid, Barcelona, and Seville. To get the best prices, try to book your tickets as soon as they're released (usually 60 days before departure), especially for popular routes. Also, consider traveling on less busy days or times, such as midweek or early in the morning, to get cheaper fares.

Discount Cards

Various cities in Spain offer discount cards, which can help you save money on attractions, public transport, and even dining. For example, the Barcelona Card offers free public transport and free or discounted entry to many of the city's top attractions. Similarly, Madrid's Tourist Card provides unlimited public transport and discounts on sightseeing tours, shows, and shopping.

Besides city cards, Spain also offers the Spain Pass for train travel, which allows a certain number of journeys within a set period, providing excellent value if you plan to travel extensively by train. Remember to compare the cost of the card with your planned activities to ensure it's worth the investment.

Off-Season Travel

Timing your trip wisely can save you a significant amount of money. Spain's peak tourist season is summer, particularly in coastal areas and popular cities. By traveling off-season (generally from October to April, excluding Christmas and Easter), you'll find lower prices on accommodation and flights, fewer crowds, and a more relaxed atmosphere.

Weather-wise, Spanish winters are relatively mild, and you can still enjoy plenty of sunshine in the south. For skiing enthusiasts, winter is the perfect time to hit the slopes in the Sierra Nevada or the Pyrenees, while autumn and spring are ideal for city trips or hiking adventures.

Final Thoughts

Traveling Spain on a budget does not mean missing out on the wonders this country has to offer. In fact, with careful planning and savvy choices, the vibrant cities, rich history, and diverse landscapes of Spain become an affordable reality. Don't forget to take advantage of Spain's delightful and affordable gastronomy, from tapas bars to local markets, where you can sample regional specialties without breaking the bank.

Remember that some of the best experiences are often free or low-cost - a walk through the historic quarters, a picnic in a beautiful park, a stunning sunset by the beach. So, embrace the adventure, for Spain is a country where priceless memories can be made, regardless of budget. With these tips in hand, the dream of a Spanish escape is well within your reach. Safe travels and enjoy every moment of your journey!

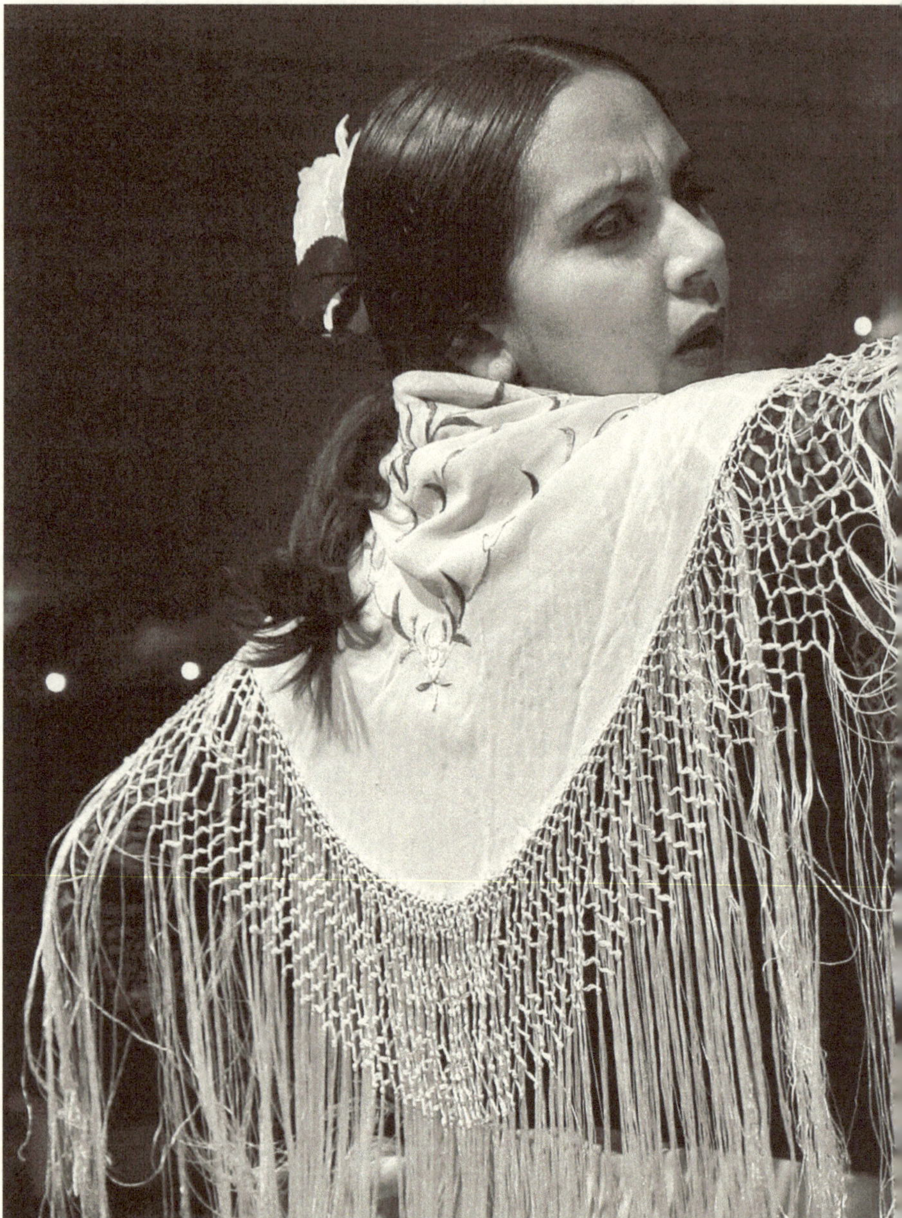

CHAPTER 12: 10 CULTURAL EXPERIENCES TO TRY

CHAPTER 12:
10 Cultural Experiences You Must Try in Spain

Embracing Spanish culture goes far beyond just visiting the sights; it's about experiencing the vibrancy and passion of Spain's traditions, arts, sports, and language. From the energetic flamenco performances and the national fervor of a football match to the nuanced flavours of Spanish wines and the country's rich artistic heritage, the Spanish culture is a lively tapestry of diverse and fascinating experiences.

Immerse yourself in the joy of Spanish festivals, filled with color, music, and a strong sense of community. Witness the controversy and tradition of bullfighting, an integral part of Spain's cultural fabric, despite the debates surrounding it. Explore the legacy of Spanish artists, whose masterpieces have left a lasting imprint on the world's art scene.

Take the opportunity to taste Spain's renowned wines in their native setting, learn about the nation's traditional crafts, and even attempt speaking Spanish. Each of these experiences offers a unique insight into the Spanish way of life, deepening your connection with the country and its people. So, let's embark on this exciting journey and explore some unforgettable cultural experiences in Spain!

1 - Flamenco Show

The pulsating rhythm of a flamenco show is an experience that captures the essence of Spain's passionate spirit. The rapid-fire footwork of the dancers, the soulful strumming of the guitar, and the powerful voice of the singer combine to create an atmosphere that's both electrifying and deeply emotional. Flamenco is not just a dance or a genre of music; it's an expressive art form that embodies the resilience, fervour, and vibrancy of the Spanish people.

Flamenco shows can be found all across Spain, but Andalusia, particularly the cities of Seville, Granada, and Jerez, is the birthplace and the heartland of flamenco. The tablaos (flamenco venues) here offer an intimate setting where the raw intensity of flamenco can be felt up close. Remember to book in advance as these shows are quite popular.

2 - Spanish Fiestas

Spanish fiestas are the epitome of Spain's exuberant culture, a splendid display of tradition, community spirit, and celebration. From the famous Running of the Bulls in Pamplona to the messy revelry of La Tomatina in Buñol and the fiery Las Fallas in Valencia, each fiesta has its unique character and allure, though all are equally vibrant and full of life.

The best way to enjoy a Spanish fiesta is to join in. Immerse yourself in the festivities, whether that means running ahead of a herd of bulls, tossing tomatoes at fellow revelers, or admiring the intricate ninots (statues) at Las Fallas. Each city and region has its own calendar of festivals, so be sure to check the local schedules when planning your visit.

3 - Bullfighting

Bullfighting, or la corrida, is one of the most traditional and controversial aspects of Spanish culture. To some, it's a captivating spectacle and an art form deeply rooted in Spanish history; to others, it's a contentious sport that raises ethical issues. Regardless of one's perspective, there's no denying the impact of bullfighting on Spanish culture.

Bullfighting season in Spain runs from March to October, with events taking place in bullrings across the country. The most famous bullring is Madrid's Las Ventas, a stunning Moorish-style arena. If you choose to attend a bullfight, be prepared for a display of dramatic theatre, skilled athleticism, and powerful emotions. However, be aware of the intense and, at times, graphic nature of the event.

4 - Spanish Art

Spain's art scene is as diverse and colourful as the country itself, boasting a rich history that has given rise to some of the world's most renowned artists. From the masterpieces of the Golden Age painters like Velázquez and El Greco to the modernist works of Picasso, Dalí, and Miró, Spanish art offers an eclectic array of styles and periods to explore.

Madrid's Golden Triangle of Art, consisting of the Prado Museum, the Reina Sofia Museum, and the Thyssen-Bornemisza Museum, is a must-visit for any art lover. However, Spanish art is not just confined to museums and galleries. The incredible architecture of Gaudí in Barcelona, the hauntingly beautiful cave paintings in Altamira, and the colourful murals in Valencia's street art district reflect the country's artistic spirit in every corner.

5 - Wine Tasting

Spain is a country of diverse landscapes, climates, and soils, a combination that makes it one of the world's top wine-producing countries. From the robust reds of Rioja and Ribera del Duero to the crisp whites of Rías Baixas and the sparkling cava of Penedès, Spanish wines are as varied as they are delicious.

The best way to appreciate Spanish wines is by visiting the country's numerous wine regions, where you can tour centuries-old vineyards, learn about the wine-making process, and, of course, sample the wines. Many bodegas (wineries) offer guided tours and tastings, often paired with local cheeses, hams, and other regional delicacies. Remember to book in advance, especially during the harvest season from September to October.

6 - Traditional Crafts

Craftsmanship in Spain is a testament to the country's rich cultural heritage. From pottery and ceramics to leather goods and lace, traditional crafts reveal the artistic skills passed down through generations. Whether it's the colourful ceramics of Talavera and Seville, the intricate lacework of Tenerife, or the elegant damascene work of Toledo, each region has its own distinctive craft traditions.

Visiting local workshops and artisan markets is an excellent way to discover and support these age-old crafts. It's not only an opportunity to buy unique souvenirs but also a chance to meet the artisans, learn about their craft, and understand the history and cultural significance of their work. Make sure to explore the local craft scene when visiting cities like Granada, Valencia, and Seville.

7 - Spanish Language

Speaking Spanish, or at least making an attempt to, can significantly enrich your travel experience in Spain. As the second most widely spoken language in the world, Spanish opens the door to a wealth of cultural experiences and interactions. Not only does it enable you to engage more deeply with the locals, but it also offers insights into the Spanish way of life.

There are many ways to immerse yourself in the language during your trip. Consider enrolling in a short language course or attend language exchange events in cities like Madrid and Barcelona. Don't hesitate to practice your Spanish at every opportunity, be it at a local mercado (market), a flamenco show, or during a friendly encounter at a tapas bar.

8 - Spanish Sports

Spain is a country where sports are deeply embedded in the culture. From the passion of a football match to the adrenaline of a bullfight, the Spanish love for sports is contagious and engaging. Football is undeniably the most popular sport, with top clubs like Real Madrid and Barcelona attracting millions of fans from around the world.

Attending a football match at one of Spain's famous stadiums, such as Camp Nou or Santiago Bernabeu, is an unforgettable experience, filled with energy and passion. If football isn't your thing, there are plenty of other sports events to check out, including the San Fermín running of the bulls in Pamplona or the Conde de Godó Tennis Tournament in Barcelona.

9 - Spanish Music

Spanish music is as varied and diverse as the country itself. From the passionate flamenco rhythms of Andalusia and the haunting tunes of Galician bagpipes to the lively indie scene of Madrid and Barcelona, Spanish music is a true reflection of the country's regional diversity and rich cultural history.

Experiencing live music in Spain is not to be missed. Attend a flamenco show in Seville, explore the vibrant nightlife and music scene of Madrid and Barcelona, or enjoy traditional Basque music in San Sebastián. There's also a host of music festivals throughout the year, catering to a wide range of musical tastes.

10 - Spanish Architecture

Spain's architecture is a captivating blend of diverse styles, reflecting the many cultures that have shaped the country's history. From the grandeur of Madrid's Royal Palace and Barcelona's stunning modernist buildings by Gaudí to the intricate Islamic designs of Granada's Alhambra and the avant-garde architecture of Bilbao's Guggenheim Museum, each city offers a unique architectural experience.

Taking a guided architectural tour can deepen your understanding of the historical and cultural contexts behind these architectural wonders. Also, don't miss the chance to explore Spain's less-touristy regions, such as Extremadura and Navarre, where you can discover Roman ruins, medieval fortresses, and charming rural architecture.

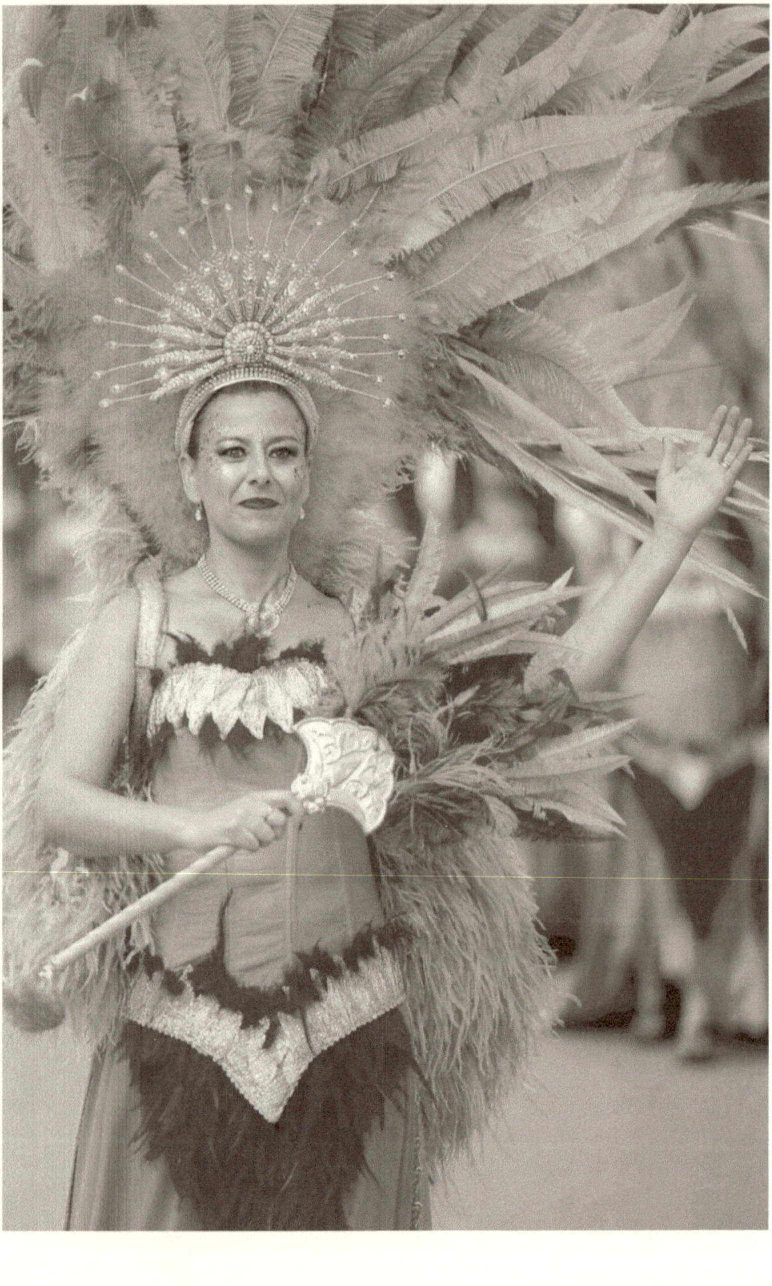

Conclusion

As we arrive at the conclusion of this guide, it's almost overwhelming to look back and reflect upon the vibrant tapestry that is Spain. Each region, each city, each tiny pueblo has its own unique allure, drawing us in with its distinct character and charm. But more than the sum of its individual parts, it's the overarching spirit of Spain - that irresistible zest for life - that truly captivates. Spain is more than a destination; it's a way of life, a sensory delight, an enchanting story written in the language of sunlit days and starry nights, reverberating Flamenco rhythms, and the warm, hearty laughter of its people.

Spain's allure is indeed intoxicating, but remember that the essence of travel isn't merely about checking off a list of sights or activities. It's about immersing yourself in the local culture, engaging with the people, and opening your senses to new experiences and perspectives. And Spain offers a myriad of opportunities for such meaningful engagements, whether it's sipping on a glass of smooth Rioja in a bustling tapas bar, soaking in the sacred aura of a centuries-old cathedral, or finding yourself lost in a cobblestoned alley adorned with vibrant ceramic tiles and hanging geraniums.

Remember that in Spain, it's not just about where you go; it's also about when you go. Time your visit to coincide with a local fiesta or a cultural event for an authentic experience that will leave a lasting impression. There's something happening all year round, from the raucous Tomatina in August and the passionate Semana Santa processions in April to the stunning fallas of Valencia in March and the vibrant Feria de Abril in Seville. These events offer an unparalleled opportunity to dive into Spanish traditions and customs, far beyond the usual tourist track.

Exploring Spain doesn't have to be an expensive affair. Embrace the local way of life to save money and enrich your experience. This could mean opting for a 'menú del día' at lunch, taking advantage of the free entrance times at many museums, shopping at local markets, or using public transport to get around. Don't hesitate to step off the beaten path - some of the most rewarding experiences often lie away from the main tourist routes.

As for the language, don't worry if you don't speak fluent Spanish. While learning a few basic phrases can go a long way in creating a connection with the locals, Spaniards are generally friendly and patient, even when faced with a language barrier. And who knows? You might find yourself picking up more Spanish than you expected by the end of your trip.

To help you along the way, here are some basic phrases that can be useful for any traveller in Spain:

- ¿Dónde está...? (Where is...?)

- ¿Cuánto cuesta? (How much does it cost?)

- ¿Habla inglés? (Do you speak English?)

- ¿Puede ayudarme? (Can you help me?)

- No entiendo. (I don't understand.)

- Estoy perdido/a. (I'm lost.)

- ¿Dónde está el baño? (Where is the bathroom?)
- ¿Podría ver el menú, por favor? (Could I see the menu, please?)
- Me gustaría... (I would like...)
- Gracias. (Thank you.)
- De nada. (You're welcome.)
- Por favor. (Please.)
- Disculpe. (Excuse me.)
- ¿Cómo se llama esto? (What is this called?)
- ¿Cómo llego a...? (How do I get to...?)

Remember, it's the effort and the intention to communicate that often matters more than perfect grammar or pronunciation. So don't be afraid to try out your Spanish - it's all part of the adventure!

Spain's culinary scene is a joy to discover, as much for the gourmet as for the casual food lover. Tapas hopping is a delicious and sociable affair, paella is a celebration in a pan, and the seafood, particularly in coastal regions, is simply out of this world. Remember that meal times in Spain are usually later than in many other countries, so adapt to the local rhythm to truly savour the gastronomic delights that Spain has to offer.

In Spain, art and culture aren't confined to museums or galleries; they're everywhere, in the flamboyant architecture, the age-old traditions, the passionate music and dance, and even in the way the Spanish enjoy their free time. Spain's cultural wealth is indeed astounding, and no matter how much time you spend here, there will always be something new to discover, to marvel at, to fall in love with.

Lastly, travel slow and savour every moment. Spain is not a place to be rushed. It's a place to linger over a leisurely lunch, to siesta in the shade of an olive tree, to stroll along a golden beach as the sun sets, to dance the night away under a sky full of stars. It's a place to live the moment, to feel the pulse of life, to breathe in the air of history and tradition, and to let the Spanish spirit seep into your soul.

With its rich cultural tapestry, mesmerizing landscapes, soul-stirring art and music, vibrant cities, and gastronomic delights, Spain promises an unforgettable travel experience. But remember, Spain isn't just a place to visit; it's a place to experience, to savour, and to love. So, pack your bags, bring an open heart, and embark on the Spanish adventure that awaits you. And as you set foot on Spanish soil, remember the words of the famous Spanish proverb: "Con paciencia y saliva, el elefante se la metió a la hormiga" - with patience and perseverance, you can achieve anything.

Here's to a journey of a lifetime in Spain, a journey that will linger in your heart and soul long after you've returned home.

PORTUGAL
Travel guide

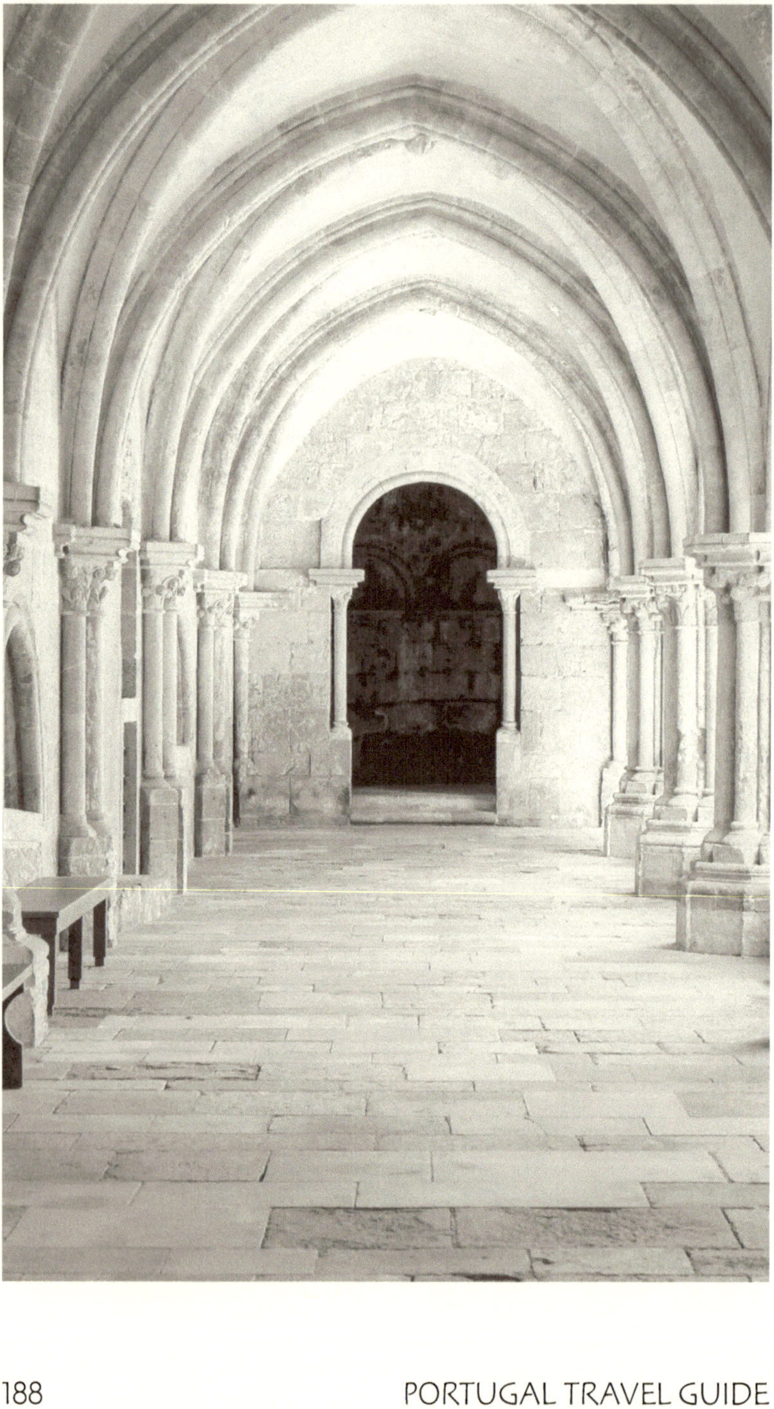

Introduction

Welcome, fellow traveler! Prepare to embark on a captivating journey through the unique allure and breathtaking beauty of Portugal, a land where the sun shines brightly on a tapestry of cultural and natural wonders. This guide aims to be your dependable and passionate travel companion, offering you an in-depth exploration of Portugal's diverse landscapes, rich history, vibrant culture, and unforgettable gastronomy.

At Journey Joy, we believe in the transformative power of travel. It's more than just visiting popular attractions or snapping photos. Traveling is about immersing oneself in the fabric of a place. It's about tasting the unique flavors of local cuisine, understanding the deep-rooted history, engaging with the warm locals, and embracing the lifestyle. We hold this belief close to our hearts as we've crafted this guide, hoping to not only inform you but also inspire you and ignite your wanderlust.

In the following chapters, we take you on an exploratory tour across the length and breadth of Portugal. We'll wander through bustling city streets and tranquil vineyards, explore centuries-old monuments and modern hubs of creativity, savor mouth-watering delicacies and world-renowned wines, and bask in the beauty of natural landscapes that leave one awe-struck.

Our journey begins in Lisbon, Portugal's radiant capital city, where the past and present interweave seamlessly against a backdrop of seven cinematic hills. Next, we sail north to the invincible city of Porto, a UNESCO World Heritage site, steeped in rich history and renowned globally for its signature Port wine.

Leaving the mainland, we'll navigate to the mesmerizing Atlantic islands of Madeira and Azores. These paradisiacal islands boast a unique blend of natural beauty and distinct culture, from the flower-laden streets of Funchal to the azure lakes and green pastures of Azores.

Heading south, we soak up the sun in the Algarve region, famed for its golden beaches, striking cliffs, and charming towns. This is a haven for those seeking sun, surf, and serene natural beauty. Beyond the coastal charm, we delve into the heart of Portugal, exploring the historical wonders of Évora and the pastoral tranquility of Alentejo. We'll immerse ourselves in academia in Coimbra, a city renowned for its ancient university, and uncover the ancient heritage of Braga and Guimarães, cradles of Portugal's rich past.

Our journey then weaves through the verdant vine-covered slopes of the Douro Valley, where the art of wine-making is as old as the culture itself. Here, the landscapes narrate a story of dedication, passion, and meticulous craftsmanship.

Portugal's cuisine is a symphony of flavors that reflects its diverse culture and geography. In a dedicated chapter, we'll dive into Portugal's culinary world, exploring everything from its emblematic bacalhau to its irresistible pastries and artisanal cheeses.

Are you a budget-conscious traveler? We've devoted a chapter to provide insightful tips and suggestions to experience the best of Portugal without straining your wallet. We cap off our journey with a selection of ten must-try cultural experiences, presenting a profound way to connect with Portugal's soul and embrace its vibrant way of life.

Each chapter of this guide is designed to be comprehensive yet engaging, filled not only with practical information but also interspersed with local tips, insightful anecdotes, and motivational prompts. Whether you are actively planning your Portuguese sojourn or simply dreaming of Portuguese landscapes, we hope this guide brings you one step closer to your journey and sparks joy and excitement in anticipation of the adventures that await.

So, buckle up, sit back, and let us navigate as we embark on this enchanting journey through the sights, sounds, flavors, and soul of Portugal. Here's to embracing the unexpected, cherishing the journey, and falling in love with Portugal, with love from Journey Joy!

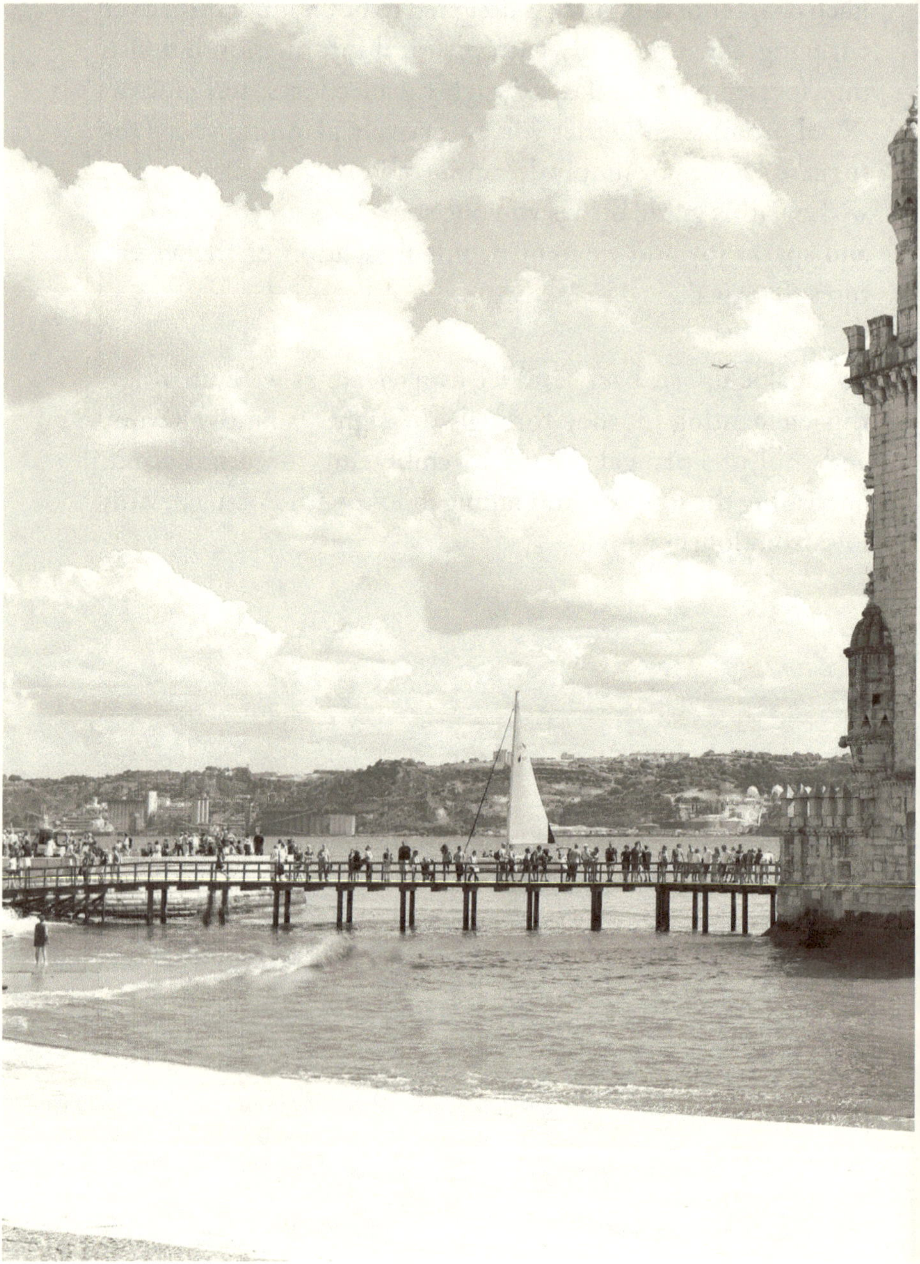

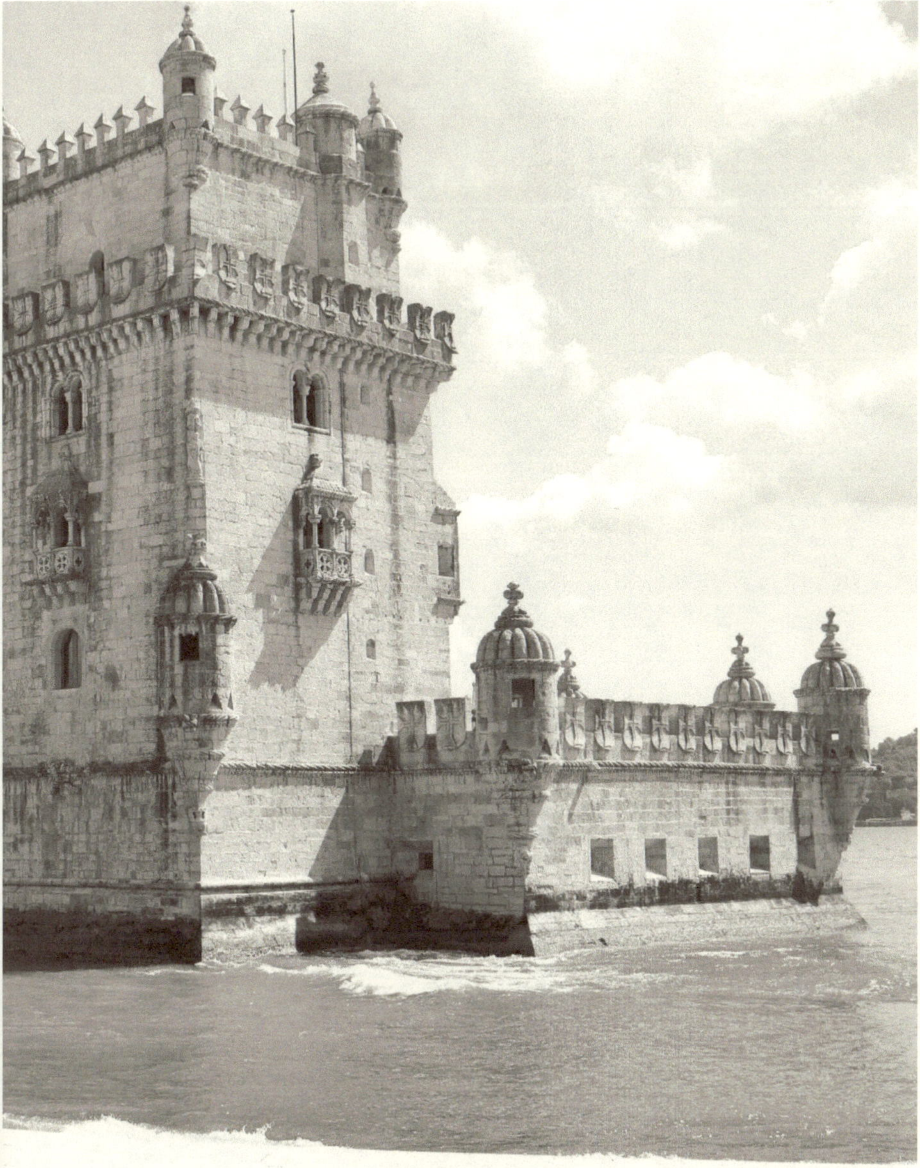

CHAPTER 1:
Lisbon

As Portugal's captivating capital, Lisbon shines brightly with a charm that is both historic and contemporary. Nestled among seven hills, this radiant city offers a collage of cultural experiences with its blend of traditional heritage and modern creativity. Here, pastel-colored houses huddle together under terracotta rooftops, and cobbled alleyways wind their way up to panoramic views, revealing the city's timeless allure.

Wandering through Lisbon's diverse districts is like walking through pages of a living history book. From the soulful Fado music that echoes in the narrow alleyways of Alfama to the vibrant street art in Bairro Alto and the creative spaces in the regenerated LX Factory, the city invites you to uncover its stories. The scent of roasting chestnuts intermingles with the salty sea breeze, adding a unique touch to the city's ambiance.

Moreover, Lisbon's gastronomy is an experience in itself, representing the city's multi-layered cultural tapestry. Freshly baked pastéis de nata, aromatic codfish dishes, and exquisite wines form a culinary map that guides you through Lisbon's rich flavors.

Let's embark on this enchanting journey, discovering the compelling mix of traditions, people, flavors, and sounds that make Lisbon an unforgettable destination. Each corner of the city has a unique tale to tell, each street a different sight to behold.

The Tower of Belém:
A Maritime Gateway to the Past

The Torre de Belém, or Tower of Belém, stands sentinel at the mouth of the Tagus River, a symbol of Lisbon's illustrious maritime past. Constructed in the early 16th century during the Age of Discovery, this fortified tower has weathered the waves of time, serving variously as a defense system, a ceremonial gateway, and a prison.

Its architecture is a testament to the richness of the Manueline style, a unique Portuguese variant of late Gothic architecture. As you walk through the tower, you can see detailed nautical motifs etched into the stonework, a tribute to Portugal's seafaring heroes. The four-story tower also offers panoramic views of the river and the city beyond, making it a photographer's paradise.

Visiting the Tower of Belém is akin to stepping back into the times when explorers like Vasco da Gama embarked on their perilous journeys, charting unknown territories and changing our understanding of the world. As such, the tower stands as a beacon of human curiosity and courage, a symbol of the exploratory spirit that drove the Age of Discovery.

Jeronimos Monastery:
Tracing the Footsteps of Portugal's Golden Age

A stone's throw from the Tower of Belém is another gem from the Age of Discovery, the Jeronimos Monastery. This grandiose structure is a masterwork of Manueline architecture, filled with intricate details that echo tales of Portugal's exploratory past.

The monastery was commissioned by King Manuel I in 1501 as a spiritual home for the Hieronymite monks, with the mandate to pray for the king's eternal soul and provide spiritual guidance to sailors. Funded by the riches flowing from Portugal's overseas colonies, the monastery embodies the country's Golden Age.

As you wander through its corridors, the building unveils its remarkable features, from the forest-like pillars of the nave to the ornate cloisters where monks once meditated. The detail in the stonework is staggering – nautical motifs of ropes, sea monsters, and other symbols that represent the exploratory voyages are woven into the architecture.

Moreover, the monastery is also the final resting place of some of Portugal's significant figures, including Vasco da Gama and poet Luis de Camões. Thus, a visit to Jeronimos Monastery offers a glimpse into the era that shaped Portugal's identity as a nation, leaving an indelible mark on global history.

Alfama District:
A Labyrinth of History and Culture

Draped over one of Lisbon's many hills, the Alfama District is a vibrant maze of narrow lanes, staircases, and charming squares, where history and culture blend seamlessly with the rhythm of everyday life. As one of the oldest districts in the city, Alfama echoes the tales of Moors and Romans, sailors and Fado singers, with each winding alley revealing a different chapter of Lisbon's past.

The streets of Alfama have a sense of timelessness, with tiled façades and iron balconies adorned with potted plants. Walking through these streets, you can hear the haunting strains of Fado music wafting from hidden taverns. This soulful music genre, a treasured symbol of Lisbon, narrates tales of love, loss, and longing, its lyrics steeped in saudade – a unique Portuguese sentiment of nostalgic yearning.

Moreover, Alfama is home to numerous historical landmarks, including the majestic São Jorge Castle and the Lisbon Cathedral, each offering captivating insights into Portugal's past. Yet, one of Alfama's most rewarding experiences is to simply lose oneself in its labyrinthine streets, soaking in the atmosphere and witnessing the enduring spirit of Lisbon's culture and community.

LX Factory:
A Creative Hub in the Heart of Lisbon

Once a thread and fabrics factory in the 19th century, LX Factory has transformed into a creative island within the city's bustling landscape. Located under the shadow of the 25 de Abril Bridge in Alcântara district, this industrial complex now teems with innovative businesses, art studios, eclectic restaurants, and charming boutiques.

Every corner of LX Factory exudes creativity. The streets are adorned with vivid murals and street art, while indoor spaces host exhibitions, fashion shows, and live music. The vibrant atmosphere is a testament to Lisbon's flourishing arts scene and the city's capacity for reinvention and innovation.

Here, you can browse through a selection of Portuguese design in charming boutiques, savor a meal in an upcycled double-decker bus, or lose yourself among the stacks of books in Livraria Ler Devagar, a bookstore housed in a former printing press. As a symbol of Lisbon's contemporary spirit, LX Factory embodies the city's dynamic blend of tradition and modernity, creativity, and entrepreneurship.

Baixa District:
The Heartbeat of Modern Lisbon

Strategically located at the heart of Lisbon, Baixa district is a vibrant area that pulses with the city's modern energy. It's here that the grandeur of neoclassical architecture meets the buzz of contemporary life, with wide boulevards lined with outdoor cafés, luxury boutiques, and elegant squares.

The district was completely rebuilt after the devastating earthquake of 1755 based on the innovative plans of Marquis de Pombal. Today, his grid-like vision can still be seen in the area's layout, making Baixa one of the first examples of earthquake-resistant construction and urban planning in Europe.

Key attractions in Baixa include the opulent Comercio Square, which opens up to the Tagus river, and the bustling Rossio Square, a traditional gathering place for locals and tourists alike. The Elevador de Santa Justa, a wrought-iron lift that offers stunning panoramic views over Lisbon, is another must-visit.

Baixa district offers the quintessential Lisbon experience – a mix of old-world charm and modern liveliness. From its neoclassical buildings to the contemporary beat of its street life, Baixa pulsates with a spirit that reflects the essence of Lisbon today.

São Jorge Castle:
Overlooking Lisbon from its Historic Heights

Perched atop Lisbon's highest hill, the São Jorge Castle is an imposing fortress that boasts a panoramic view over the city and the shimmering Tagus River. This iconic castle's fortified walls and watchtowers have stood guard over Lisbon since the medieval period, and its historical significance is deeply intertwined with Portugal's storied past.

Visitors to the castle can explore the Moorish fortifications, stroll through the verdant gardens filled with native Portuguese trees, and lose themselves in the labyrinth of narrow alleyways within the castle walls. You can discover the archaeological site, which unveils layers of history, from Iron Age remnants to Moorish residential traces.

Remember to take the castle's multimedia guide. This narrated history brings alive tales of the Visigoths, Moors, and Christians who once dwelled within these walls. For a special experience, consider visiting the castle at sunset. The changing hues cast a magical glow over the cityscape, offering a breathtaking sight.

Fado Music:
The Soulful Sounds of Lisbon

The stirring melodies of Fado, a traditional form of Portuguese music, are a testament to Lisbon's rich cultural heritage. Characterized by soulful vocals and accompanied by the melancholic sounds of the Portuguese guitar, Fado music encapsulates saudade - a uniquely Portuguese expression of deep, nostalgic longing.

Fado houses, typically intimate venues, are scattered throughout the city, with many concentrated in the Alfama and Mouraria districts. At these establishments, you can savor a traditional Portuguese meal while immersing yourself in the moving performances of Fado singers.

For first-time listeners, the Fado Museum is a worthwhile stop. The museum offers an in-depth exploration of Fado's history, its greatest personalities, and its cultural significance. When visiting a Fado house, remember that these performances are deeply personal and respected. It's customary to maintain silence during the songs, a quiet nod to the deep emotions being shared.

Tram 28:
A Vintage Journey through Lisbon's Streets

A ride on Tram 28 is a delightful throwback to a bygone era and one of the most authentic ways to explore Lisbon. This vintage yellow tram meanders through the city's steep, narrow streets, offering a unique vantage point to observe Lisbon's daily life and architectural splendor.

Starting in Graça, the tram takes you on a journey through popular neighborhoods like Alfama, Baixa, and Estrela, passing notable landmarks such as the São Jorge Castle and the Lisbon Cathedral along the way. With its old-world charm and scenic route, Tram 28 is not just a mode of transportation, but a charming attraction in its own right.

If planning to hop on the Tram 28, be mindful of the timings. The trams are often packed during peak tourist hours. Therefore, consider boarding early in the morning or later in the evening for a more leisurely experience. Also, be wary of pickpockets who might take advantage of the tram's popularity with tourists. Keep your belongings secure and enjoy the picturesque journey through Lisbon's storied streets.

Lisbon Oceanarium:
Delving into the Depths of the Sea

Lisbon's Oceanarium, one of the largest and most spectacular aquariums in Europe, is a marvel for both children and adults alike. Situated in the modern district of Parque das Nações, the oceanarium is a tribute to the world's diverse marine ecosystems, emphasizing the importance of their conservation.

The centerpiece of the oceanarium is an enormous central tank, teeming with a variety of marine species from around the globe. Here, you can observe a range of fascinating creatures – from sleek sharks and elegant rays to colorful schools of tropical fish. Encircling the central tank, four additional habitats replicate the ecosystems of the Atlantic, Pacific, Indian, and Antarctic oceans. A visit to the temporary exhibitions is a must, showcasing unique marine creatures and offering interactive learning experiences. Also, consider attending a feeding session where you can witness the vibrant marine life in action.

While it's easy to lose track of time mesmerized by the underwater world, it's recommended to set aside at least two to three hours for your visit. To make the most out of your experience, consider hiring an audio guide, which provides a wealth of information about the marine species and their habitats.

Day Trip to Sintra:
A Royal Retreat on Lisbon's Outskirts

Just a short train ride away from Lisbon, Sintra offers an enchanting escape from the hustle and bustle of the city. This picturesque town is a UNESCO World Heritage Site, renowned for its fairy-tale palaces, opulent manors, and lush gardens.

The must-see landmark is the Pena Palace, an astonishing romanticist castle that seems to have leaped straight out of a storybook with its vividly painted terraces and mythical statues. Don't miss the Moorish Castle, a hilltop medieval fortress that offers stunning panoramic views. The labyrinthine Quinta da Regaleira, with its grottoes and hidden tunnels, is also a sight to behold.

When planning your trip to Sintra, make sure to arrive early to avoid the afternoon rush, and wear comfortable shoes for exploring the hilly terrain. Bear in mind, Sintra deserves more than a rushed visit. Consider dedicating a full day to truly appreciate the town's rich architectural and natural beauty.

Lisbon Cuisine:
A Melting Pot of Flavors and Traditions

Portuguese cuisine, while often overshadowed by its Mediterranean neighbors, is a gastronomic delight that leaves food-lovers raving about its diverse flavors and time-honored traditions. Lisbon, being the capital, naturally offers a wide variety of Portuguese culinary experiences, with a unique mix of Atlantic influences and southern European tastes.

Seafood is at the heart of Portuguese cuisine, and in Lisbon, you'll find it at its freshest. Bacalhau (salted cod), prepared in countless ways, is a national staple. For a unique Lisbon treat, sample sardinhas assadas (grilled sardines), especially during the popular Saints' Festival in June.

However, Lisbon's culinary scene extends beyond seafood. Try cozido à Portuguesa, a hearty stew of vegetables and various meats, a delicious testament to the country's farming traditions. No gastronomic journey in Lisbon would be complete without tasting the iconic pastel de nata, a creamy egg custard tart that has won over dessert-lovers worldwide. Visit the historic Pastéis de Belém bakery, where these famed tarts have been produced using a secret recipe since 1837.

Wash it all down with a glass of Ginjinha, a sour cherry liqueur native to Lisbon, or dive into Portugal's extensive wine culture with a glass of Vinho Verde or a rich Douro red.

When dining in Lisbon, adopt the local leisurely pace. Portuguese meals are a time for relaxation and conversation. Look for local tascas (taverns) where traditional dishes are served, and don't hesitate to ask for the prato do dia (dish of the day) – often the freshest and best value option.

Also, don't forget to explore Lisbon's vibrant market scene. Visit Mercado da Ribeira, also known as Time Out Market, where you can try dishes from numerous local chefs all under one roof.

From its seafood-rich diet to its tantalizing pastries, Lisbon offers a culinary adventure that's deeply rooted in the city's culture and traditions, providing an authentic taste of Portugal that lingers long after the meal is over.

Final Thoughts:
Lisbon, A City of Seven Hills and Endless Charm

As you come to the end of your journey through Lisbon, you realize that this city is much more than a sum of its parts. The charm of Lisbon lies not only in its grand monuments, rich history, or delicious cuisine but also in its everyday scenes – the clatter of trams navigating narrow lanes, the poignant strains of Fado echoing in the streets, the aroma of roasting chestnuts filling the air.

To fully experience Lisbon, it's advisable to walk its streets as much as possible. Yes, the city is famously built on seven hills, which can make for some steep climbs, but these often lead to spectacular miradouros, or viewpoints, each offering a unique panorama of the city and the Tagus River. Don't be afraid to lose yourself in the winding alleys of Alfama or Mouraria – often, the best discoveries are the unexpected ones.

However, getting to know Lisbon is not just about sightseeing. It's also about connecting with its people, the Lisboetas. Take the time to chat with the locals, whether it's the vendor selling you pastéis de nata or the friendly old man at the neighborhood tasca. Their stories and insights will enrich your understanding of the city and its culture.

When it comes to dining, while there are numerous high-end restaurants in Lisbon, some of the most memorable meals can be had in simple tascas, where traditional dishes are prepared with love and served without pretense. Also, make a point to try the local wines, as Portugal's vineyards produce some exceptional varieties that are not as well-known as they deserve to be.

Plan your visit around the city's festivals if you can. Whether it's the popular Saints' Festivals in June, the contemporary art and music events of the LX Factory, or the lively street parties of Bairro Alto, these vibrant celebrations offer a glimpse into the city's pulsating heart.

Lastly, allow for some flexibility in your itinerary. One of Lisbon's greatest delights is its proximity to a variety of day-trip destinations. Whether it's the fairy-tale palaces of Sintra, the surf beaches of Cascais, or the traditional fishing villages of Setúbal, there's a whole world to explore just outside the city.

Discovering Lisbon is like unraveling a complex tapestry woven with threads of history, culture, gastronomy, and human warmth. Whether you're drawn to its sun-drenched plazas, its ancient streets humming with life, or its stunning seascapes, Lisbon has a way of capturing your heart. It's a city that invites you to return, promising new discoveries and deeper connections each time you walk its seven-hilled landscape.

CHAPTER 1: LISBON 207

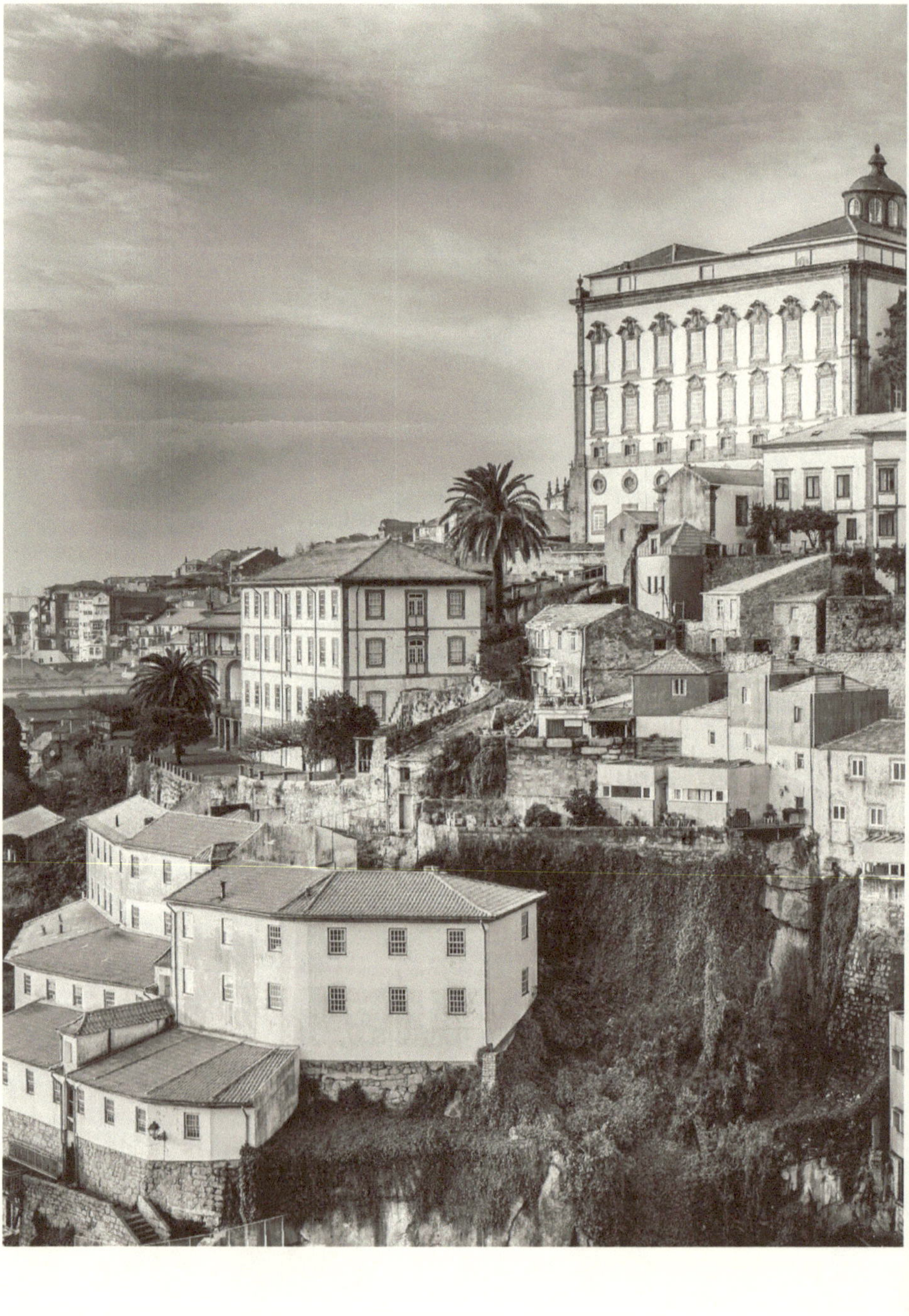

CHAPTER 2: PORTO 209

CHAPTER 2:
Porto

As the second-largest city in Portugal, Porto, often referred to as 'Oporto' by English speakers, is a vibrant blend of old-world charm and contemporary dynamism. Situated along the Douro River, the city's undulating landscape, punctuated by historic buildings, iconic bridges, and steep, narrow lanes, is a testament to its rich cultural heritage. From its legendary Port wine cellars to its bustling marketplaces, from its ornate churches to its charming riverside district, each aspect of Porto invites exploration, promising a captivating journey into Portugal's northern heartland.

At first glance, Porto's character is revealed in its architectural diversity. The city's historic heart, the Ribeira district, a UNESCO World Heritage site, is a maze of medieval streets, lined with colorful, tile-fronted houses. Ascending from the riverbank, the district offers stunning vistas at every turn, from the graceful arches of the Dom Luís I Bridge to the imposing façade of the Church of São Francisco. Not far from here, the Livraria Lello, one of the world's most beautiful bookstores, enchants with its neo-Gothic interiors and its rumored inspiration for the "Harry Potter" series.

Yet Porto is not just a city trapped in time. Its forward-looking spirit is evident in its modern architectural wonders, such as the Serralves Museum of Contemporary Art, an art-deco masterpiece nestled within a verdant park. This innovative streak extends to Porto's culinary scene, where chefs deftly combine tradition with creativity, producing dishes that are deeply rooted in local flavors yet strikingly original.

Moreover, the city's appeal goes beyond its physical boundaries. A short distance from Porto, the historic city of Guimarães beckons, offering a journey into the birthplace of Portugal. Also, the charming seaside neighborhood of Foz do Douro, where the river kisses the Atlantic, provides a tranquil retreat from the city's hustle and bustle.

However, what truly sets Porto apart is its indomitable spirit. Known as 'Cidade Invicta' or 'The Unvanquished City' for its tenacity during the Siege of Porto in the 19th-century Liberal Wars, this resilience is reflected in its people, the Portuenses. Their warmth, hospitality, and pride in their city are infectious, making a visit to Porto not just a trip, but an immersion into a way of life that values tradition, cherishes history, and embraces change.

So, ready your senses for a rich tapestry of experiences as we delve into the invincible city of Porto. Whether you're a history buff, a food lover, a culture enthusiast, or an urban explorer, Porto promises to charm and delight in equal measure. Let's embark on this journey together, unveiling the many layers of this remarkable city, one step at a time.

Ribeira District:
The Historic Heart of Porto

Your Porto adventure begins in the Ribeira District, a UNESCO World Heritage site brimming with historical allure and vibrant life. As you wander through its narrow, winding cobblestone streets, you'll stumble upon a cascade of colorfully painted houses, centuries-old monuments, and bustling squares teeming with locals and tourists alike.

Start at the heart of the district, the Praça da Ribeira, a lively square bursting with traditional Portuguese eateries. Don't miss trying a Francesinha, a Porto specialty sandwich layered with meats and smothered in a rich beer sauce. Pair it with a glass of local Super Bock beer for an authentic Porto lunch.

For a serene moment, stroll along the Douro River where Rabelo boats, traditionally used for transporting Port wine, create a picturesque scene against the backdrop of the iconic Dom Luís I Bridge. The riverside, especially during sunset, offers a breathtaking panorama that is a feast for photography enthusiasts. Remember, the district can be crowded, so early mornings or late evenings provide a more relaxed atmosphere.

Livraria Lello:
Inside One of the World's Most Beautiful Bookstores

Prepare to step into a world of literary fantasy at Livraria Lello, one of the most beautiful bookstores globally. This century-old bookstore is more than a place to buy books; it's a journey into the heart of Porto's art and culture.

From the moment you approach its neo-Gothic façade, you're treated to an artistic spectacle. Inside, marvel at the stunning stained glass skylight, ornate wood carvings, and the grand red staircase resembling a flowing ribbon, reportedly an inspiration for J.K. Rowling's Harry Potter series.

Due to its popularity, Livraria Lello often teems with visitors. To beat the crowds, consider purchasing your tickets online beforehand. Plus, your ticket cost is deducted if you buy a book - a perfect memento from Porto. Remember to respect the quiet atmosphere and limit photography, as this is a place of literature, after all.

Porto Wine Cellars:
A Journey Through Portugal's Iconic Wine

Cross the river to Vila Nova de Gaia, home to Porto's famous wine cellars. Here, you'll embark on an intoxicating journey through the history, production, and taste of Portugal's iconic Port wine.

Begin your visit by delving into the cool, damp cellars housing enormous barrels of aging wine. The informative tours not only illuminate the meticulous winemaking process but also the rich history and tradition of Port wine. And of course, no tour is complete without a tasting session. Savor the diverse flavors, from the rich, fruity Ruby Port to the complex, nutty Tawny Port.

There are several renowned cellars to choose from, including Sandeman's and Graham's, but also consider smaller, family-run cellars for a more personalized experience. Remember to book in advance, especially during the busy summer months, and keep in mind, Port is a fortified wine - it's stronger than it tastes, so savor it responsibly!

Church of São Francisco:
A Gothic Marvel in the Heart of Porto

Hidden among Porto's vibrant cityscape, you'll find the Church of São Francisco, an awe-inspiring monument of Gothic architecture and Baroque interior. From the outside, its somber facade barely hints at the opulence within.

Step inside and prepare to be dazzled by the breathtaking interior, coated from floor to ceiling with intricate golden gilding. Exquisite wood carvings depict scenes from the life of St. Francis and biblical stories, each meticulously detailed and bathed in an ethereal glow. Don't miss the unique Tree of Jesse, an extraordinary genealogical representation of Jesus Christ's ancestry.

For those fascinated by the macabre, the church's catacombs offer a unique perspective into Porto's history. Here, the eerie ossuary and ancient tombs paint a compelling picture of the city's past. Note: the catacombs have limited access, so try to arrive early or consider booking a tour for a more insightful visit.

Dom Luís I Bridge:
Bridging Porto's Past and Present

Dominating Porto's skyline is the Dom Luís I Bridge, a magnificent double-deck metal arch bridge that spans the Douro River. Whether you're a history buff, an architecture enthusiast, or a casual traveler, this impressive feat of engineering is not to be missed.

The bridge offers two levels for crossing. The lower level gives you a close-up view of the fast-moving river below, while the upper level (exclusively for pedestrians and the metro), approximately 44 meters above, offers panoramic views of Porto and Gaia's sprawling cityscapes. As you stroll across, take a moment to appreciate the ingenuity of its 19th-century design and the stunning views it provides.

Walking the bridge at different times of day offers varying experiences. Early morning gives you a peaceful start to your day, while sunset paints the sky with a breathtaking palette of colors. And as night falls, the illuminated cityscape creates an unforgettable sight.

Serralves Museum:
A Contemporary Art Oasis

Away from Porto's historic streets, the Serralves Museum provides a refreshing burst of modernity. As the most visited museum in Portugal, it's an essential stop for art and architecture lovers.

Designed by the renowned architect Álvaro Siza Vieira, the minimalist white building is a piece of art itself, beautifully contrasting with the surrounding lush green gardens. Inside, the museum houses an impressive collection of contemporary art from Portugal and around the world. The exhibitions are continually rotating, ensuring there's always something new to discover.

Don't skip a visit to the Serralves Gardens, an expansive 18-hectare oasis filled with themed gardens, quirky sculptures, and even a farm. It's the perfect spot for a leisurely stroll or a peaceful picnic. Note: the museum offers free entry on the first Sunday of each month, but it can get quite busy, so plan your visit accordingly.

Foz do Douro:
Where the River Meets the Sea

At the point where the Douro River mingles with the Atlantic Ocean, Foz do Douro is a beloved gem in Porto's crown. This affluent seaside district presents a blend of maritime charm and modern sophistication, making it a favored escape from the city's busy core.

Stroll along the breezy seafront promenade, lined with palm trees and dotted with historic fortresses and lighthouses. Watch the sunset from one of the beachfront bars, its vibrant hues mirrored by the shimmering ocean. Don't miss the iconic Felgueiras Lighthouse, a popular spot for capturing the ocean's raw power during high tide.

Foz do Douro also boasts some of Porto's most enticing eateries. Whether you're craving the day's fresh catch, a traditional Portuguese dish, or modern fusion fare, you're in for a culinary treat. A word of advice: seafood tastes even better when paired with a glass of local Vinho Verde.

Bolhão Market:
A Feast for the Senses in Porto

Immerse yourself in Porto's vibrant local culture at the Bolhão Market, the city's most famous food market. Housed in a striking neoclassical building, this bustling hub is a sensory delight of sights, sounds, and aromas that perfectly encapsulate Porto's food scene.

Meander through the maze of stalls brimming with fresh produce, locally made cheeses, aromatic herbs, and a spectacular array of seafood, from sardines to octopus. Friendly vendors are always ready to share stories, tips, or even a sample or two. Don't shy away from trying something new!

Beyond shopping, Bolhão is also a fantastic place to enjoy a simple, delicious meal. Grab a stool at one of the market's small eateries and watch as the chef prepares your dish using ingredients sourced directly from the market. It's a truly authentic culinary experience.

Day Trip to Guimarães:
Cradle of Portugal

Just a short trip from Porto, Guimarães is a city steeped in history and charm. Known as the "Birthplace of Portugal", it's here that the country's first king, Afonso Henriques, was born. With its well-preserved medieval architecture, quaint cobbled streets, and imposing castle, a visit to Guimarães feels like stepping back in time.

Start your exploration at the iconic Guimarães Castle, a symbol of the nation's formation. Venture inside to discover its austere chambers and climb the towers for a panoramic view of the city. Nearby, the Palace of the Dukes of Braganza, with its grand rooms and extensive gardens, offers further insight into Portugal's early history.

After visiting the landmarks, lose yourself in the city's old quarter. Its narrow lanes are lined with ancient houses, charming cafes, and artisanal shops. Pause for a meal in one of the traditional taverns serving Vinho Verde and local dishes for a truly authentic taste of northern Portugal. A day trip to Guimarães is a delightful detour into Portugal's rich past.

Porto Cuisine:
The Savory Secrets of Northern Portugal

Embarking on a culinary journey in Porto is an unforgettable adventure filled with delightful flavors and age-old traditions.

The cuisine of northern Portugal is a gastronomic treasure trove, teeming with hearty dishes that reflect the region's fertile lands and coastal bounty.

The city's iconic dish, Francesinha, is a must-try. This meaty sandwich, smothered in a rich, spicy beer sauce and crowned with a layer of melted cheese, is comfort food at its best. Paired with a glass of Super Bock beer, it's a meal that embodies Porto's robust culinary spirit.

Another beloved local staple is Bacalhau, dried and salted cod, prepared in myriad ways. Whether it's Bacalhau à Brás, shredded cod mixed with onions and crispy potatoes, or Bacalhau à Gomes de Sá, a satisfying casserole with potatoes and olives, these cod dishes are a testament to Porto's deep connection to the sea.

Porto's vibrant food markets, like the Bolhão and Mercado da Foz, offer an abundance of fresh produce and artisanal goods. Don't miss the opportunity to try local cheeses, smoked meats, and the famous Pastel de Nata, a creamy custard tart that is a Portuguese culinary icon.

And, of course, no culinary exploration of Porto would be complete without experiencing its world-renowned Port wine. Visit one of the numerous wine cellars for a tour and tasting session, where you'll learn about the meticulous process of producing this sweet, fortified wine. Alternatively, enjoy a glass by the Douro River, watching the world go by as you savor the rich, complex flavors.

Final Thoughts:

Porto, A City of Tradition and Transformation

Wandering the streets of Porto, it's impossible not to be captivated by the city's unique blend of history and modernity.

As the sun sets, painting the Douro River in hues of gold and crimson, one can't help but reflect on Porto's enchanting mix of resilience and charm.

Exploring Porto is about immersing oneself in its vibrant culture and witnessing the harmony between past and present. It's about navigating the narrow, winding streets of Ribeira, getting lost in the chatter of local markets, and pausing to listen to the haunting melodies of Fado music wafting from a neighborhood tavern.

Remember, the best way to experience Porto is at your own pace. Take time to sit in a cafe, savor the local cuisine, and simply watch life unfold around you. Visit the city's landmarks, but don't overlook the lesser-known gems. The true essence of Porto is found not only in its iconic structures but also in its intimate corners where everyday life carries on, steeped in tradition and community spirit.

As a visitor, let yourself be led by curiosity and embrace the unexpected. Seek out conversations with locals, be open to new flavors, and take part in traditions. In Porto, every stone tells a story, and every story adds a new layer to your travel experience. While it's essential to plan your trip, remember that some of the most memorable experiences come from spontaneity. A missed turn might lead to a beautiful hidden square, an unplanned meal might turn into a culinary revelation, and a chance encounter could lead to a lasting friendship.

So, as you plan your visit to Porto, remember that this city is more than a destination—it's a journey into a rich tapestry of culture, history, and human connection. Porto isn't just a place to visit, it's a place to experience, a place to feel. And that, more than anything, is the magic of travel. Let Porto leave its indelible mark on your traveler's soul. In doing so, you'll be taking a piece of Porto with you, forever.

CHAPTER 2: PORTO 221

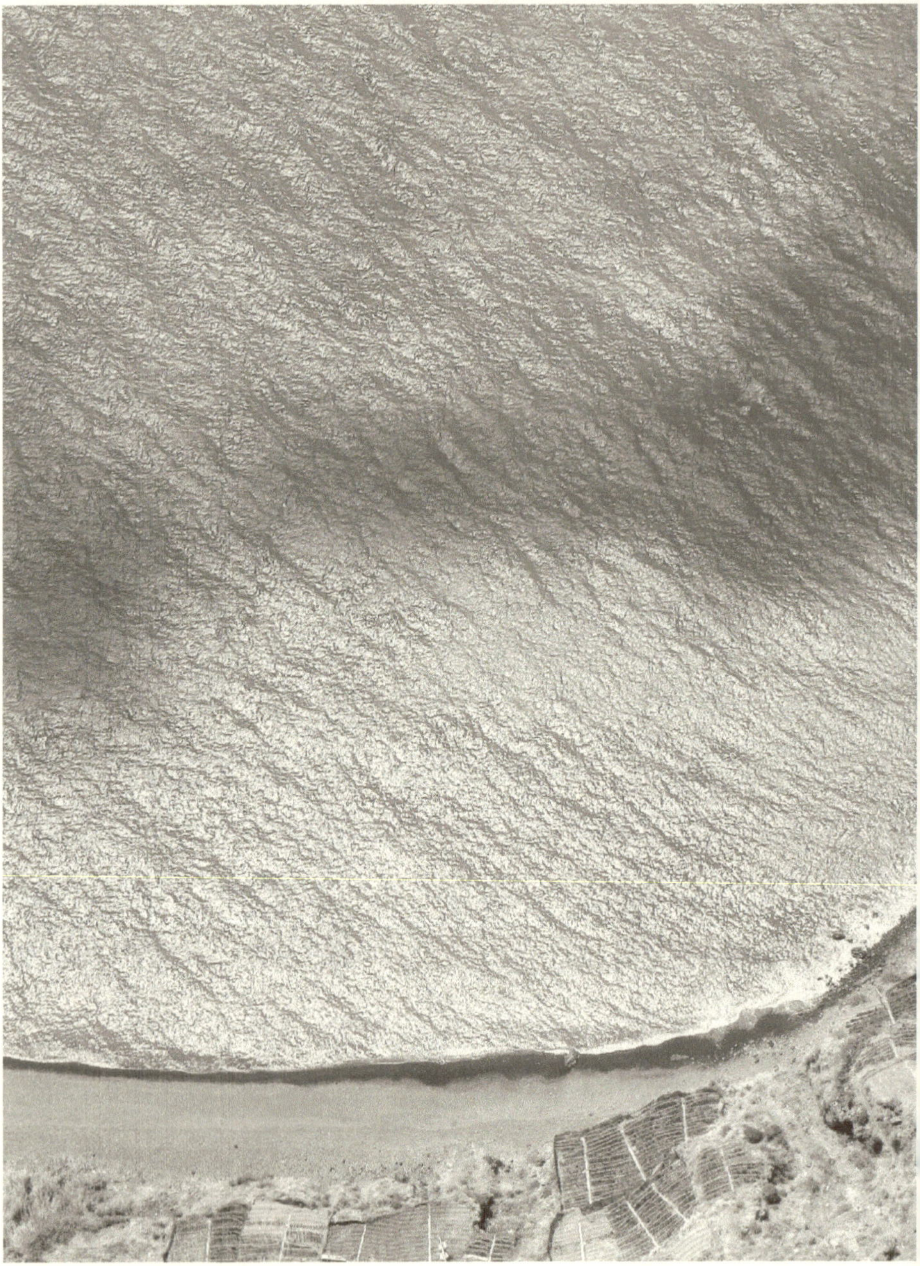

CHAPTER 3: MADEIRA

CHAPTER 3:
Madeira

Immersed in the sapphire-blue Atlantic Ocean, the volcanic island of Madeira blooms with an enchanting mix of lush vegetation, dramatic landscapes, and cultural richness. Known as the "Island of Eternal Spring", Madeira beckons travelers with its temperate climate, which nurtures a stunning array of botanical wonders year-round, resulting in a kaleidoscope of colors and fragrances that captivate the senses.

Emerging from the sea as a result of volcanic activity over millions of years, Madeira's awe-inspiring topography is a paradise for nature enthusiasts and adventure seekers. Its jagged cliffs tower over the sea, offering panoramic vistas that are sure to leave an indelible imprint on your memory. The island's heart is a rugged, mountainous terrain etched with 'levadas' - ancient irrigation channels turned hiking trails that unravel across the island, leading you through emerald green forests, alongside gurgling streams, and unveiling mesmerizing views.

At the heart of Madeira is Funchal, a charming city that seamlessly weaves the old and the new. You'll find centuries-old cathedrals and fortresses nestled among trendy restaurants, boutiques, and art galleries. Its vibrant streets, filled with the melodious chatter of locals, are a gateway to the island's storied past and cosmopolitan present.

Yet, Madeira's allure extends beyond its physical beauty and cultural charm. This island is a gastronome's paradise, offering a rich culinary tradition that mirrors the island's diverse natural environment. Fresh seafood from the Atlantic, exotic fruits from the fertile soil, and world-renowned Madeira wine contribute to a flavorful journey that will titillate your taste buds.

Embarking on a trip to Madeira is more than just a holiday; it's a sensory experience. Every corner of the island resonates with the gentle hum of nature, the whispers of history, and the warmth of its people. And as you navigate through Madeira, you'll soon discover that the island, in its humble yet profound way, touches your soul, forever transforming your concept of travel.

Welcome to Madeira, the Island of Eternal Spring - a place where nature and culture meet to create a mesmerizing symphony that celebrates the joy of discovery and the spirit of exploration.

Funchal's Old Town:
Strolling Through History

Embarking on a journey through Funchal's Old Town is like opening a timeless book filled with stories of past generations. Known locally as Zona Velha, this district is the heart and soul of the city, its cobbled streets and traditional architecture resonating with the echoes of Funchal's rich seafaring past.

As you wander through the narrow alleys, you'll discover centuries-old houses with triangle-shaped rooftops and distinctive exterior walls, which local artists have transformed into vibrant canvases. This open-air art gallery, called the Arte de Portas Abertas project, infuses Funchal's history with a modern, creative spirit. Don't forget to make a stop at the Mercado dos

Lavradores, a lively farmers' market brimming with exotic fruits, fresh fish, and traditional Madeiran crafts.

Your journey wouldn't be complete without visiting the Fortaleza de São Tiago, a 17th-century fortress that once guarded Funchal against pirate attacks. Today, its mustard-yellow walls house the Contemporary Art Museum, bridging the past with the present. Grab a cup of poncha, Madeira's traditional drink, at one of the outdoor cafes, and let the charm of Funchal's Old Town seep into your senses.

Madeira Botanical Garden:
A Colorful Paradise

Madeira Botanical Garden, or Jardim Botânico da Madeira, is a living canvas of colors, fragrances, and textures that encapsulate Madeira's abundant biodiversity. Nestled on a hillside overlooking Funchal, this garden is home to over 2,000 exotic plant species collected from all corners of the world, creating a mesmerizing tapestry of nature's beauty.

As you explore the terraced gardens, you'll encounter vibrant flowerbeds, lush tropical forests, and cactus gardens that stretch out beneath the bright Madeiran sky. Pause at the Loiro Park, a sanctuary for exotic birds, where colorful parrots, cockatoos, and lovebirds add a dash of liveliness to your visit.

Every step within this botanical wonderland unravels a different facet of Madeira's natural heritage. Whether you're an avid gardener, a nature enthusiast, or simply a traveler seeking tranquility, Madeira Botanical Garden offers a refreshing escape into a world brimming with life, color, and serenity.

Monte Palace Tropical Garden:
A Zen Escape

High above Funchal, tucked within the hills of Monte, you'll discover the Monte Palace Tropical Garden, an oasis of tranquility that offers a serene escape from the city's hustle and bustle. Once a luxurious hotel in the 18th century, today this enchanting garden showcases Madeira's natural beauty intertwined with oriental influences.

Stroll through the garden's meticulously manicured landscapes, where Madeiran and Azorean indigenous plants coexist harmoniously with heather shrubs from Scotland and protea flowers from Africa. Glistening ponds filled with Koi fish and adorned with oriental sculptures create an atmosphere of zen, transporting you to the tranquil gardens of Japan and China.

One of the garden's highlights is its impressive tile collection, consisting of traditional Portuguese azulejos panels, which depict scenes from Portugal's history, culture, and mythology. Don't miss a ride on the Monte Cable Car, offering a breathtaking panoramic view of Funchal on your journey up or down. A visit to Monte Palace Tropical Garden is more than just a stroll through a garden; it's a soothing journey that transcends borders, uniting the East and the West, the past and the present, nature and art, in a harmonious symphony.

Levadas of Madeira:
Nature's Aquatic Trails

If Madeira is a canvas painted by nature, then the levadas are its master strokes. These centuries-old irrigation channels, originally created to distribute rainfall from the wetter northern regions to the sun-drenched southern slopes, are now an integral part of Madeira's cultural heritage and a unique way to explore the island's breathtaking landscapes.

Imagine hiking alongside these narrow watercourses, under the cool shade of laurel and heather trees, while the gentle murmur of flowing water becomes the soundtrack to your adventure.

From the serene Levada dos Tornos offering panoramic views of Funchal, to the more challenging Levada do Caldeirão Verde taking you through deep emerald green forests and dramatic waterfalls, there's a levada walk for every fitness level and interest.

Remember to pack a waterproof jacket as Madeira's weather can change quickly, and a headlamp if your chosen levada walk includes tunnels. Always respect the nature around you, stick to the marked paths, and prepare to be enchanted by the idyllic scenery that awaits you on the levadas of Madeira.

Cabo Girão:
Standing at the Top of the World

At Cabo Girão, the sky touches the sea at one of the highest sea cliffs in Europe. Standing 580 meters above the shimmering Atlantic, the viewpoint at Cabo Girão offers heart-stopping, panoramic views that are nothing short of spectacular. On a clear day, you can see Funchal to the east, the stark cliffs of Câmara de Lobos to the west, and the distant outline of the Desertas Islands on the horizon.

An adrenaline-pumping glass skywalk extends over the cliff edge, offering the thrill of walking on air with the vast ocean beneath your feet. Though it might seem daunting, take a deep breath and step onto the transparent platform; the view from this unique perspective is absolutely worth conquering your fears for.

While the viewpoint can get crowded during midday, visit early in the morning or late in the afternoon for a more peaceful experience. Whether you're a thrill-seeker or a nature lover, Cabo Girão offers a heady mix of breathtaking vistas, towering cliffs, and endless ocean, making it a must-visit spot on your Madeiran itinerary.

Santana's Traditional Houses:
A Peek into Madeira's Past

Santana, a small picturesque town nestled in the northern part of Madeira, is famed for its traditional A-frame houses, locally known as 'Casas de Colmo.' These charming dwellings with their steep, thatched roofs and colorful red, blue, or yellow walls, seem straight out of a storybook, offering a glimpse into Madeira's pastoral past.

Although originally built as farmer's dwellings, today, a few of these iconic houses have been converted into shops selling local handicrafts and products. You can even tour the inside of some, which have been preserved to showcase traditional Madeiran life. Don't miss the opportunity to take some photos outside these adorable houses; their distinctive architecture set against the backdrop of Santana's lush landscapes makes for a perfect memento of your Madeira trip.

Visiting Santana also offers you a chance to explore the nearby Laurissilva Forest, a UNESCO World Heritage site, or take a thrilling cable car ride to the Rocha do Navio Nature Reserve. Combining history, culture, and nature, Santana provides a uniquely Madeiran experience that's sure to leave a lasting impression.

Pico do Arieiro:
Conquering Madeira's Third Highest Peak

If your idea of a perfect holiday includes exhilarating hikes and sweeping panoramas, then a trek up Pico do Arieiro, Madeira's third highest peak, should definitely be on your itinerary. Standing tall at 1,818 meters above sea level, Pico do Arieiro offers breath-taking vistas of craggy mountains, deep valleys, and the endless blue of the Atlantic.

The hike to the summit can be challenging with its steep inclines, but your efforts are rewarded tenfold when you reach the top and are greeted by a sunrise that paints the sky in a riot of colors, or a sunset that bathes the island in a warm, golden glow. On clear days, you can even see the island's highest peak, Pico Ruivo, and the sprawling central mountain range.

Dress in layers as temperatures at the peak can be significantly cooler than at sea level and carry plenty of water. Whether you're an experienced hiker seeking a thrill or a nature lover in search of stunning landscapes, conquering Pico do Arieiro promises to be an unforgettable experience.

Day Trip to Porto Santo:
Madeira's Golden Sister

A trip to Madeira would be incomplete without a visit to its sunny sibling, Porto Santo. Known for its golden, sandy beaches and crystal-clear waters, this tranquil island is a paradise for sun-worshippers and beach lovers. Hop on a ferry from Funchal and within a few hours, you'll be stepping onto the sands of Porto Santo's 9 km long beach, a perfect escape from the hustle and bustle of everyday life.

While the beach is undoubtedly the star attraction, there's more to Porto Santo than just sun and sand. Explore the charming town of Vila Baleira with its quaint houses and historical sites, try your hand at golf at Porto Santo Golfe, or hike up to Pico do Castelo for stunning views of the island. Remember to apply lots of sunscreen, as the island's sunny weather can be quite deceptive!

The Basket Toboggan Ride:
A Unique Madeiran Experience

For an adrenaline-packed end to your day, try a truly unique Madeiran experience: a toboggan ride down the steep streets of Funchal in a wicker basket sled. Originally a fast means of transport for locals, these "carros de cesto" have become one of Madeira's most popular tourist attractions.

Steered by two "carreiros" dressed in traditional white uniforms and straw hats, these toboggan rides are an exciting, if unconventional, way to navigate the city's winding streets. You'll find yourself laughing with exhilaration as you slide down the steep slopes, take sharp turns, and race down the narrow roads at thrilling speeds.

Remember that the toboggan ride ends at Livramento, from where it's a bit of a walk or a short taxi ride back to the city center. The ride is perfectly safe, but do hold on tight when your toboggan gathers speed. Whether you're a thrill-seeker or simply a tourist looking for a fun experience, this unique ride promises to be a highlight of your Madeiran adventure.

Madeira Cuisine:
A Blend of Land and Sea

Madeiran cuisine is a mouth-watering mix of flavors from the land and the sea, reflecting the island's fertile soil and abundant oceans. One of the must-tries is 'Espetada', skewers of succulent beef rubbed in garlic and salt, grilled over wood or charcoal, and served on a bay leaf stick. Enjoy it with 'Bolo do Caco', a round bread made with sweet potatoes and cooked on a flat basalt stone.

From the sea comes 'Peixe Espada Preto com Banana', a unique dish featuring the local black scabbardfish served with fried banana and passionfruit sauce. For those who love seafood, 'Lapas grelhadas', grilled limpets with garlic and butter, are an absolute delight.

Don't leave without trying 'Poncha', a potent alcoholic drink made with aguardente de cana (sugarcane rum), honey, sugar, and lemon juice. And for dessert, 'Bolo de Mel', a rich, dark, and spicy honey cake that's traditionally enjoyed during Christmas, is an absolute must.

Remember, Madeiran dining is not just about the food; it's about the experience. Savor your meals at a leisurely pace, accompanied by the local wines, and let the island's culinary magic work its charm.

Final Thoughts:
Madeira, A Jewel in the Atlantic

As we conclude our journey through Madeira, the words that come to mind are awe-inspiring and captivating. Madeira is not just an island; it's a canvas painted with the vibrant colors of exotic flowers, the deep blue of the Atlantic, the ruggedness of the mountains, and the warm hues of its heritage buildings.

Whether you've spent your days hiking through lush landscapes, discovering the unique traditions, savoring the tantalizing cuisine, or simply basking in the island's eternal spring, Madeira is a destination that invites exploration and rewards curiosity.

When planning your trip, remember that Madeira is a year-round destination, thanks to its mild climate. While the weather is usually pleasant, it's worth packing a light jacket for cooler evenings or visits to higher altitudes. It's also a good idea to pack sturdy walking shoes, especially if you plan to explore the levadas or the island's mountainous terrain.

For an authentic experience, don't shy away from trying the local cuisine and participating in local traditions. And, most importantly, take the time to enjoy the simple pleasures - the scent of exotic flowers in the air, the taste of a freshly caught seafood meal, the breathtaking views around every corner, and the warm hospitality of the Madeiran people.

Madeira, with its blend of natural beauty, rich heritage, and friendly locals, is indeed a jewel in the Atlantic. Its lure lies in its simplicity and its ability to offer something for everyone. Whether you're an adventure enthusiast, a nature lover, a foodie, or a history buff, Madeira invites you to explore, enjoy, and embrace its charm. As you depart, you'll carry with you memories of a magical island that promises to draw you back again and again. The beauty of Madeira awaits you – come, explore, and lose yourself in this Atlantic paradise.

CHAPTER 3: MADEIRA 235

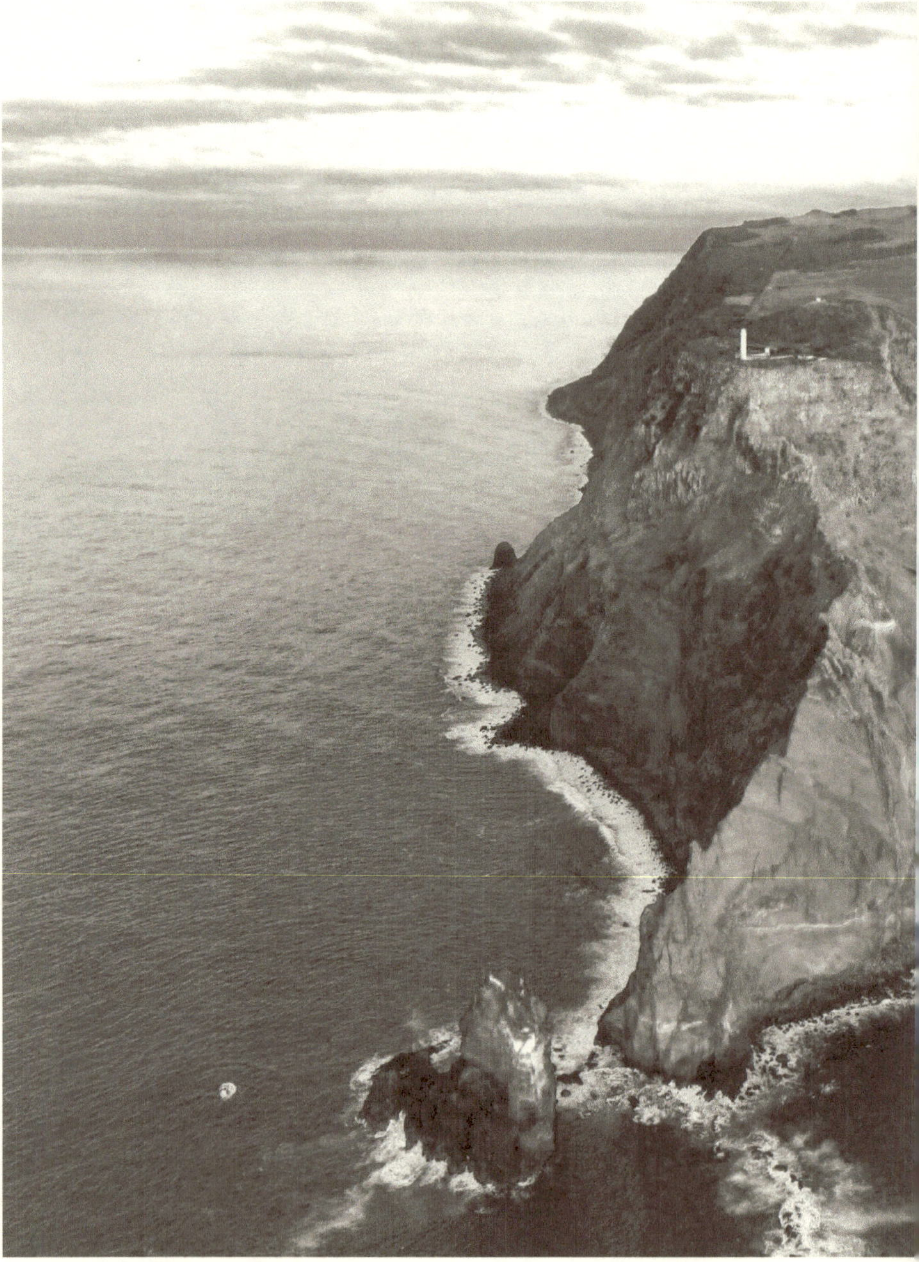

CHAPTER 4: AZORES

CHAPTER 4:
Azores
. . . .

Welcome to the Azores, a lush and vivid Eden located in the heart of the Atlantic Ocean. These nine volcanic islands, still a secret to many travelers, emerge like emerald gems from the azure waters, beckoning explorers with their blend of dramatic landscapes, rich wildlife, and timeless culture. Here, verdant pastures blend seamlessly with sapphire waters, creating a tableau so mesmerizing it seems to leap straight out of a fairytale.

As we embark on our journey through these captivating islands, we will dive deep into their unique geological formations, uncover their rich history, and explore their cultural heritage. Each island offers a distinct experience, from hiking Portugal's highest peak on Pico Island, tracing the paths of discovery in Terceira, to basking in the beauty of the aptly named Flower Island, Flores.

We will traverse the beautiful trails of São Miguel, taste the unique flavors of Azorean cuisine, and experience the thrill of spotting whales and dolphins in their natural habitat. We'll delve into the past at the UNESCO World Heritage Site of Angra do Heroísmo and immerse ourselves in the maritime charms of Faial Island.

The Azores offer a vibrant blend of unspoiled natural beauty and rich, layered history, complemented by a friendly and welcoming local culture. The islands are a paradise for nature lovers, adventure seekers, and anyone longing for a place where time seems to slow down, and the frenetic pace of modern life feels a world away.

As we navigate through this guide, let's remember that travel is as much about immersing ourselves in new experiences as it is about seeing new places. The Azores invite us not just to observe but to participate, to taste, to listen, to feel the wind in our hair, the volcanic soil under our feet, and the thrill of discovery in our hearts.

So, get ready to step into the green and blue Eden that is the Azores - an enchanting world of volcanic landscapes, azure lagoons, charming coastal towns, and delicious culinary delights. This is a journey of exploration and awe, a tribute to the breathtaking power and beauty of nature. Pack your bags and join us on this exciting adventure as we uncover the many charms of the Azores.

São Miguel Island:
The Allure of the Green Island

Often called the "Green Island", São Miguel is the largest and most populous island in the Azores archipelago. Blessed with lush landscapes, stunning lagoons, and a vibrant culture, this island is a paradise for nature lovers. Let's start our exploration in the island's capital, Ponta Delgada, where you'll find charming cobblestone streets, beautifully preserved Baroque churches, and a bustling marina lined with enticing restaurants.

However, it's beyond the city where São Miguel truly shines. Venture out to the stunning Lagoa das Sete Cidades, a massive, twin-lake crater that's among the most beautiful natural sights in Portugal. Here's a tip: for the best views, follow the walking trail to Vista do Rei, a lookout that offers breathtaking panoramas of the lagoon and beyond.

Don't miss the iconic Gorreana Tea Plantation, where you can sample locally grown tea, or the geothermal cooking spots at Furnas, where you can taste the unique cozido das Furnas, a stew cooked in volcanic steam vents. São Miguel is truly a feast for the senses, offering a mix of natural beauty, rich flavors, and cultural insights.

Pico Island:
Conquering Portugal's Highest Peak

On Pico Island, the adventure starts high above the clouds. Dominating the landscape is Mount Pico, Portugal's highest peak, standing at an impressive 2,351 meters (7,713 feet) above sea level. The island invites adventurers to take the challenging yet rewarding hike to the summit, offering unparalleled views of the surrounding islands on clear days. Remember, safety comes first: always check the weather conditions and hire a local guide if you're not an experienced hiker.

But Pico Island isn't just about the mountain. It's also renowned for its vineyards, which are so unique they've been designated a UNESCO World Heritage Site. Here, the vines are planted in black, volcanic rock, which retains heat and protects the plants from the Atlantic winds. Don't miss a visit to a local adega (wine cellar) to taste the exquisite Verdelho wine, renowned for its crisp, volcanic minerality.

Faial Island:
The Blue Island's Maritime Charms

Also known as the "Blue Island" due to the abundant blue hydrangeas that bloom in the summer, Faial offers a maritime charm that's hard to resist. The island's capital, Horta, is a popular stop for yachts crossing the Atlantic, giving the town an exciting, cosmopolitan feel. Don't forget to stop by Peter's Café Sport, a famous sailors' pub, where you can hear tales of high seas adventures and admire the impressive scrimshaw collection.

One of Faial's most captivating sites is the Capelinhos Volcano. It erupted in 1957-58, creating a dramatic, lunar-like landscape that extends the island's western coast. Visit the underground Interpretation Centre to learn about the Azores' volcanic history.

And for a slice of tranquility, stroll around the lush Caldeira, a massive crater at the heart of the island. Faial combines its natural attractions with a unique seafaring spirit, offering visitors a chance to experience the Azorean charm in all its blue and green glory.

Terceira Island:
Tracing the Paths of Discovery

Terceira Island, aptly named as it was the third island discovered in the Azores archipelago, is a place of rich history and cultural significance. Angra do Heroísmo, the island's main city, has been a UNESCO World Heritage Site since 1983, thanks to its beautiful Renaissance architecture and its important role during the Age of Discovery. You'll find a blend of history, nature, and tradition here, embodied in the colorful imperial chapels, bullfighting events, and distinctive local cuisine.

For a journey into the past, a visit to the fortifications of São Sebastião and São João Baptista is a must. These historic forts stand as a testament to the island's strategic importance in the Atlantic. But Terceira isn't just about human history.

The island's natural wonders, such as the Algar do Carvão, an ancient lava tube, and the stunning vistas from Serra do Cume, make it a well-rounded destination with something for everyone.

Flores Island:
Basking in the Beauty of Portugal's Flower Island

As its name suggests, Flores Island is like a floating garden in the middle of the Atlantic. It is the westernmost point of Europe, and perhaps the most breathtakingly beautiful of all the Azorean islands. Its lush landscapes, dotted with countless waterfalls, emerald-green crater lakes, and charming villages, seem to belong more to a fairytale than to reality.

The island's numerous trails make it a paradise for hikers. Trails like the Rocha dos Bordões, with its distinctive columnar basalt formations, or the Poço da Alagoinha, a magical spot with cascading waterfalls, are not to be missed.

And for birdwatchers, Flores is a heaven. It's the perfect place to spot rare seabirds like the Cory's Shearwater or the Roseate Tern. While you're here, don't forget to try the local cheese, Queijo do Fio, a string cheese that's a delicious Flores specialty.

Angra do Heroísmo:
Walking Through a UNESCO World Heritage Site

Angra do Heroísmo, the historic capital of Terceira Island, is more than just a town. It's a journey through time, a place where history lives in the streets. As you stroll through the cobbled streets, every corner reveals a bit more of the town's rich past. From the grand Cathedral of Angra do Heroísmo to the fortifications of the 16th-century Forte de São João Baptista, there's history at every turn.

One of the highlights is the Paços do Concelho, the Town Hall, an exquisite example of 19th-century architecture. Don't miss a walk up Monte Brasil for a fantastic view of the city and its surrounding landscape. But Angra isn't just about sightseeing. It's also about experiencing the Azorean culture. Visit the lively market, taste the local pastries like the Donas-Amélias, and enjoy the friendly vibe of the local cafés. Angra do Heroísmo is more than just a city; it's a testament to the Azorean spirit, filled with beauty, history, and charm.

Azorean Whaling:
Insights into a Bygone Era

In the Azores, the history of whaling is a story of survival, tradition, and transition. For more than a century, whaling was an essential part of Azorean life, providing both a livelihood for the islanders and a significant connection to the sea that surrounds them. The island of Pico was once known as the "Island of the Whalers", and today, the whaling museums in Lajes and São Roque offer a glimpse into this challenging way of life.

In these museums, you can learn about the courage and resilience of the Azorean whalers and the evolution of whaling techniques over the years. You'll see the historic whaling boats, called 'whaleboats,' and learn about the transition from hunting whales to conserving and appreciating them. The transition from a whaling culture to a culture of conservation has been a remarkable one, reflecting a deep respect for the ocean and its inhabitants.

Whale and Dolphin Watching:
Encounters with Majestic Marine Life

The Azores is one of the best places in the world for whale and dolphin watching. Here, in the deep and nutrient-rich waters of the Atlantic, you can spot about a third of the world's cetacean species. The islands have transformed from a whaling culture to one of the world's leading destinations for responsible whale and dolphin watching.

Species like the enormous blue whale, the acrobatic common dolphin, or the mysterious sperm whale can be spotted here. Whether you embark on a boat trip from Pico, São Miguel, or Faial, the sight of these majestic creatures breaching the water is unforgettable.

Remember, always choose companies that follow responsible wildlife-watching guidelines to ensure minimal disturbance to these magnificent animals. In the Azores, you can witness the beauty of life in the ocean, leaving with unforgettable memories and a deeper understanding of why we must protect these creatures.

The Geothermal Wonders of the Azores:
Exploring Volcanic Landscapes

The Azores is a land born of fire and brimstone, molded over millennia by the relentless power of the Earth's inner heat. This volcanic origin is still very much alive today and is evident in the stunning geothermal landscapes that dot the islands. From bubbling hot springs to steam vents and mud pots, the Azores is a geologist's dream come true.

One of the must-see geothermal wonders is the Furnas Valley on São Miguel Island, where geysers hiss, and hot springs bubble. Don't miss the experience of tasting a "Cozido das Furnas", a stew cooked underground by volcanic steam. On Terceira Island, you can venture inside the Algar do Carvão, an ancient lava tube.

And on Faial Island, the Capelinhos Volcano provides a lunar-like landscape, a testament to the island's most recent volcanic eruption. These unique landscapes remind us of the Azores' fiery birth and the continuing dynamism of our living planet.

Azorean Cuisine:
A Feast from the Atlantic Depths

Azorean cuisine is a testament to the islands' rich marine resources and fertile volcanic soil. Hearty, simple, and deeply satisfying, the food here captures the spirit of the Azorean people - resourceful, hospitable, and closely tied to the land and the sea.

From the sea comes a bounty of fish and seafood. Tuna, mackerel, limpets, and octopus are staples of the Azorean table, prepared in various ways - grilled, stewed, or served as a ceviche-style dish known as "cracas". However, the Azores' culinary repertoire isn't confined to the sea alone. From the land comes fresh cheese, yams, sweet pineapples, and the famous spicy "linguiça" sausage.

One must-try delicacy is the 'Cozido das Furnas,' a rich and hearty stew cooked underground by volcanic steam in Furnas Valley on São Miguel Island. The meal takes on a smoky flavor that is unlike anything else you'll taste, a literal taste of the island's volcanic nature.

Azorean wines, too, are unique, grown on volcanic soil and imparting a distinct minerality. The verdelho wines of Pico Island are particularly noteworthy, grown in unique, UNESCO-listed, rock-walled vineyards.

Final Thoughts:
Azores, A Green Pearl in the Atlantic

The Azores is an archipelago of discovery, of adventure, and of remarkable beauty. A place where nature reigns supreme, and the pace of life is dictated by the rhythms of the land and sea. Here, in this emerald Eden set amidst the Atlantic's sapphire expanses, the journey becomes a destination, and every moment is an opportunity to connect more deeply with the world around you.

Every island in this archipelago has its unique charm, from the verdant vistas of São Miguel, the mountainous heights of Pico, to the floral paradise of Flores. Wherever you go, you'll find yourself in landscapes that both humble and inspire. The volcanic craters, the undulating pastures, the thunderous waterfalls, the azure lakes - each natural wonder is a testament to the Earth's creative force.

But the Azores is more than just a natural paradise. It's a place where history and tradition echo in every corner, from the cobblestone streets of Angra do Heroísmo to the seaside hamlets of Faial. Where the cuisine tells stories of the sea and the fertile land. Where every local you meet treats you not as a visitor, but as a friend.

In terms of practical advice, be prepared for changing weather, as the islands can experience all four seasons in a day. Pack comfortable hiking shoes for exploring the beautiful landscapes. Always respect local customs and natural environments, and opt for sustainable choices wherever possible. This is a place of astounding natural beauty, and it's up to us to help keep it that way.

The Azores invites you to slow down, to breathe, and to truly live in the moment. So as you embark on your journey, let the beauty of these islands remind you of the wonders that await when we venture beyond the familiar. In the Azores, every path is a journey, every moment a story, and every day a treasure. Embrace the adventure, and let the Azores show you the joy of discovering not just a new destination, but a new way of seeing the world.

CHAPTER 4: AZORES

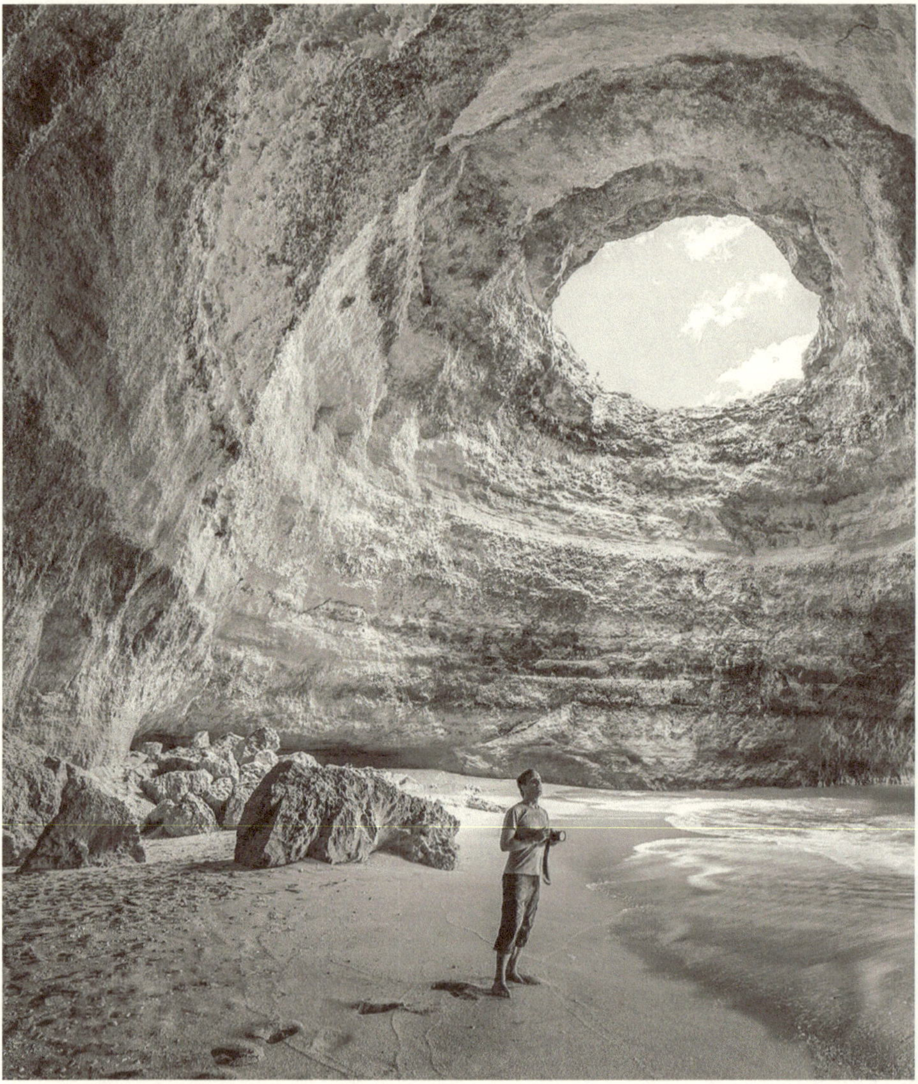

CHAPTER 5: ALGARVE 251

CHAPTER 5:
Algarve

Sun-drenched and graced with enchanting coastlines, Algarve is a slice of paradise tucked away in Portugal's southernmost region. Known for its golden sand beaches, dramatic cliffs, and azure waters, Algarve holds the secret to an idyllic beach getaway. However, the charms of Algarve go beyond its scenic landscapes. With a rich maritime history, Moorish roots, gastronomic delights, and some of Europe's most celebrated golf courses, Algarve encapsulates a well-rounded and captivating travel destination.

There's a palpable sense of serenity as you step into the cobbled lanes of Algarve's old towns, echoing tales of sailors and explorers of yesteryears. The region's strategic location on the Atlantic has made it a significant maritime hub since the Age of Discoveries. Yet, there is an even older history etched into Algarve's identity - the Moorish influence, which is reflected in the region's architecture, culture, and even food.

Outdoor enthusiasts will find Algarve to be their playground. The iconic Benagil Cave, the unspoiled trails of Ria Formosa, and the panoramic views from Cape St. Vincent – these natural attractions make Algarve a place of endless adventures. And for those drawn to the fairways, the region's golf courses promise not only challenging play but also sweeping sea views.

A trip to Algarve is also a culinary journey. The region's cuisine is a delectable medley of the Atlantic's bounty. With a glass of vinho verde or a cup of almond-flavored amarguinha, seafood in Algarve is best enjoyed with a backdrop of the setting sun.

In Algarve, the warmth of the sun is matched only by the hospitality of its people. This is a place where every beach hides a paradise, every town holds a story, and every meal is a celebration. Welcome to Algarve - Portugal's southern jewel. Here's to the memories and experiences waiting to unfold, as golden and unforgettable as Algarve's sandy shores.

Lagos:
Tracing the Maritime Legacy of Algarve

A city drenched in history and washed by the sun-kissed beaches of the Algarve, Lagos is the perfect marriage of the past and the present. This picturesque seaside town played a significant role in Portugal's Age of Discovery, serving as a launching point for voyages to Africa and the New World.

Roam the cobbled streets of the historic old town, where whitewashed houses and colorful facades stand in stark contrast to the azure sky. The fortress-like walls whisper tales of old, while the bustling marina brings you back to the present. And standing guard over the town is the imposing Lagos Castle, its towers offering a bird's-eye view of the city and the sea.

Of course, no visit to Lagos is complete without basking on its beautiful beaches. Meia Praia, with its long stretch of golden sand, is a sunbather's dream. For a taste of local cuisine, visit one of the beachfront eateries. They're the perfect places to enjoy fresh seafood paired with a chilled glass of vinho verde, all while watching the sun set over the Atlantic.

Benagil Cave:
A Sea Cave Paradise

Emerging from the emerald waters of the Algarve coast, the Benagil Sea Cave is a natural wonder that has captured the hearts of locals and travelers alike. Formed by the relentless forces of the ocean, the cave is a dramatic showcase of nature's artistry, where the play of light and shadow creates a spectacle worth witnessing.

Access to the cave is only possible by water, adding to the adventure. Several boat tours depart from nearby beaches, providing safe and knowledgeable navigation. Once inside, you'll be in awe of the cathedral-like dome, the golden sand beach, and the natural skylight opening to the blue sky above.

Remember to plan your visit according to the tides and weather conditions, as the sea can be quite unpredictable. It's also worth noting that swimming to the cave is not recommended due to strong currents. The best time to visit is in the morning, when the cave is less crowded and the light creates enchanting patterns on the walls.

Faro:
The Gateway to the Algarve

As the capital of the Algarve region, Faro often serves as the first glimpse of southern Portugal for many travelers. But beyond being a gateway, Faro is a destination in its own right, with a wealth of history, charming architecture, and a vibrant cultural scene.

Wandering through Faro's old town, you'll encounter an array of historic buildings, from the medieval city walls to the beautiful Faro Cathedral. Visit the Municipal Museum to delve into the city's Roman past, or unwind in one of the city's picturesque squares, basking in the sun and the laid-back Algarve vibe.

As the sun sets, make your way to the marina, a lively area teeming with restaurants and bars. This is the time to relish Faro's culinary offerings, whether it's a plate of fresh clams, a hearty cataplana, or a simple grilled sardine. Accompany it with a glass of local wine for a delightful end to your Faro exploration.

The Ria Formosa:
Algarve's Natural Wonder

The Ria Formosa lagoon is a mesmerizing network of canals, islands, marshlands, and sandy beaches that span 60 km along the Algarve coast. Recognized as a Natural Park, this unique ecosystem is a haven for a variety of wildlife, particularly migratory birds that use it as a stopover during their lengthy flights.

A visit to the Ria Formosa is a wonderful opportunity to immerse yourself in nature. Take a boat tour to explore the lagoon's picturesque waterways, or rent a bicycle and ride along the trails that crisscross the park. The barrier islands of Farol and Deserta are also worth a visit, each boasting pristine beaches and inviting waters.

If you're a birdwatcher, don't forget your binoculars. With over 200 species recorded in the park, you're bound to spot flamingos, spoonbills, and a variety of waders. And for a tasty break, stop at one of the local seafood restaurants. Try the clams or oysters; they're harvested directly from the lagoon and are a true Algarvian delicacy.

Sagres and Cape St. Vincent:
At the Edge of the World

At the southwesternmost point of mainland Europe, Sagres and Cape St. Vincent stand as sentinels over the tumultuous Atlantic. Often called the "End of the World", this is a place of raw, natural beauty, steeped in history and mystery.

Start in Sagres, a town that is intimately tied to Portugal's Age of Discovery. Visit the imposing Sagres Fortress, thought to be the site of the legendary nautical school founded by Prince Henry the Navigator. From its cliffs, enjoy a sweeping view of the endless ocean and the rugged coastline.

Then, make your way to Cape St. Vincent and its iconic lighthouse. As you stand on the windswept cliffs, watching waves crash against the rocks below, it's easy to see why ancient mariners thought this was the end of the world. Be sure to stay for the sunset; witnessing the sun sink into the Atlantic from this dramatic vantage point is a truly unforgettable experience.

Silves:
Algarve's Moorish Gem

In the heart of the Algarve, Silves invites visitors to delve into the region's rich past. As the former capital of the Moorish Algarve, Silves is home to some of the best-preserved Islamic architecture in Portugal.

The city's crowning glory is the red sandstone Silves Castle, a testament to the artistic and military prowess of the Moors. As you wander its robust walls and towers, you'll be rewarded with panoramic views of the town and the surrounding countryside. Don't miss the underground cistern, a testament to the advanced engineering of the Moors.

The winding streets of Silves are a joy to explore, with their whitewashed houses, flower-filled balconies, and historic buildings like the Gothic Cathedral and the Bridge of Silves. Take a moment to relax in one of the local cafes and savor a traditional pastel de nata. With its rich history and tranquil ambiance, Silves offers a delightful contrast to the bustling beach resorts of the Algarve.

Algarve's Beaches:
Basking in the Southern Sun

The Algarve is renowned for its stunning coastline, a captivating blend of golden sands, azure waters, and dramatic cliffs. With over 150 beaches to choose from, you're sure to find your perfect spot under the southern sun.

Praia da Marinha, often hailed as one of the most beautiful beaches in the world, is a must-visit. Nestled between towering cliffs, this idyllic cove is perfect for swimming and snorkeling in the clear, calm waters. For a more secluded experience, consider a boat trip to the uninhabited islands of Ria Formosa Natural Park, where the beaches are as pristine as they come.

Each Algarvian beach has its unique charm. Some, like Praia da Rocha, offer a lively atmosphere with beach bars, water sports, and plenty of amenities. Others, like Praia do Beliche, are tranquil hideaways, perfect for a quiet day by the sea. Whichever you choose, the Algarve's beaches are the region's undeniable highlights.

Golfing in Algarve:
Chasing Par Under the Algarve Sun

With over 40 golf courses, exceptional weather, and breathtaking scenery, the Algarve is a golfer's paradise. The region's world-class courses, designed by legendary names like Sir Nick Faldo and Jack Nicklaus, promise a memorable golfing experience.
Courses like the Oceanico Victoria and Quinta do Lago have hosted international tournaments, drawing professional players from around the world. But it's not just about the challenge; the stunning landscapes, with views of the sea, mountains, and verdant countryside, make for a round that is as scenic as it is rewarding.
Remember, golf in the Algarve isn't just for the pros. With a range of courses to suit all abilities, beginners can also enjoy the game. Most clubs offer equipment rental and lessons, so why not give it a swing? After your round, enjoy a meal at one of the clubhouses, where the region's culinary delights are sure to hit the mark.

Day Trip to Tavira:
Algarve's Historic Town

Tavira is one of the Algarve's most enchanting towns. Straddling both sides of the Gilão River, this tranquil town is a step back in time, with its cobblestone streets, medieval castle, and historic churches.
Begin your visit at the Tavira Castle, where you can explore the remnants of the Moorish fortress and enjoy panoramic views from the walls. Nearby, the Santa Maria do Castelo Church houses the tombs of seven Christian knights killed during the Reconquista.

Take a leisurely stroll along the river, crossing the Roman Bridge and watching the boats go by. Explore the town's backstreets, lined with traditional houses adorned with the region's characteristic tilework. If you need a break, the pristine beaches of Ilha de Tavira are just a short ferry ride away.

Tavira is also known for its gastronomy. Visit the local market for fresh produce, or sit down in one of the riverside restaurants to sample the seafood stew, a regional specialty. A day trip to Tavira offers a delightful blend of culture, history, and Algarvian charm.

Algarve Cuisine:
A Seafood Paradise

If there's one thing the Algarve is as famous for as its beaches, it's the cuisine. In this region, the Atlantic Ocean doesn't just provide a beautiful backdrop - it also fills the local kitchens with a bounty of seafood, resulting in dishes that are as flavorful as they are fresh.

A classic starter is the "Ameijoas à Bulhão Pato" - clams cooked in white wine, garlic, and coriander. For the main course, you can't miss the "Cataplana de Marisco", a delightful medley of seafood cooked in a clam-shaped copper pan. Grilled sardines, a summer favorite, and "Arroz de Marisco", a savory seafood rice dish, are other must-tries.

While seafood dominates, the Algarve's culinary scene is not without variety. Taste the "Frango da Guia", a spicy, piri-piri chicken dish, or the "Feijoada de Porco Preto", a hearty stew made from black Iberian pork and beans. End your meal on a sweet note with the "Dom Rodrigo", a traditional dessert made of egg yolk and almond.

Pair your meal with a local wine - the Algarve has four wine regions producing excellent vintages. Whether you're dining in a high-end restaurant or a seaside shack, the Algarve's gastronomic delights will make every meal an occasion to remember.

Final Thoughts:
Algarve, The Southern Jewel of Portugal

The Algarve, with its sun-drenched landscapes, historical towns, and delectable cuisine, has a unique allure. Its golden beaches, towering cliffs, and azure seas create a paradise for sun-seekers. At the same time, its Moorish past, maritime heritage, and rural heartlands offer a rich tapestry of culture and history to explore. Getting around the Algarve is relatively easy. The region has an extensive bus network, and most towns have train stations. However, renting a car will give you the freedom to discover the Algarve's less-trodden paths and hidden gems at your own pace. The region's size makes it possible to base yourself in one place, like Faro or Lagos, and take day trips to other towns and attractions.

The Algarve is a region for all seasons. While summer is a popular time for beach vacations, the mild winters make it an ideal destination for golfing, hiking, or simply enjoying the quieter side of Algarvian life. No matter when you visit, the region's warm hospitality will make you feel at home.

The Algarve is more than a destination; it's an experience. It's the feeling of the warm sun on your skin as you stroll along a sandy beach, the thrill of discovering a secluded cove at the end of a cliff-top trail, the pleasure of a fresh seafood feast after a day of exploration. It's the moments of unexpected beauty, the encounters with local culture, the simple joy of being in a place that is as welcoming as it is enchanting.

From the sunsets over Sagres to the whitewashed houses of Tavira, the Algarve leaves a lasting impression. It beckons with the promise of discovery and the allure of the extraordinary. So come and explore, indulge, and lose yourself in the southern jewel of Portugal. Because in the Algarve, every moment is a postcard from paradise.

CHAPTER 5: ALGARVE

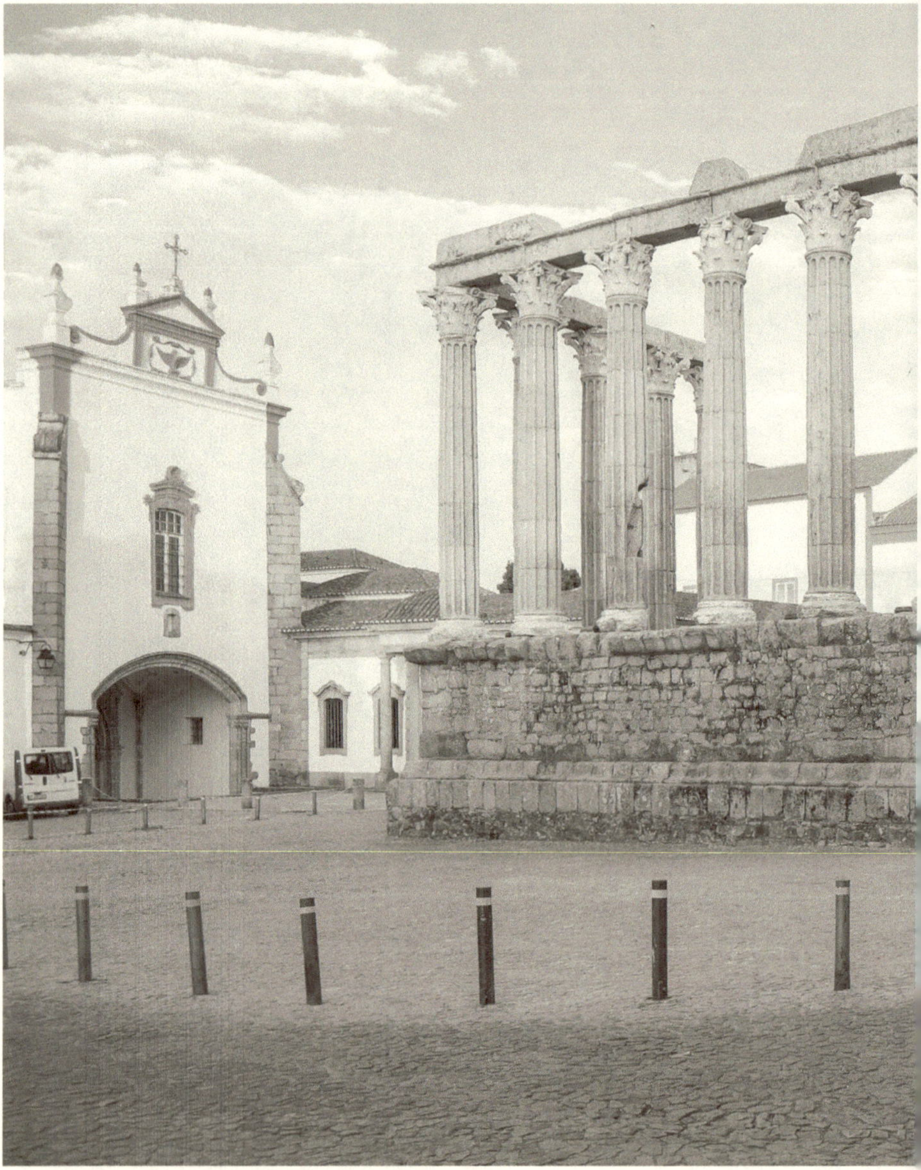

CHAPTER 6: ÉVORA AND ALENTEJO

CHAPTER 6:
Évora and Alentejo

With its sun-baked plains, rolling vineyards, and hilltop villages, Alentejo captures the soul of Portugal in its most unvarnished form. This vast region, often likened to a breadbasket, stretches across the south-central part of Portugal, from the Spanish border to the Atlantic Coast. At the heart of Alentejo lies Évora, a charming city steeped in history and infused with a timeless allure. Together, Évora and Alentejo form a captivating tapestry of history, culture, and gastronomy that rewards the discerning traveler.

As you approach Évora, its medieval walls and the towering spires of its cathedral beckon you into a city where the past feels wonderfully alive. From the Roman Temple's ancient ruins to the evocative Chapel of Bones, Évora is a treasure trove of historical landmarks. But it's not all about history. The city's bustling markets, family-run taverns, and vibrant arts scene ensure that modern life thrives amidst the heritage.

Venturing beyond Évora, Alentejo unfolds like a scenic storybook. The region's rustic charm is found in the whitewashed houses of hilltop villages, the majestic castles that tell tales of past struggles and conquests, and the ancient megaliths that hint at prehistoric life. It echoes in the haunting melodies of the Cante Alentejano, a traditional form of polyphonic singing.

Alentejo's gastronomic scene is a celebration of the region's abundant produce. From robust wines and flavorful cheeses to hearty stews and rich desserts, Alentejo's cuisine is a feast for the senses.

Embarking on a journey through Évora and Alentejo is not merely about traversing a geographical region. It's about stepping into a world where time seems to slow down, where life's simple pleasures are savored, and where every landscape, every bite of food, and every note of music narrates a story. So, prepare to immerse yourself in the rhythms of this region, as we delve into the manifold charms of Évora and Alentejo.

Évora Cathedral:
A Blend of Gothic and Manueline Styles

In the heart of Évora stands a stunning testament to Portugal's architectural grandeur, the Sé de Évora or Évora Cathedral. Constructed from local rose granite, this imposing structure seamlessly blends Romanesque, Gothic, and Manueline styles, painting a vivid portrait of Portugal's architectural evolution.

Enter the cathedral, and you'll find yourself beneath a forest of stone columns and pointed arches, characteristic of the Gothic aesthetic. Don't miss the chance to climb the cathedral's tower; the view from the top is simply sublime, providing a panoramic vista of Évora and the sprawling Alentejo plains.

If you're a lover of sacred music, be sure to check the cathedral's schedule for choral concerts. There's something profoundly moving about experiencing the cathedral's incredible acoustics as voices echo throughout the vaulted nave. Remember to dress respectfully as you're entering a place of worship, and consider hiring a guide to fully appreciate the cathedral's rich history.

Évora's Roman Temple:
A Glimpse of the Roman Past

One cannot visit Évora without being drawn to the city's Roman Temple. Also known as the Temple of Diana, it's one of the best-preserved Roman structures in the Iberian Peninsula, offering an insight into the city's ancient roots.

Marvel at the Corinthian columns standing tall against the sky, and imagine the temple as it might have been nearly 2000 years ago. Come at sunset to capture stunning photographs, when the warm glow enhances the temple's already impressive façade. The temple's vicinity also offers a handful of charming cafes where you can savor a cup of coffee or a glass of Alentejo wine. The regional tart, Queijada de Évora, made with cheese, is a local favorite, pairing perfectly with a strong bica, the Portuguese version of espresso.

Chapel of Bones:
Confronting Mortality in Évora

Tucked behind the Church of St. Francis, the Chapel of Bones (Capela dos Ossos) presents a chilling yet intriguing aspect of Évora's historical narrative. The walls of this 16th-century chapel are lined with thousands of human bones, serving as a sobering memento mori — a reminder of our mortality.

Upon entering, you're greeted with the ominous inscription, "We bones that here are, for yours await". While not for the faint of heart, this chapel offers a profound reflection on life and death that's rare in its frankness.

After visiting the Chapel, lighten the mood by exploring the beautiful gardens of Jardim Publico, a short walk away. Its tranquil paths, shaded by towering trees, are the perfect respite after the weighty visit to the Chapel of Bones. The garden's peacocks and ducks are an added delight, especially if you're traveling with children.

Monsaraz:
Journey to a Hilltop Village

Perched atop a hill with commanding views over the Alentejo plains, Monsaraz is a charming medieval village that seems frozen in time. From its cobblestone streets to whitewashed houses and the mighty castle, everything in Monsaraz whispers tales of a bygone era.

The village's elevated position means you can enjoy panoramic views of the surrounding countryside and the Alqueva dam, Europe's largest artificial lake. Take a leisurely stroll around the village, visit the local artisan shops, and try the olive oils and wines that Alentejo is famous for.

Before leaving, make sure to enjoy a meal in one of the local restaurants. Lamb stew and pork with clams are regional dishes that you shouldn't miss. And remember, Monsaraz's beauty shines brightest under the moonlight, so consider staying till dusk for a truly magical experience.

Evoramonte Castle:
Panoramic Views and a Slice of History

Emerging on the horizon like a vision from a fairy tale, the Evoramonte Castle (also known as Évora Monte Castle) is an intriguing fusion of Gothic and Manueline architectural styles.

Constructed in the 12th century, the castle was later modified in the 16th century, giving it its unique appearance today.
Climb the castle's towers and walk along the ramparts to appreciate the breathtaking 360-degree views of the Alentejo landscape. Be sure to bring your camera, as the panoramic vistas make for excellent photo opportunities.
A tip for history enthusiasts: delve into the castle's historical significance by exploring its connection to the 1834 Convention of Evoramonte, which ended the Portuguese civil wars. And remember, the castle can get quite hot during summer afternoons, so try to plan your visit for earlier in the day.

Vila Viçosa and its Ducal Palace:
A Trip to the House of Braganza

Vila Viçosa, often overlooked by visitors, is a treasure trove of art and history. The town's crown jewel is the Ducal Palace, the former seat of the House of Braganza, the last royal family of Portugal.

Step into the Palace, and you'll be swept into a world of opulence and grandeur. From exquisite tile work to intricately carved ceilings and invaluable art pieces, the Palace provides a glimpse into the life of Portuguese nobility.

When visiting the Palace, take advantage of the guided tours. They provide an excellent overview of the history and the fascinating anecdotes that make the Palace come alive. After your visit, enjoy a relaxing stroll in the town's quiet streets, and perhaps treat yourself to a meal in one of the local restaurants. Traditional Alentejo bread soup, paired with a glass of regional wine, is a must-try.

Marvão:
Discovering One of Portugal's Most Impressive Villages

Tucked away in the highlands of Alentejo and surrounded by medieval walls, Marvão is an enchanting village that offers panoramic views of the region from every corner. Its narrow streets, white houses, and centuries-old castle are a testament to the region's rich history.

Your journey through Marvão should begin at the Castle, where you'll find stunning vistas of the surrounding landscape and neighboring Spain. Inside the village, the Church of Santa Maria, with its quaint museum, is another must-visit spot.

A word of advice for photography enthusiasts: the views from Marvão at sunset, with the golden light bathing the Alentejo plains, are a sight you won't want to miss. Also, consider visiting in November, when the annual chestnut festival fills the village with joyful celebration and delicious treats.

Cante Alentejano:
Echoes of Alentejo's Musical Heritage

A visit to Alentejo wouldn't be complete without experiencing its soulful traditional music, Cante Alentejano. Recognized by UNESCO as an Intangible Cultural Heritage of Humanity, this polyphonic singing style has deep roots in the region and is a cherished part of local identity.

Often performed a cappella by amateur groups in local taverns and during festivals, the haunting melodies of Cante Alentejano express themes of rural life, love, and longing. For a truly immersive experience, look for live performances in Evora's

local taverns or music festivals across Alentejo.
Whether you're a music lover or not, listening to Cante Alentejano is an unforgettable way to connect with Alentejo's cultural heritage. So when the opportunity arises, sit back, enjoy a glass of local wine, and let the music touch your soul.

The Megalithic Monuments of Alentejo:
Prehistoric Wonders

For a fascinating journey back in time, Alentejo's megalithic monuments are a must-visit. Spread across the region, these ancient stone structures, including dolmens and menhirs, date back thousands of years and provide intriguing insights into prehistoric Portugal.

Among these, the Almendres Cromlech, located just outside of Évora, stands out. Considered one of the most important megalithic clusters in Europe, the site features nearly 100 standing stones arranged in an elliptical shape.

Remember to bring your walking shoes as some monuments require a short hike to reach. The best time to visit these sites is during sunrise or sunset, when the soft light adds an air of mystery to these already intriguing structures. And don't forget, these sites hold significant cultural importance, so please respect the monuments and their surroundings.

Alentejo Cuisine:
A Taste of Portugal's Breadbasket

When it comes to the culinary scene, Alentejo does not hold back. Portugal's breadbasket takes you on an unmatched gastronomic journey, revealing the richness of its soil and the soul of its people through each bite. Embodying generations of tradition and infused with unmistakable love for the land, Alentejo cuisine is comfort food at its finest.

To truly understand Alentejo's culinary culture, one must start with the bread. Its simplicity belies its significance - served at every meal, 'pão alentejano' is a testament to the region's agricultural heritage. Warm, crusty, and perfect with a smear of local butter, it's a delightful introduction to Alentejo's gastronomy.

Cheese is another highlight of Alentejo's cuisine. Explore the varieties from smooth and creamy to pungent and crumbly, each representing a different village's take on this beloved staple. 'Queijo de Serpa' and 'Queijo de Évora', made from sheep's milk, are must-tries, delivering a burst of flavor that pairs brilliantly with Alentejo's wines.

Speaking of wines, Alentejo's vineyards produce some of Portugal's best. Whether you're a novice or a connoisseur, wine tasting in Alentejo is an enriching experience. From the robust reds to the refreshing whites and fruity rosés, each glass offers a snapshot of Alentejo's diverse terroir.

The region is also known for its delectable meats and hearty stews. 'Porco Preto' (black pork), a local breed fed on acorns, and 'migas à alentejana', a delightful medley of bread, garlic, and pork, are classics that never fail to impress.

Eating in Alentejo is not just about the food, but also about the setting. Enjoy your meals in rustic taverns, family-run eateries, or amidst the vineyards under the vast Alentejo sky. Remember, in Alentejo, food is not hurried. It is savoured with joy and gratitude, much like the region itself.

Final Thoughts:
Évora and Alentejo, A Trip Through History and Gastronomy

Stepping into Évora and Alentejo is like walking into a living, breathing tapestry that weaves together historical wonders, enchanting landscapes, and soulful gastronomy. Each city, town, and village tells a tale, each monument holds a secret, and each meal invites you to partake in a tradition.

Whether you're tracing the lines of the Manueline style on Évora Cathedral, exploring the formidable walls of Evoramonte Castle, or immersing yourself in the hypnotic rhythm of Cante Alentejano, the experiences are boundless. These, combined with the warm hospitality of the Alentejanos, make every visit a remarkable adventure.

Embrace the Alentejo pace of life when you visit. Stroll through the streets of Évora, the whitewashed villages of Monsaraz and Marvão, taking in the architecture and the unchanging rhythms of local life. Get lost in the narrow, winding alleyways, browse through the local markets, or simply find a quiet spot to soak in the view of the undulating plains and cork forests. The tranquility of Alentejo has a way of slowing down time, turning every moment into a cherished memory.

Consider planning your trip to coincide with the changing seasons. Witness Alentejo in the vibrant hues of spring wildflowers, the golden warmth of summer, the festive bounty of autumn's harvest, or the calm serenity of winter. Each season paints the region in its unique palette, promising a different yet equally enchanting experience.

The beauty of Évora and Alentejo lies in their ability to transport visitors through time and introduce them to a lifestyle intimately tied to nature and tradition. These are lands that inspire, excite, and welcome, offering the traveler not just a journey, but a profound understanding of Portugal's heartland. As you conclude your trip, it's this sense of connection and discovery that will stay with you, reminding you of the joy of exploring new cultures, histories, and flavors. So, here's to Évora and Alentejo, where every path leads to a story, every meal to a celebration, and every moment to a memory.

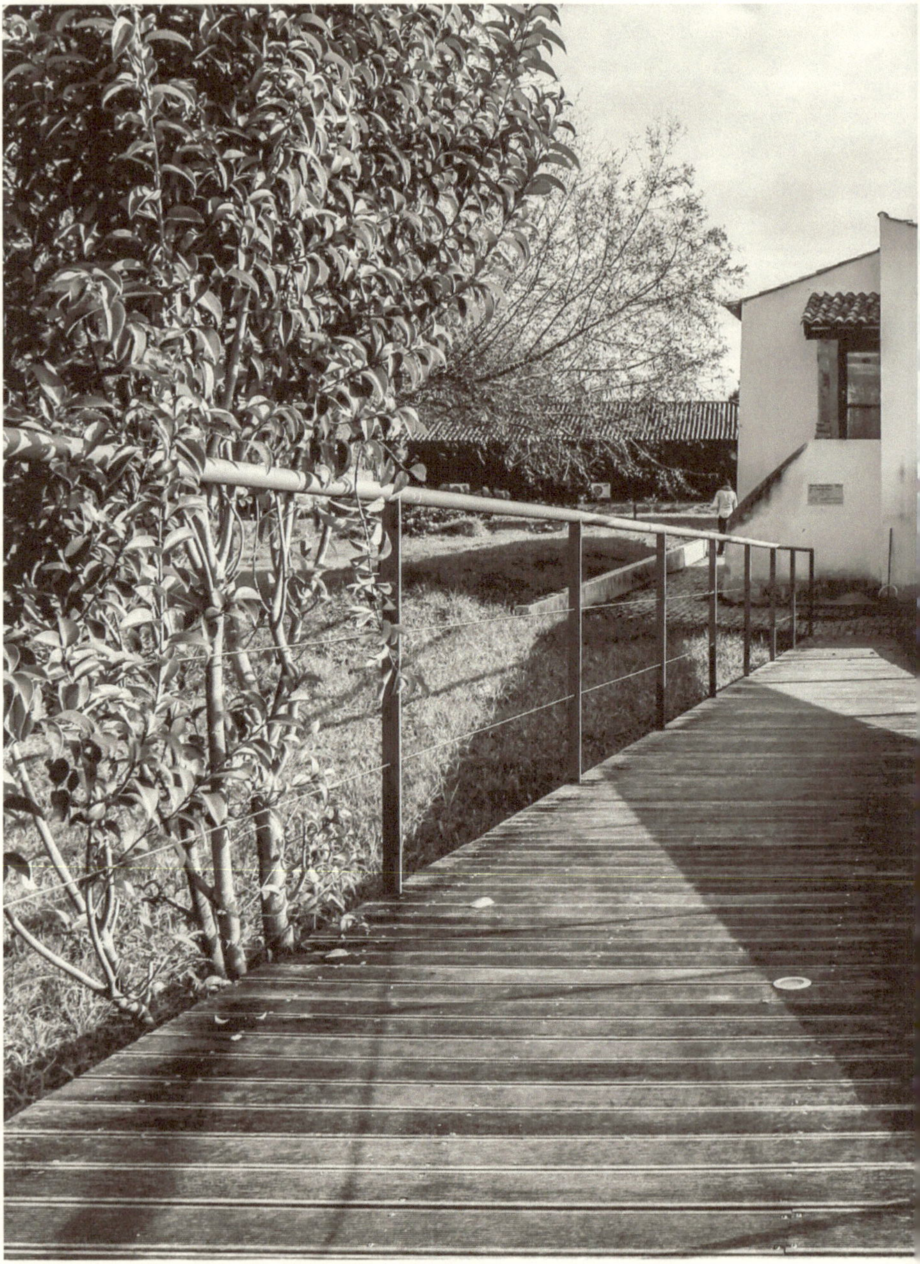

CHAPTER 7: COIMBRA

CHAPTER 7:
Coimbra

Nestled in the central region of Portugal, stretching along the banks of the Mondego River, lies Coimbra - a city where tradition and knowledge harmoniously intertwine. As one of the oldest university towns in Europe, Coimbra is characterized by a profound academic legacy, its timeworn streets bearing testament to the intellectuals who once traversed them. Yet, beyond its scholastic roots, the city teems with architectural treasures, verdant parks, and rich gastronomic delights that make every visit an exploration of Portugal's cultural heart.

Once the country's capital, Coimbra is divided into two distinct areas: the Cidade Alta (Upper Town) and the Cidade Baixa (Lower Town). The Upper Town, known as the historic hilltop university district, offers panoramic vistas of the Mondego River and beyond. Here, the grand structures of the University of Coimbra stand, whispering stories of the past. As you meander through its cobbled lanes, you're treated to a delightful architectural palette, spanning Romanesque churches to Manueline masterpieces.

On the other hand, the Lower Town, the commercial hub of Coimbra, buzzes with a dynamic energy. Quaint cafes, local boutiques, and bustling markets weave in and out of ancient buildings and modern establishments, painting a lively cityscape that encapsulates Coimbra's spirit. Here, the pulse of city life blends seamlessly with the echoes of the past, creating an atmosphere that is quintessentially Coimbra.

Yet, Coimbra is more than a convergence of the old and new. It's a city steeped in folklore and tradition, where student serenades resonate through ancient archways, and the centuries-old 'Queima das Fitas' (Burning of the Ribbons) still colors the city in vivacious hues every year. This deep-rooted academic and cultural identity, coupled with its rich history and charming landscapes, sets Coimbra apart, turning every visit into an immersive journey into the heart of Portugal.

Whether you're a history buff, a nature lover, or a food enthusiast, Coimbra has something to offer. Prepare to be drawn in by the city's intellectual charm, captivated by its storied structures, and enamored by its vibrant local life. Welcome to Coimbra - where every stone tells a story, every path leads to a discovery, and every visit leaves an indelible imprint on your heart.

University of Coimbra:
The Cradle of Knowledge

Dominating the city's skyline from its hilltop position, the University of Coimbra is a beacon of knowledge and a testament to the city's academic prestige. Established in the 13th century, it's one of the oldest universities in continuous operation in the world, inviting you to traverse the footsteps of scholars past. The grand buildings, perched high on the hill, echo stories of intellectual pursuits and scientific discoveries.

The university is home to a series of historical landmarks worth exploring. The intricate beauty of the Pátio das Escolas, the main courtyard, sets a grand stage for your exploration. Don't miss the opportunity to climb the iconic University Tower. While its 180 steps might seem challenging, the panoramic view of the city and the Mondego River from the top is rewarding.

Visiting the university isn't just about appreciating its architectural grandeur—it's also about immersing in academic tradition. Witness the students, robed in their traditional black capes, engaging in debates, making music, and contributing to the rich tapestry of university life. It's a living testament to Coimbra's deep-rooted love for knowledge and learning.

Joanina Library:
A Literary Jewel in Coimbra

Beyond the classrooms and lecture halls of the University of Coimbra lies the Joanina Library, a veritable temple to knowledge. Known as Biblioteca Joanina in Portuguese, it's a Baroque masterpiece that houses a precious collection of books dating back to the 16th century.

The moment you step inside, the library's grandeur unfolds. It's a work of art, with lavishly decorated interiors featuring intricate wood carvings, gilded archways, and frescoed ceilings, embodying the perfect marriage of aesthetic beauty and intellectual prowess.

Its collection comprises around 200,000 works, covering medicine, geography, and history—many of which are rare and invaluable. A visit to the Joanina Library isn't just for bibliophiles. It's for anyone who appreciates the marriage of history, architecture, and the enduring power of knowledge. Don't forget to observe the library's quiet guardians— the colony of bats that protect the books from insects during the night, an example of nature and culture living in harmony.

Monastery of Santa Cruz:
Paying Homage to Portugal's First Kings

Located in the heart of Coimbra, the Monastery of Santa Cruz serves as a sacred repository of Portugal's early history. Founded in 1131, this Augustinian monastery is a place of monumental importance, housing the tombs of Portugal's first two kings, Afonso Henriques and Sancho I.

From the outside, the Monastery presents an elegant facade of Manueline style, a stark contrast to the austere Romanesque architecture that dominates Coimbra. Once inside, however, you're treated to an impressive array of ecclesiastical art and architecture.

Pay a visit to the main chapel, where the tombs of the kings rest. The magnificent tombs, embellished with ornate sculptures, offer a poignant glimpse into Portugal's past. Don't miss the chance to explore the Church's chancel, adorned with striking azulejos (traditional ceramic tiles) that narrate biblical stories.

As you wander through this historical gem, spare a moment to soak in the peaceful atmosphere. Whether you're an architecture lover, a history buff, or simply a curious traveler, the Monastery of Santa Cruz offers a serene yet insightful foray into Portugal's early history.

Quinta das Lágrimas:
A Walk Through a Love Story

Set on the outskirts of Coimbra, the Quinta das Lágrimas estate encapsulates a heart-rending tale of love and tragedy, deeply ingrained in the nation's collective memory. It's here where the ill-fated romance of Prince Pedro and Inês de

Castro, the woman he loved against all odds, unfolded in the 14th century.

Strolling through the estate feels akin to leafing through the pages of a love story etched in time. The "Fonte das Lágrimas" (Fountain of Tears) stands as a poignant monument to their tale, where it's said Inês wept her last tears before being tragically murdered.

Beyond its tragic legend, Quinta das Lágrimas boasts splendid gardens dotted with native and exotic plants, century-old trees, and tranquil ponds. The estate is also home to a golf course and a luxurious hotel. As you navigate the manicured pathways and historical landmarks, let yourself be transported back to an epoch of intense passion and heartbreaking romance.

Portugal for Little Ones:
The Magic of Portugal dos Pequenitos

Tucked away in Coimbra is a unique attraction that delights visitors of all ages - Portugal dos Pequenitos. This miniaturized park, whose name translates to "Portugal for the Little Ones", is an endearing exploration of Portugal's cultural and architectural heritage, presented in a delightful, child-friendly manner. Stroll through the park to discover diminutive versions of Portugal's most famous landmarks, from the historic towers of Coimbra to the palaces of Sintra. The park also showcases miniature versions of traditional houses and cottages from across Portugal's diverse regions, providing a charming and educational snapshot of the country's regional heritage.

Remember to take your camera along. Whether it's your child standing next to a tiny version of Lisbon's Belem Tower or posing with a small-scale cod fisherman, these memorable moments are sure to make your visit to Portugal dos Pequenitos a highlight of your Coimbra adventure.

Botanical Garden of Coimbra:
A Green Oasis in the City

Stepping into the Botanical Garden of Coimbra, you're welcomed by a tranquil oasis, a welcome respite from the city's hustle and bustle. Established in the 18th century by the University of Coimbra, it's one of the oldest botanical gardens in Portugal and serves as a living museum of plant species from across the globe.

The garden is a perfect blend of science and serenity, organized into several sections, each dedicated to different types of flora. Wander through the systematic beds, greenhouses brimming with tropical plants, and a collection of medicinal plants that hark back to the garden's academic origins.

The "Garden of Aromas", home to a variety of aromatic and medicinal plants, is a sensory delight, while the bamboo grove offers a touch of the exotic. And don't miss the "Valley of Ferns", a cool, shaded area that's the perfect spot to unwind on a sunny day.

A visit to the Botanical Garden of Coimbra isn't just about enjoying its verdant surroundings—it's about understanding the intricate world of plants and the importance of biodiversity. Whether you're a nature lover or a curious traveler, the garden offers a peaceful and educational retreat.

The Old Cathedral of Coimbra:
A Romanesque Relic

The Old Cathedral of Coimbra, locally known as Sé Velha, is one of the city's most enduring symbols. Erected in the 12th century, during the reign of the first Portuguese king, Afonso Henriques, this fortress-like cathedral encapsulates the spirit of Romanesque architecture in Portugal.

Stepping inside the cathedral, visitors are welcomed by a nave and two aisles, defined by stout columns and rounded arches, characteristic of Romanesque style. The captivating wooden ceiling, the ornate main chapel, and the elegant cloister all contribute to its historical charm.

Don't miss the chance to climb to the upper level for panoramic views of Coimbra. As you gaze at the city stretching out below, surrounded by the solemn stone walls of Sé Velha, you're not just seeing Coimbra—you're experiencing a living slice of Portugal's historical heritage.

The New Cathedral of Coimbra:
A Testament of the Jesuit Legacy

Contrasting the antiquity of the Old Cathedral, Coimbra's New Cathedral, or Sé Nova, tells a different chapter of the city's ecclesiastical history. Originally built in the 16th century as the Jesuit Church of the Holy Name of Jesus, it became the city's new cathedral in the 18th century, following the Jesuits' expulsion from Portugal.

The exterior, adorned with a beautifully carved portal and an imposing bell tower, embodies the sober grandeur of the Mannerist style. Inside, the gilded woodwork and blue and white "azulejos" (Portuguese tiles) adorning the walls and ceiling represent the baroque splendor of Portuguese religious art.

Sé Nova is not just a cathedral—it's a testament to the city's ever-evolving religious and architectural narratives. Here, you can absorb the ambiance of devotion, trace the influences of the Jesuits, and admire some of the finest examples of religious art in the city.

Exploring the River Mondego:
Coimbra's Lifeline

Coimbra and the River Mondego are inextricably entwined, with the river playing an integral role in the city's identity. The Mondego, the longest river running entirely within Portugal, breathes life into Coimbra, its waters reflecting the city's grandeur and its banks serving as a meeting point for locals and visitors alike.

A walk along the riverfront promenade is a must. Here, you can take in the picturesque vista of the cityscape, with the University's tower watching over the old city, while rowing boats glide peacefully on the river. The riverside park, Parque Verde do Mondego, is perfect for picnics, leisurely strolls, or bike rides.

For an unforgettable Mondego experience, hop on a traditional wooden boat, or "barco moliceiro", for a leisurely tour of the river. As you drift along, you'll have a unique perspective on Coimbra's historic sites and charming riverside neighborhoods. The river Mondego isn't just a waterway—it's the fluid, vivacious pulse of Coimbra.

Coimbra Cuisine:
A Taste of Academic Life

One can't truly know Coimbra without indulging in its culinary culture, which, like the city itself, is rich in tradition and full of soul. As home to one of the world's oldest universities, Coimbra's gastronomy reflects its academic heritage, offering flavors that have satisfied the palates of scholars for centuries.

Start your culinary journey with "Chanfana", a classic dish that has its roots in the city's student culture. This hearty stew, made with goat meat, red wine, and a mix of aromatic spices, is traditionally slow-cooked in a black clay pot, resulting in a deeply flavorful dish that warms the soul. Pair it with a glass of Dão wine, a robust red that originates from the nearby Dão region, and you have a meal fit for an academic.

Street food also thrives in Coimbra, with "Bifanas", or pork cutlet sandwiches, being a local favorite. For a quick snack, try the "Pastel de Santa Clara", a sweet custard tart named after Coimbra's Santa Clara Convent.

When it comes to dining venues, Coimbra offers everything from historical taverns to modern eateries. One of the most iconic places is the Antiga Casa dos Leitões, famous for its roasted suckling pig, or "leitão assado". For something a little different, head to Ze Manel dos Ossos, a quirky eatery decked out with hand-written notes from patrons and serving rustic Portuguese dishes.

To experience Coimbra's vibrant student culture, join the locals at one of the many student bars, or "Repúblicas", where cheap beer, lively chatter, and traditional "fado" music combine to create an ambiance filled with youthful energy and academic camaraderie.

In Coimbra, food isn't merely sustenance—it's an embodiment of the city's history, a testament to its academic spirit, and a tantalizing journey of flavors that resonates with every bite.

Final Thoughts:
Coimbra, A City Steeped in Tradition and Knowledge

As we draw this chapter to a close, it's clear that Coimbra is more than just a city—it's a custodian of Portugal's academic traditions, a bastion of centuries-old architecture, and a vibrant cultural hub. Each cobblestone street, ancient edifice, and traditional "fado" song tells a story, painting a vivid picture of the city's rich past and dynamic present.

If you're planning a visit, take the time to truly absorb the city's scholarly spirit. Immerse yourself in its vibrant student culture, explore the hallowed halls of the University, and lose yourself in the maze of ancient streets. When the golden light of dusk falls on Coimbra, and the strains of "fado" echo through the air, you'll find yourself in the heart of Portugal's soulful academia.

But Coimbra isn't just about living in the past—it's a city that balances tradition and modernity with grace. Alongside the ancient monuments, you'll find bustling cafes, contemporary restaurants, and innovative art spaces. And amidst the academic rigor, there's a sense of joy and celebration, best seen in the lively student festivals and vibrant nightlife.

When it comes to gastronomy, Coimbra offers an immersive experience. From traditional dishes steeped in history to innovative fusion cuisine, the city's food scene is a reflection of its diverse cultural influences and its academic heritage.

While exploring, don't forget the River Mondego, Coimbra's lifeline. A boat trip along the river, a leisurely walk along its banks, or a picnic in the riverside park offer unique ways to appreciate the city's beauty.

Lastly, remember that the beauty of traveling lies in immersing oneself in the local culture. Listen to the stories the locals tell, join in their celebrations, and take a moment to appreciate the timeless traditions. This is Coimbra—a city that educates, inspires, and enthralls.

So, are you ready to step into a world steeped in tradition and knowledge? Coimbra awaits, with its arms open and its stories ready to be told. Prepare for a journey that's as enriching as it is unforgettable. Coimbra, the city of scholars, is ready to teach you its history, share its culture, and welcome you with open arms. Be prepared to learn, for Coimbra is not just a city, but a lifelong lesson in history, culture, and life itself.

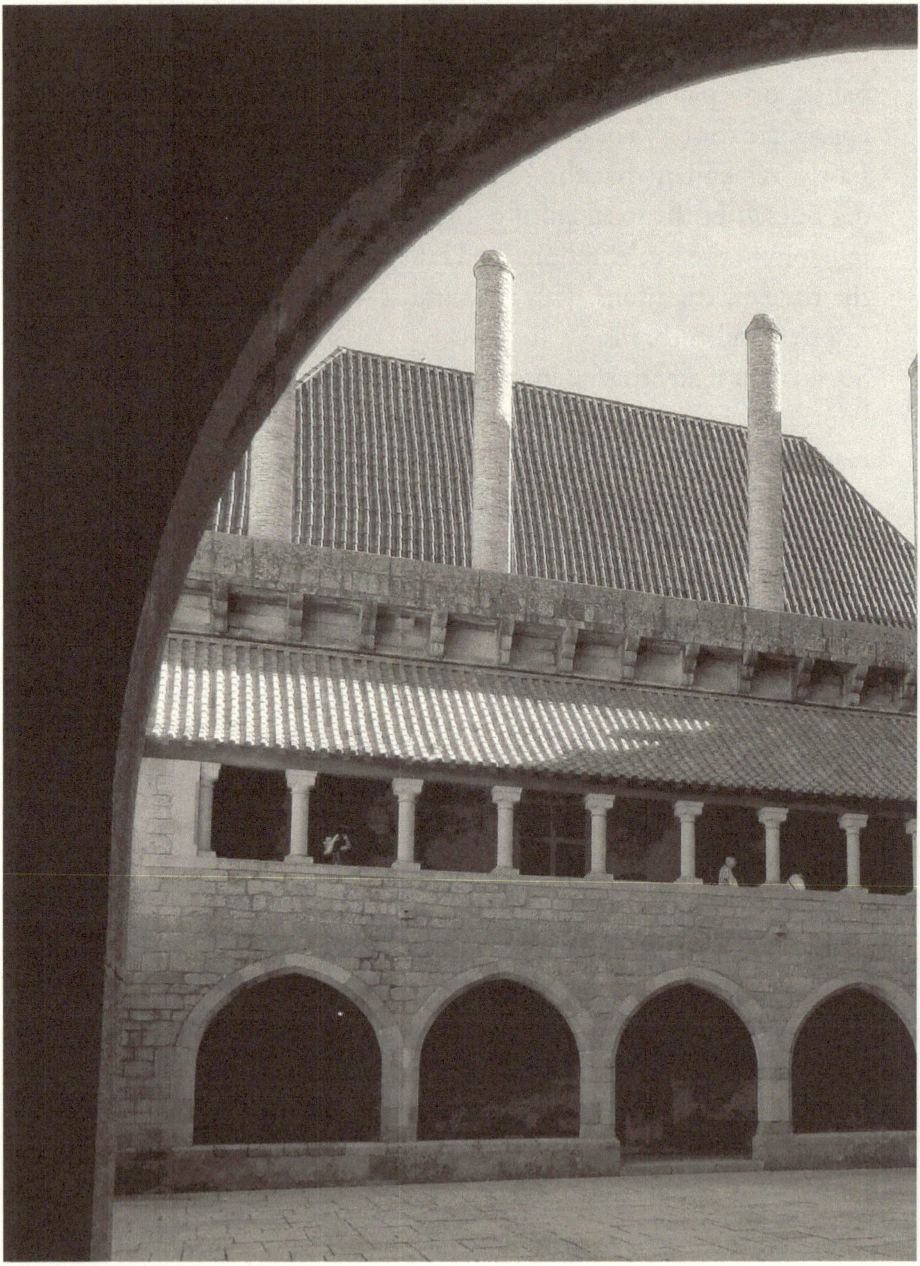

CHAPTER 8: BRAGA AND GUIMARÃES

CHAPTER 8:
Braga and Guimarães

Welcome to the land where Portugal's heart beats - the ancient cities of Braga and Guimarães. Rich in historical significance and bursting with cultural treasures, these two northern gems stand as proud custodians of the nation's heritage, each echoing tales of kings, saints, and age-old traditions.

Braga, one of the oldest Christian cities in the world, serves as a spiritual beacon, where ancient and modern faith intertwines amidst towering cathedrals, grand sanctuaries, and beautiful baroque architecture. Time spent here reveals a rich tapestry of history, as every cobblestone, monument, and church is imbued with stories spanning over 2,000 years.

At the heart of Braga, you'll find the Sé, Portugal's oldest cathedral, which weaves a tangible narrative of religious art and architectural styles that have evolved over the centuries. Meanwhile, outside the city center, the magnificent sanctuaries of Bom Jesus do Monte and Sameiro offer stunning panoramas that match their spiritual significance.

Just a short distance from Braga lies Guimarães, often referred to as the "birthplace of Portugal". This city was the first capital of Portugal and the birthplace of Afonso Henriques, the country's first king. Its historic center, a UNESCO World Heritage site, is a captivating maze of medieval lanes, ancient buildings, and impressive monuments.

The imposing Guimarães Castle and the luxurious Palace of the Dukes of Braganza tell tales of regal power and nobility, while the archaeological site of Citânia de Briteiros offers a glimpse into the region's distant Celtic past.

In the culinary scene, Braga and Guimarães serve hearty Minho fare, with dishes that comfort the soul and tickle the palate. These cities are also renowned for their vibrant festivals, where traditions are kept alive with colorful processions, traditional music, and joyous celebrations.

Braga and Guimarães are more than historical repositories – they are living, breathing testament to Portugal's rich past, vibrant present, and hopeful future. As we delve deeper into these cities, prepare yourself for a journey through time, where centuries of stories, traditions, and flavors are waiting to be discovered. Welcome to Braga and Guimarães, where every corner echoes with the heartbeats of Portugal's history.

Bom Jesus do Monte:
Ascending Braga's Spiritual Hill

Perched on a hilltop just outside Braga, the Sanctuary of Bom Jesus do Monte is more than just a place of worship—it's a testament to religious devotion and architectural grandeur. Ascending the sanctuary is a spiritual journey that begins at the foot of its iconic Baroque staircase, which symbolically guides pilgrims through the stages of the Cross.

The climb, although challenging, rewards visitors with stunning views of the city and the surrounding countryside. Yet, if you prefer a less strenuous ascent, the century-old funicular—the oldest water-powered funicular in the world—is ready to ease your journey.

At the top, the church itself is a masterpiece of Neoclassical design, filled with intricate religious artworks. But don't stop there. Explore the beautiful gardens, tranquil ponds, and hidden grottoes that surround the sanctuary. It's a slice of heavenly peace, a perfect spot to reflect and enjoy the serene beauty of nature.

Braga Cathedral:
Tracing Centuries of Religious Art and Architecture

Braga Cathedral, or Sé de Braga, is a cornerstone of Portugal's religious history. As the oldest cathedral in the country, it's a tapestry of architectural styles, reflecting the many periods it has witnessed since its construction began in the 11th century. From its imposing Romanesque exterior to the richly decorated Gothic main chapel, every corner tells a story. Discover the organ decorated with Chinese motifs—a tribute to the early Portuguese explorations in Asia—or admire the stunning Baroque additions from the 18th century.

Don't forget to visit the Cathedral's Treasury, which houses an impressive collection of ecclesiastical art, relics, and manuscripts. Here, the history of the church—and Braga itself—is beautifully preserved, offering a deep insight into Portugal's religious evolution.

Guimarães Castle:
Walking Through the Birthplace of Portugal

Steeped in history and heritage, Guimarães Castle stands as a proud symbol of Portugal's origin. Constructed in the 10th century to protect the region from Moorish and Norman invasions, it was within these walls that Portugal's first king, Afonso Henriques, was supposedly born.

The imposing fortress, with its crenelated towers and fortified walls, exudes a strong medieval charm. Venture inside to explore its compact yet intriguing interiors, where you can climb the towers and walk the battlements, imagining the fervor of battles past.

Take a moment to marvel at the beautiful views of Guimarães from the castle walls. The panorama of terracotta rooftops, ancient buildings, and narrow alleys encapsulates the medieval spirit of the city. A visit to Guimarães Castle is a journey to the very roots of the Portuguese nation, a step back in time to the birth of a kingdom.

Palace of the Dukes of Braganza:
A Dive into Portuguese Nobility

A stone's throw away from Guimarães Castle, the Palace of the Dukes of Braganza is a formidable reminder of Portugal's noble history. Built in the 15th century by Afonso, the first Duke of Braganza, the stately mansion showcases the grandeur of Portuguese nobility during the Middle Ages.

As you wander through the palace's 39 rooms, you'll discover an impressive collection of tapestries, paintings, and antique furniture. Pay special attention to the Great Hall, where the enormous chimneys and wooden ceiling are a testament to medieval luxury.

The palace also hosts a museum with fascinating exhibitions that change throughout the year, providing insight into the life of the nobility. Don't miss the beautiful gardens that surround the palace—a perfect spot for a leisurely stroll. The Palace of the Dukes of Braganza is not just a museum; it's a window into the past, and a vital part of the historical narrative of Portugal.

São Martinho de Tibães Monastery:
Braga's Monastic Life

Located just outside Braga, the São Martinho de Tibães Monastery offers a glimpse into Portugal's monastic tradition. Dating back to the 11th century, it served as the mother house for the Benedictine Order in Portugal and Brazil during the colonial period.

From the moment you enter, the monastery captivates you with its grandeur. The ornate Rococo church, featuring stunning gold leaf work and intricate wood carvings, is a highlight of any visit. Equally impressive are the cloisters, where you can stroll in peace and quiet, surrounded by beautiful baroque tile work.

Venture further to explore the kitchen, refectory, and the monks' cells. Don't forget to visit the remarkable surrounding gardens, complete with a lake and several Baroque fountains. A visit to São Martinho de Tibães Monastery is a journey into a tranquil past, offering a fascinating look at monastic life in Portugal.

Guimarães Historical Center:
A UNESCO World Heritage Site

A stroll through the Historical Center of Guimarães is like stepping into a time capsule. This UNESCO World Heritage site, often referred to as the cradle of Portugal, preserves a rich collection of well-preserved medieval buildings, narrow cobblestone streets, and quaint squares.

Begin your journey at the Largo da Oliveira, the town's central square, which is bustling with cafes, shops, and a Gothic shrine in its middle. From there, lose yourself in the maze of ancient alleys, each one revealing a new piece of the city's history.

While you explore, look out for the iconic inscription "Aqui nasceu Portugal" (Portugal was born here) on the old city walls—a reminder of the city's significance in the country's history. After a day of exploration, sit back at a local café and watch the world go by. The historical center of Guimarães, with its unique charm and rich history, promises an unforgettable journey through time.

Sameiro Sanctuary:
Panoramic Views from Braga's Holy Site

Perched atop a mountain, the Sanctuary of Our Lady of Sameiro, or simply Sameiro Sanctuary, is one of the most important Marian shrines in Portugal. But besides being a place of religious devotion, it offers breathtaking panoramic views of Braga and the surrounding region.

As you climb the granite staircase, adorned with statues of saints, you'll reach the grandiose neoclassical church. Inside, you'll find a richly decorated interior with a high altar in polished granite and an image of the Virgin Mary, said to have been brought from Rome in the 19th century.

Don't miss the opportunity to ascend to the top of the sanctuary's two towers. The sweeping vistas are worth every step. Whether you're a devotee seeking solace or a traveler in search of beauty, the Sameiro Sanctuary provides a peaceful retreat, high above the hustle and bustle of city life.

Citânia de Briteiros:
Unearthing Guimarães' Celtic Past

Step back in time with a visit to Citânia de Briteiros, an archaeological site located just outside Guimarães. This ancient settlement, known as a 'citânia', was home to the Celtic Bracari people around 2,000 years ago.

Walking through the site, you'll encounter the remnants of ancient stone structures, which include circular dwellings, bathhouses, and a council house, giving you a tangible sense of life in a pre-Roman Celtic village. Signposts and information boards around the site help piece together the story of this fascinating civilization.

Make sure to visit the on-site museum, where artifacts discovered during excavation—like pottery, tools, and jewelry—are on display. To truly appreciate Citânia de Briteiros, wear comfortable shoes, bring water, and allow yourself plenty of time to wander and explore this gateway into Portugal's ancient history.

Raio Palace:
A Jewel of Braga's Baroque Architecture

In the heart of Braga stands Raio Palace, an exquisite example of late Baroque and Rococo architecture. Built in the 18th century for João Duarte de Faria, a prominent merchant, the palace's striking blue façade with its ornate white decorations instantly draws the eye.

Step inside to explore the beautifully restored rooms, each one showcasing a different aspect of 18th-century noble life. The palace also hosts a museum dedicated to the history of the hospital and medical practices, making it a unique cultural experience in Braga.

Despite its grandeur, Raio Palace often flies under the radar of many visitors, making it a hidden gem waiting to be discovered. After your visit, take a moment to enjoy a coffee at one of the nearby cafés and take in the beauty of this architectural masterpiece.

Braga and Guimarães Cuisine:
A Tale of Two Cities

Both Braga and Guimarães, while close in proximity, each offer unique flavors and culinary experiences that highlight the diversity and richness of Northern Portugal's cuisine. This regional fare is deeply influenced by the land's agricultural abundance, treasured family recipes, and centuries-old traditions.

In Braga, indulge in the city's signature dish, 'Bacalhau à Braga'. This codfish delicacy is typically served with thinly sliced fried potatoes and a garnish of onions and peppers. The city is also known for its 'frigideiras', a type of meat pie, and 'Pudim Abade de Priscos', a heavenly dessert made by combining egg yolks, sugar, and pork fat, infused with a touch of Port wine.

Guimarães, on the other hand, boasts hearty meat dishes. Try 'Roasted Kid Goat' or 'Posta à Mirandesa', a thick-cut steak from a local cattle breed. 'Tortas de Guimarães' and 'Toucinho do Céu' are two delightful pastries not to be missed.

When it comes to drinks, both cities offer excellent Vinho Verde. This young, slightly effervescent wine pairs perfectly with the local cuisine and is best enjoyed in one of the many traditional taverns. Make your culinary journey complete by visiting local markets, where you can buy fresh produce, cheeses, and cured meats. Here, the vendors' friendly banter and the array of local products truly encapsulate the region's gastronomic spirit.

Final Thoughts:
Braga and Guimarães, Where Portugal's Heart Beats

Braga and Guimarães, two cities steeped in history, culture, and tradition, are the pulse of Portugal's soul. They captivate visitors with their blend of medieval charm, religious fervor, and vibrant culinary scenes.

To truly savor these cities, take your time. Wander their ancient streets, pause in their tranquil squares, and take a moment to breathe in the timeless ambiance. Visit their markets, indulge in their gastronomy, and converse with the locals, who are always eager to share stories of their cities' proud heritage.

When in Guimarães, pay attention to the small details—the cobbled streets, the medieval buildings, the ambiance of its historic center. They all whisper tales of the birth of a nation. In Braga, feel the city's spiritual heartbeat in its churches, sanctuaries, and religious festivals.

Remember, every corner of Braga and Guimarães offers a slice of Portuguese history and culture, making them not just destinations, but gateways to understanding Portugal itself. Whether you are a history enthusiast, a food lover, or simply a curious traveler, Braga and Guimarães promise an unforgettable journey where you'll witness Portugal's heart beating in every nook and corner.

As you leave these cities, you'll carry with you not just photographs or souvenirs, but a piece of Portugal's vibrant spirit. So, embark on this journey, open your heart to new experiences, and let Braga and Guimarães charm you, just as they have charmed generations of travelers before you.

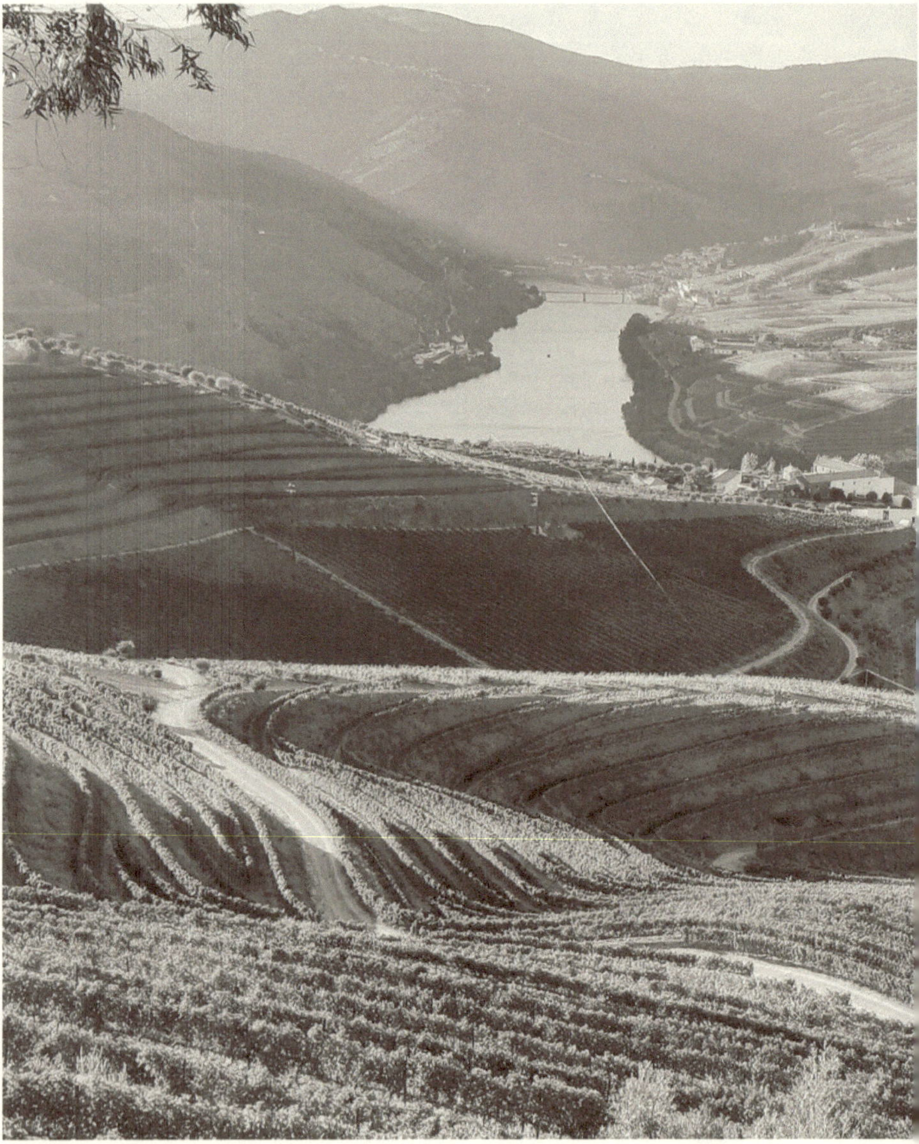

CHAPTER 9: DOURO VALLEY 307

CHAPTER 9:
Douro Valley

There's a serene rhythm to life in the Douro Valley, a place where nature and man have harmoniously shaped the land over the centuries. The valley's terraced vineyards, carved into the rugged hillsides, create a mesmerizing patchwork of greens and golds that has captivated artists, poets, and travelers alike. Stretching from the coastal city of Porto to the Spanish border, the Douro Valley is not just Portugal's, but the world's oldest demarcated wine region, internationally recognized for its fine Port and Douro wines.

But there's more to this valley than its world-renowned wines. The Douro River, which shapes the valley, snakes its way through a landscape dotted with quaint towns, opulent manor houses, and tranquil monasteries. Its slopes and valleys are home to a rich variety of flora and fauna, and its people, always warm and welcoming, carry with them centuries-old traditions and customs.

This chapter invites you to embark on a journey through the Douro Valley, a place where each bend in the river unveils a new panorama, where every sip of wine tells a story, and where the essence of Portugal can be experienced in its purest form. Whether you're a wine connoisseur, a lover of natural beauty, a history enthusiast, or a gastronome, the Douro Valley promises a multitude of enchanting experiences. So, pack your bags, open your senses, and get ready to dive deep into the heart of Portugal's wine country.

Régua:
Douro's Unofficial Capital

Régua, also known as Peso da Régua, is often referred to as the unofficial capital of the Douro Valley. It's an important hub for the wine industry and the point from which many Douro adventures begin. Its charming riverside location and historical significance make it a delightful stopover.

Visitors to Régua can stroll along the scenic riverfront, lined with traditional rabelo boats, once used for transporting wine barrels down the river. The Douro Museum, located in a beautifully restored 18th-century building, provides an insightful look into the region's wine culture. Besides, the town's numerous wine shops and cellars offer a chance to taste a wide variety of Douro wines.

Régua's train station connects it to other major towns in the valley, making it an accessible base for exploration. Don't miss out on a visit to the Douro Museum to gain a deep understanding of the region's wine heritage.

Douro River Cruise:
Sailing Through Vineyard-Covered Slopes

One of the most memorable ways to explore the Douro Valley is undoubtedly by a river cruise. A Douro River Cruise offers an immersive perspective of the region's vineyard-covered slopes, meandering waterways, and picturesque quintas (wine estates).

The slow-paced journey allows you to soak in the panorama of terraced vineyards rising from the river banks, traditional rabelo boats floating gently by, and hilltop villages adding charm to the landscape. Some cruises also provide on-board wine tastings and gourmet meals, enhancing the overall experience.

River cruises range from a few hours to multi-day voyages. Consider the time you have at your disposal when booking. An early morning or late afternoon cruise can offer breathtaking views of the sunrise or sunset over the valley.

Wine Tasting in Douro:
Savoring Portugal's Wine Heritage

The Douro Valley's most irresistible attraction is undoubtedly its wine. A tasting session in Douro not only satiates the palate but also provides a deep understanding of the region's wine-making traditions. From robust reds to crisp whites and the ever-popular Port, the wines of Douro are as diverse as they are delightful.

Many quintas offer guided tours, where you can walk through lush vineyards, visit age-old cellars, and learn about the wine-making process from passionate vintners. These tours are usually rounded off with a tasting session, often accompanied by local cheese and charcuterie.

Booking a wine tasting session in advance is highly recommended, especially during the peak season. Don't shy away from asking questions during the tour - vintners are usually more than happy to share their knowledge and passion for wine. And remember, it's perfectly okay to spit the wine out during a tasting – it's a sign of a discerning palate, not rudeness!

Mateus Palace:
A Grand House in the Douro Valley

An emblematic symbol of the region, the Mateus Palace in Vila Real is one of the finest examples of baroque civil architecture in Portugal. Recognizable from the labels of the famous Mateus Rosé wine, this grand manor house is a spectacle to behold with its ornate granite facade and imposing watchtowers. The palace's elegant interiors, adorned with 17th and 18th-century furniture, family portraits, and valuable works of art, offer a fascinating insight into Portugal's aristocratic past.

The palace grounds feature beautifully manicured gardens, reflecting pools, and cedar-lined paths, offering a serene retreat. For wine aficionados, the palace cellars offer a taste of the family-owned Mateus wine. It's advisable to book a guided tour for a deeper understanding of the palace's history and architecture.

Pinhão and its Train Station:
Art and Views in the Douro

Nestled on the banks of the Douro River, Pinhão is known for its serene river views and picturesque landscapes. But the star attraction of this small town is undoubtedly its historical train station. The station's main building is adorned with twenty-four blue and white tile (azulejo) panels depicting scenes from the daily life and harvest in the Douro Valley, offering a wonderful glimpse into the region's past.

The charming town of Pinhão also serves as a perfect base for vineyard visits, with several quintas located just a short drive away. The surrounding hills offer stunning viewpoints, perfect for catching a panoramic sunset over the Douro.

Vineyard Visits:
Immersion in the Wine Making Process

Visiting a quinta (wine estate) in the Douro Valley is an immersive journey into the world of wine-making. Walking amidst rows of vine-laden terraces, visitors can gain insights into the labor-intensive process of growing grapes on these steep slopes. In addition to learning about the different grape varieties and the intricacies of the terraced vineyards, visitors can delve into the wine-making process, from grape harvesting and crushing to fermentation and aging. Some quintas offer the opportunity to participate in grape harvesting and stomping – a unique and fun experience, especially during the vendimia (harvest season). After the tour, it's time to savor the fruits of these labors with a wine tasting session. Sampling the wines in the very place they are produced, often in the company of the wine-makers themselves, is a truly special experience. Booking in advance is generally recommended as many quintas are not open for impromptu visits. Remember to wear comfortable shoes as the terrain can be quite uneven.

Miradouro de São Leonardo de Galafura:
Breathtaking Views of the Douro Valley

If you're seeking the most breathtaking panoramas of the Douro Valley, look no further than the Miradouro de São Leonardo de Galafura. Located approximately halfway between Régua and Pinhão, this viewpoint offers unparalleled vistas of the winding Douro River and the valley's terraced vineyards. The dramatic landscape stretching out beneath your feet is a sight to behold and a photographer's dream.

Visitors can also enjoy a serene chapel, a picnic area, and a restaurant with equally stunning views. Don't forget to pack your camera and make sure you arrive in time for the sunset when the valley is bathed in a warm, golden light.

Lamego:
A Blend of Baroque and Gothic Splendors

Steeped in history, Lamego is an ancient city renowned for its cultural and architectural riches. A fusion of Gothic and Baroque splendors, the city is home to the magnificent Shrine of Our Lady of Remedies. This towering structure is adorned with exquisitely designed azulejos and offers a fantastic view of the city below. To reach the shrine, prepare yourself for a climb up the double zigzag stairway of 686 steps - a journey worth every step.

Lamego's old town is replete with historic landmarks like the Castle of Lamego, Lamego Cathedral, and the Ribeiro Conceição Theatre. Wandering the narrow, winding streets of Lamego, you'll discover a range of traditional shops selling local specialties such as Bôla de Lamego (a type of bread filled with smoked ham), and Raposeira, the local sparkling wine.

Harvesting Grapes:
Experiencing the Vendimia

The grape harvest or vendimia, typically between September and October, is the most exciting time of year in the Douro Valley. It's when the region comes alive with activity as locals and visitors alike gather to participate in the centuries-old tradition of grape harvesting.

Participating in the vendimia is a hands-on experience. From the early morning picking of the ripe grapes, to the traditional grape stomping in large granite lagares, you'll be part of a vibrant, festive atmosphere filled with camaraderie and often accompanied by folk music and traditional dances. It's a chance to experience firsthand the labor and love that goes into every bottle of Douro wine.

Several quintas offer grape harvesting experiences which typically need to be booked in advance. This is not only a unique opportunity to learn about the winemaking process but also a way to deeply connect with the local culture and traditions. Ensure you're dressed comfortably for the day in the vineyard - a hat and sunblock are a must.

Douro Valley Cuisine:
Pairing Food with Douro Wines

Exploring the Douro Valley isn't just a visual feast, it's a culinary journey too. This region's cuisine is as rich and diverse as its landscape, with deeply rooted traditional recipes passed down through generations. Here, food is a celebration, and wine is its inseparable companion, creating a symphony of flavors that sings the song of the region's history and culture.

The Douro Valley's cuisine is hearty, reflecting the lifestyle of its vineyard laborers. Dishes like Feijoada Trasmontana (a kind of bean stew with various meats), Cabrito Assado (roast kid), and Posta Mirandesa (a traditional steak dish) are staples. These robust flavors find their perfect match in the full-bodied, complex red wines of the Douro.

But the pairing doesn't stop there. The region's delicate white wines are ideal companions to its rich fish dishes, particularly the Bacalhau à Braga, a cod dish unique to the region. For dessert, indulge in the doces conventuais, traditional pastries dating back to convent and monastery kitchens. The slight sweetness of a Douro Moscatel or a Late Harvest wine pairs excellently with the richness of these pastries.

Many quintas and local restaurants offer food and wine pairing experiences. Remember, while a particular pairing suggestion may enhance your culinary experience, the best pairing is one that caters to your personal preference. In the end, wine and food pairing is a journey, not a destination, one that unfolds beautifully in the bountiful Douro Valley.

Final Thoughts:
Douro Valley, A Symphony in Green and Gold

Your journey through the Douro Valley is akin to stepping into a vivid painting, a landscape beautifully brushed with the vibrant hues of green vineyards and golden sunlight. The river Douro, the lifeblood of the region, serenely snakes its way, while the terraced vineyards stand as a testament to human tenacity and creativity. It's not just a visit; it's an immersion into a way of life that has been shaped by the rhythm of nature and the love for wine.

Plan your visit keeping in mind the seasonality. While every season in the Douro has its charm, the harvest season brings a unique vitality to the region. If you're planning on a river cruise or a train journey, remember to book in advance as they tend to fill up quickly, especially during peak season.

Douro Valley is not a place to rush through. It's a destination to be savored, just like its wines. Take time to walk through the vineyards, enjoy a leisurely picnic by the river, lose yourself in the timeless beauty of the landscapes, and let the local cuisine surprise you at every meal. Most importantly, open yourself up to the people you meet - their stories and their smiles. It's in these personal encounters that you truly experience the heart and soul of this extraordinary region.

The Douro Valley is not merely a destination. It's a melody composed by the strumming river, the whispering vines, and the bustling wineries. A song that, once heard, echoes in your heart long after you've left. The Douro is more than just a valley; it's a symphony in green and gold, an ode to the art of wine, and a testament to human perseverance and passion. In the Douro Valley, you'll find that beauty is indeed an endless river.

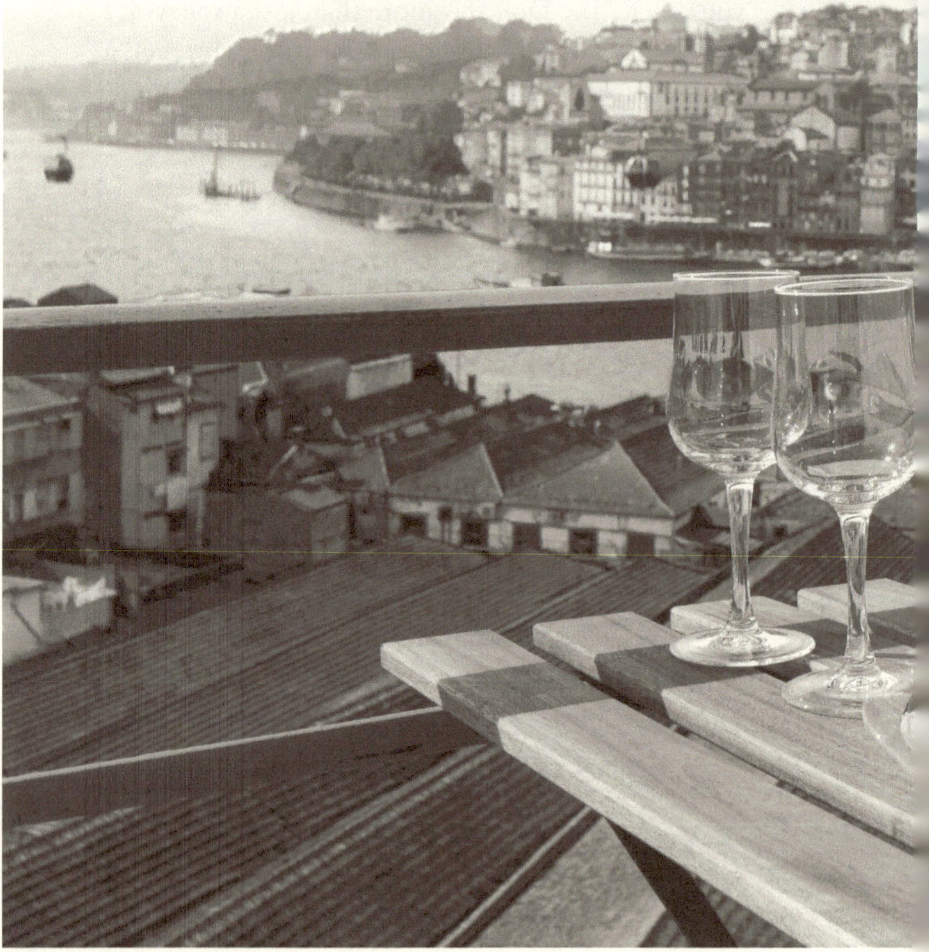

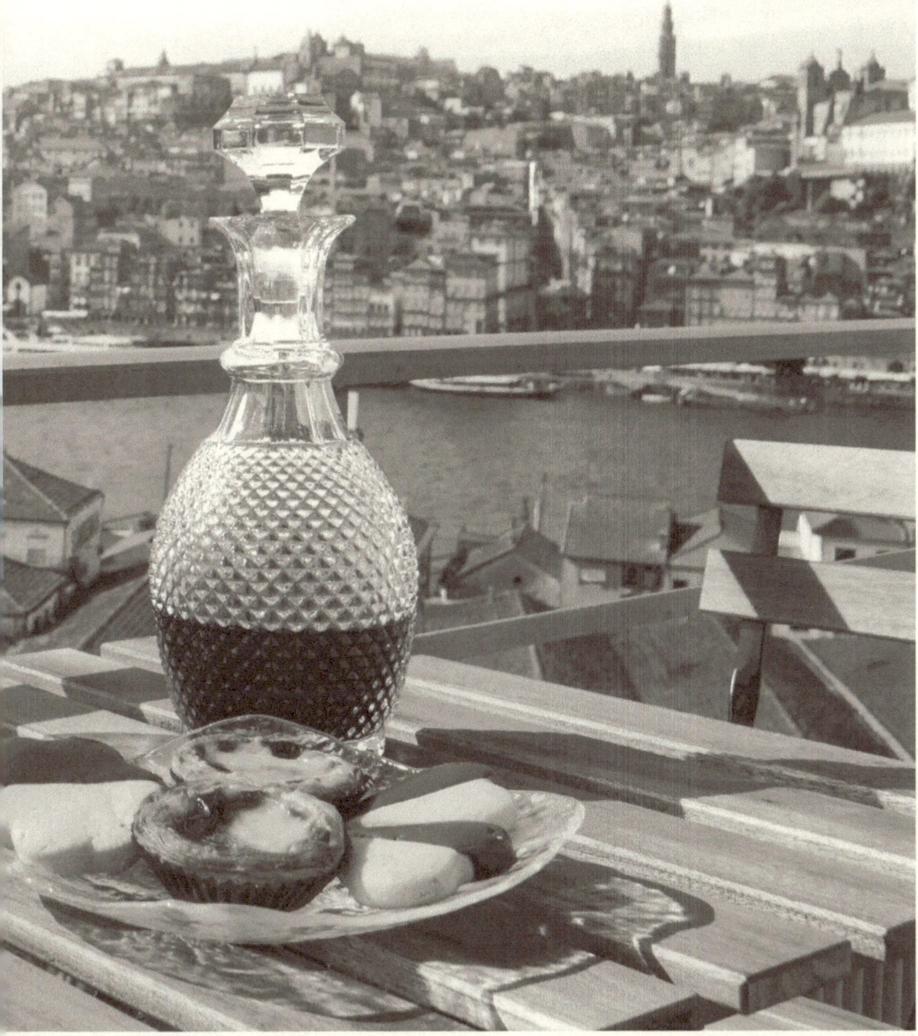

CHAPTER 10:
Portuguese Cuisine

Embarking on a culinary journey through Portugal is much like unfolding a historical tapestry of cultures, influences, and landscapes. Portuguese cuisine is an exquisite reflection of the country's diverse geography and rich past. Every bite tells a story, every sip sings a melody. Food here is not just a necessity, it's a deeply ingrained part of the cultural fabric, woven with threads of tradition and innovation. This chapter, a deep dive into the flavoursome world of Portuguese food, aims to guide you through the culinary marvels that await.

An old Portuguese saying goes, "A barriga cheia, coração contente", which translates to "A full belly, a happy heart". This saying encapsulates the essence of Portuguese cuisine and reflects the nation's love for food, serving as a testament to the importance of hearty meals in shaping daily life in Portugal. Portuguese cuisine is characterized by its straightforwardness, yet it never fails to delight with its array of flavors.

The backbone of Portuguese gastronomy is the holy trinity of bread, wine, and olive oil - ingredients deeply rooted in the country's farming past and still indispensable on every Portuguese table. However, what truly elevates Portuguese cuisine is the philosophy with which it's prepared and savored - meals here are much more than sustenance, they are a time for conviviality and joy.

In Portugal, tradition meets innovation in a tantalizing gastronomic dance. As we delve deeper into the different facets of this cuisine, we'll explore both timeless classics and innovative creations that are pushing the boundaries of Portuguese food as we know it. From rustic family-run tascas serving comfort food that warms your soul to Michelin-starred restaurants offering a refined culinary experience, Portuguese cuisine is as diverse as it is delightful.

As we traverse through this gastronomical landscape, one bite and one sip at a time, we invite you to not only taste but also understand the culture, the history, and the love infused into every Portuguese dish. So let's raise a glass to the cuisine of Portugal, where indeed, a full belly means a happy heart.

Bacalhau:
The National Dish of Portugal

Bacalhau, or codfish, is the undisputed star of Portuguese cuisine. They say there are 365 ways to prepare bacalhau, one for each day of the year. This is a testament to its versatility and the creativity of Portuguese cooks. The love affair between Portugal and bacalhau dates back centuries, and despite the codfish being a cold-water species not native to Portugal's waters, it has become the nation's culinary icon.

The most traditional preparation is "bacalhau à Brás", a comforting dish where the cod is shredded and sautéed with onions, garlic, and thinly sliced potatoes, then bound with beaten eggs. "Bacalhau com Natas", or codfish with cream, is another beloved recipe, delivering a gratifying richness that will delight your palate.

When ordering bacalhau in a restaurant, don't be surprised if it comes served with potatoes and collard greens, a typical side.

But if you really want to cook it like a local, try soaking it in water at home to rehydrate and reduce the salt - a step in many Portuguese households before cooking this beloved dish.

Portuguese Pastries:
The Sweet Gems of Portugal

If you have a sweet tooth, Portugal is your paradise. Portuguese pastries, or pastéis, are a crucial part of the country's culinary scene. Each pastry carries a story, often linked to specific monasteries and convents where nuns and monks used egg yolks, leftover from starching clothes, to create these delicious treats.

The most famous pastry is the Pastel de Nata, a creamy custard tart with a flaky crust that's best enjoyed warm, sprinkled with cinnamon and powdered sugar. Other popular pastries include the Pão de Ló, a soft sponge cake, and the Travesseiro de Sintra, a puff pastry pillow filled with almond cream.

Exploring Portugal's pastry shops, or pastelarias, is a joy. Be sure to arrive early for the freshest selection and savor your chosen pastry with a bica, the Portuguese version of an espresso, for the quintessential Portuguese sweet experience.

Seafood in Portugal:
The Ocean's Bounty

Given Portugal's expansive coastline, it's no surprise that seafood plays a significant role in its culinary landscape. Portugal has one of the highest per capita seafood consumption rates worldwide. Whether it's sardines, octopus, clams, or the prized goose barnacle, the Portuguese know their seafood and prepare it exceptionally well.

One of the must-try seafood dishes is the Arroz de Marisco, a flavorful seafood rice brimming with various shellfish in a rich, tomato-based sauce. Cataplana de Marisco, named after the traditional copper cookware it's cooked in, is another seafood lover's delight, combining a plethora of seafood with ham, sausage, and a tangy tomato sauce.

If you're dining by the coast, don't miss the opportunity to try the daily catch, grilled to perfection and served with boiled potatoes and a simple salad. It's the perfect way to appreciate the freshness and quality of Portugal's seafood offerings. Remember, seafood is best paired with a crisp vinho verde or a light, refreshing white from the Douro Valley.

Portuguese Cheese:
A Cheesy Affair in Portugal

Portugal's love for cheese is deeply ingrained in its culture, boasting an impressive variety of regional cheeses. From creamy to crumbly, mild to sharp, there is a Portuguese cheese to satisfy every palate.

In the mountainous region of Serra da Estrela, you'll find the eponymous Queijo Serra da Estrela, often considered the king of Portuguese cheeses. This creamy, slightly tangy sheep's milk cheese is traditionally made by hand and has a unique soft texture that practically begs to be spread on a piece of bread. Another must-try is Azeitão, a buttery and slightly spicy cheese from the Setúbal Peninsula, best enjoyed with a slice of pear or a dollop of jam.

Venture to the Azores islands, and you'll discover Queijo São Jorge, a firm, sharp cheese with a peppery finish that's ideal for grating over dishes. Cheese in Portugal is often enjoyed as an appetizer, accompanied by bread and olives, or as a dessert, paired with quince jam or honey. So don't hesitate to ask for a cheese plate on your next Portuguese dining experience.

Portuguese Wines:
Portugal's Bottled Poetry

Portugal's winemaking tradition dates back thousands of years, and today, it's home to hundreds of indigenous grape varieties, producing an impressive array of wines. From the effervescent Vinho Verde in the Minho region, to the robust reds of the Douro Valley, and the sweet, fortified Port Wine famous worldwide, Portugal's wines are as diverse as the country itself.

One cannot discuss Portuguese wines without mentioning Madeira, a fortified wine from the Madeira Islands that was a favorite of the American Founding Fathers. It's known for its unique aging process, known as estufagem, which involves heating the wine and deliberately exposing it to some levels of oxidation.

While visiting vineyards and wineries is a fantastic way to learn about Portugal's wine heritage, simply visiting local wine shops or restaurants can be just as educational. Don't be shy to ask for recommendations — Portuguese people are proud of their wines and more than happy to share their knowledge with curious travelers.

Alentejo Bread:
More Than Just a Side Dish

Bread in Portugal is not just an accompaniment to meals, it's a celebrated part of the culinary fabric. One of the best places to experience this is in Alentejo, Portugal's breadbasket. Here, bread goes beyond the simple combination of flour, water, and salt. It's a testament to tradition, history, and regional identity.

Alentejo bread, or pão Alentejano, is a hearty, sourdough-type bread made from wheat flour. It's traditionally baked in a wood-fired oven, lending it a slightly smoky flavor and a delightful crust. Notably, it's also a key ingredient in many Alentejano dishes, such as açorda, a bread soup made with garlic, coriander, olive oil, and sometimes eggs or fish.

Visiting a traditional bakery, or padaria, in Alentejo and witnessing the bakers at work is a wonderful way to understand the importance of bread in Portuguese cuisine. Don't leave without trying a fresh-out-of-the-oven slice of Alentejano bread, drizzled with local olive oil. It's the epitome of simple, soulful Portuguese cuisine.

Portuguese Olive Oil:
Liquid Gold of Portugal

Portuguese cuisine is synonymous with olive oil, or azeite, used abundantly in almost every dish, from soups and stews to salads and desserts. This "liquid gold", as it's often called, lends a distinct richness and depth of flavor to the food.

Portugal's temperate climate and varied terrain provide ideal conditions for olive cultivation, particularly in the Alentejo region where vast olive groves stretch as far as the eye can see.

The oils produced here range from delicate and fruity to more robust and peppery, reflecting the diversity of the region's olive varieties.

Olive oil tasting is an immersive experience that's gaining popularity in Portugal. Many olive oil producers offer guided tours of their olive groves, followed by tastings where you can learn to appreciate the color, aroma, and taste of different oils. When buying Portuguese olive oil, look for the DOP label (Denominação de Origem Protegida), which guarantees the product's quality and origin. Drizzle it over fresh bread, grilled fish, or a bowl of soup to truly appreciate its exceptional flavor.

Azeitão Cheese:
An Unforgettable Taste

Azeitão is a cheese that makes a strong case for the brilliance of Portugal's artisanal cheese-making tradition. Named after the small town of Azeitão in the Setúbal Peninsula, south of Lisbon, this cheese is one of Portugal's gastronomic treasures.

Azeitão cheese is made from raw sheep's milk, rennet derived from cardoon thistles, and salt, following a centuries-old recipe. The result is a semi-soft, creamy cheese with a slightly sour, buttery taste and a faintly herbal aroma, reflecting the diet of the grazing sheep.

The cheese is typically molded into small, round shapes and ripened for at least 20 days. Once cut open, the rich, creamy interior oozes out invitingly, making it a perfect spread on crusty bread. Pair it with a glass of local red wine for a match made in heaven. Azeitão cheese is a PDO product (Protected Designation of Origin), so rest assured that every bite is an authentic taste of Portugal.

Portuguese Coffee Culture:
A Caffeinated Journey

Coffee holds a special place in Portuguese daily life. It's more than just a morning pick-me-up; it's a moment of pleasure, a reason for social gatherings, and a ritual deeply ingrained in the culture. Portuguese coffee is strong and aromatic, with the most popular style being the espresso-like "bica" in Lisbon or "cimbalino" in Porto.

Portuguese coffee houses, or pastelarias, are not just places to grab a quick caffeine fix, they're also community hubs where locals catch up over a cup of coffee and a pastry. These establishments often have an old-world charm, with mirrored walls, marble counters, and an array of delicious pastries on display.

When ordering coffee in Portugal, note that "uma bica" will get you a strong espresso, while "uma garoto" is a lighter version with more milk. For a latte-style coffee, ask for "uma meia de leite". Remember, enjoying coffee in Portugal is not about rushing but savoring the moment. So, take a pause from your sightseeing, watch the world go by, and immerse yourself in Portugal's coffee culture.

Portuguese Cuisine:
A Vegetarian Perspective

While traditional Portuguese cuisine is known for its seafood and meat dishes, the country's vegetarian food scene is on the rise, offering an exciting array of options for vegetarians and vegans alike. From vegetable-centric dishes to innovative plant-based alternatives, exploring the vegetarian side of Portuguese cuisine can be an enriching experience.

Vegetables, legumes, and fruits have always had a place in Portuguese cooking, featuring in soups, stews, salads, and side dishes. Staples like "sopa de legumes", a nourishing vegetable soup, and "salada de grão-de-bico", a chickpea salad, are delicious examples of plant-based Portuguese fare. Also, Portugal's wide variety of bread and cheeses, as well as olive oil and olives, offer vegetarian-friendly options that are easy to enjoy.

In recent years, vegetarian and vegan restaurants have become more prevalent, particularly in larger cities like Lisbon and Porto. Here you can find everything from traditional Portuguese dishes reinvented with plant-based ingredients to international vegetarian cuisine. It's worth exploring local farmers' markets too, where you can find fresh, locally-sourced fruits, vegetables, and artisanal plant-based products.

Another aspect worth mentioning is Portugal's wines. Many Portuguese wineries are adopting organic and biodynamic practices, producing wines that are not only excellent in taste but also better for the environment. Look for "vinho biológico" (organic wine) in wine shops or when ordering at restaurants.

Final Thoughts:
Savoring the Flavors of Portugal

Exploring the culinary landscape of Portugal is like embarking on a grand adventure. Each region, each city, and each village offers a unique tapestry of flavors and textures, reflecting the rich history and diverse influences that have shaped this nation's food culture.

From the ubiquitous bacalhau, prepared in a multitude of ways across the country, to the Alentejo bread, an understated yet indispensable part of Portuguese meals, the cuisine of Portugal is an expression of its land and its people. The sweetness of Portuguese pastries is a testament to the nation's love for indulgence, while the robustness of its cheeses reflects a tradition honed over centuries.

Let the diversity of Portuguese wines enchant you, each variety from the crisp Vinho Verde to the complex Douro reds, and of course, the unique Port wine, narrates a story of its terroir. Enjoy a cup of strong Portuguese coffee, ideally paired with a pastel de nata, and you're participating in a ritual that locals hold dear.

In Portugal, food is a celebration of life. It's deeply woven into the country's fabric, a daily affirmation of its history, culture, and community spirit. As you journey through Portugal, allow your taste buds to guide you. Savor the moment, be it at a bustling city café, a rustic countryside tavern, or a serene seaside eatery. Each bite, each sip, is a connection with the soul of Portugal.

And if you're a vegetarian, fear not. Portugal's culinary scene is evolving, embracing the vegetarian ethos, and offering a palette of flavors that are as vibrant and inviting as the country itself.

As you venture forth, remember that in Portugal, eating is much more than mere sustenance. It's an experience to be savored, a delight to be shared, and above all, a journey to be treasured. Here's to the unforgettable flavors of Portugal, "Bom apetite!"

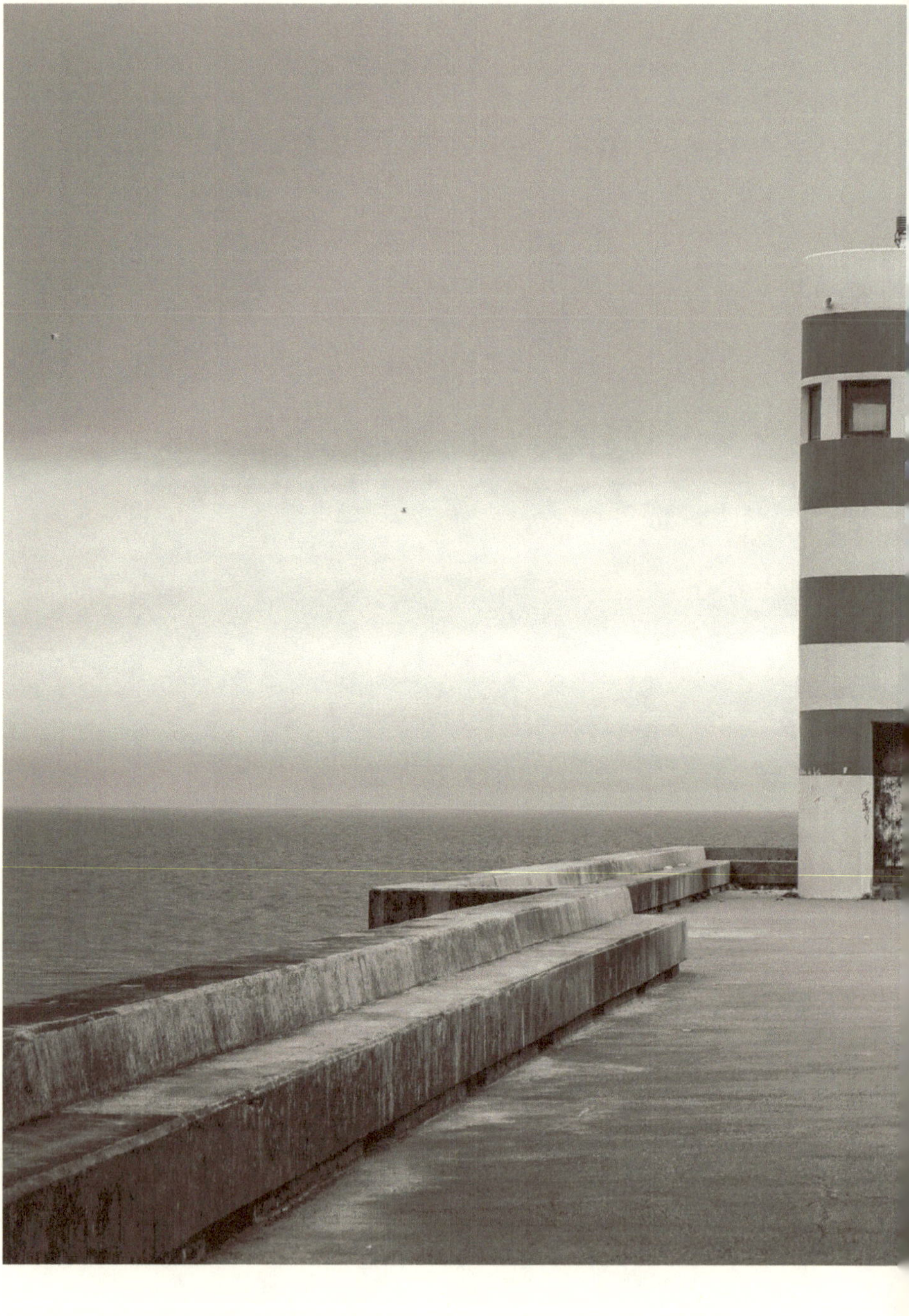

CHAPTER 11: HOW TO TRAVEL ON A BUDGET

CHAPTER 11:
How to Travel Portugal on a Budget

As we've journeyed through the various regions and flavors of Portugal, it's clear that the allure of this country extends far beyond its sun-drenched coastlines, historical cities, and mouthwatering cuisine. With its rich culture, vibrant traditions, and warm hospitality, Portugal is a country that welcomes every traveler, regardless of budget.

In this chapter, we delve into the practical aspects of travel planning, focusing on how you can experience the best of Portugal without breaking the bank. Exploring Portugal on a budget doesn't mean missing out on the country's best offerings. On the contrary, it can often mean a more authentic, immersive, and rewarding experience, as you get to engage more with local culture, savor home-cooked meals, and discover off-the-beaten-path attractions.

From timing your trip to maximize savings, finding affordable accommodations, and navigating the public transportation system, to savoring inexpensive local cuisine and finding cheap or free attractions, this chapter will provide you with an array of tips and advice on how to make your euros go further in Portugal.

Whether you're a solo backpacker, a family on a summer vacation, or a couple on a romantic getaway, this guide will help you plan a trip that's not only affordable but also unforgettable. Let's begin this journey into the art of discovering Portugal on a budget.

Timing Your Trip:
Maximizing Your Budget

Planning your trip can make a big difference to your budget. Generally, the summer months, from June to August, are the most expensive time to travel in Portugal, as they coincide with the European summer holidays and the demand for flights, accommodation, and tourist activities is high. To save, consider traveling during the off-peak season, from November to March, when prices for accommodation and flights tend to be lower.

However, it's worth noting that during the off-peak season, some tourist attractions may have shorter opening hours, and in more remote areas, some services may be limited. Therefore, if your heart is set on exploring every corner of Portugal, the shoulder seasons, namely April to May and September to October, can provide the perfect balance. They offer more moderate weather, fewer crowds, and reasonable prices, while ensuring that all attractions are accessible.

Affordable Accommodations in Portugal:
Staying Comfortable on a Budget

Accommodation can be one of the biggest expenses when traveling. Fortunately, Portugal offers a range of budget-friendly options. Hostels are plentiful, especially in larger cities like Lisbon and Porto. They provide affordable beds, often in dormitory-style rooms, and are a great way to meet fellow travelers.

For those seeking more privacy, guesthouses or "pensões" are an excellent option. They offer private rooms at a fraction of the cost of a hotel. Self-catering accommodation, like apartments or holiday homes, can also be a good choice, particularly for longer stays or for those traveling in groups. These often come equipped with kitchen facilities, allowing you to save on meals by cooking your own food. Also, don't forget to check out online platforms like Airbnb for unique and budget-friendly accommodation options.

Portuguese Food on a Shoestring:
Eating Well Without Splurging

Eating out in Portugal can be surprisingly affordable. Traditional Portuguese eateries, known as "tascas", serve hearty and inexpensive meals, with daily specials often available for under 10 euros. Seafood dishes, soups, and stews like "caldo verde" or "bacalhau à brás" are common features on these menus. Also, many restaurants offer a "prato do dia" (dish of the day), which usually includes a soup, main dish, drink, and sometimes even dessert at a fixed and affordable price.

For on-the-go meals, look out for "pastelarias" or bakeries, which offer delicious pastries, sandwiches, and often, coffee, at wallet-friendly prices. Don't miss out on trying a pastel de nata, the iconic Portuguese custard tart. Local markets are also worth a visit. They offer fresh produce, cheese, bread, and often have food stalls where you can grab a quick, inexpensive bite. For a fun and budget-friendly dining experience, consider a picnic with local produce in one of Portugal's many beautiful parks or beaches. Remember, when it comes to food in Portugal, it's entirely possible to eat well without breaking the bank!

Free and Affordable Attractions:
Sightseeing Without Breaking the Bank

Portugal brims with affordable attractions and activities that can enrich your travel experience without straining your wallet. Many museums and monuments, such as the Museu Coleção Berardo in Lisbon, offer free entry on certain days of the week or month. Churches, like the Sé Cathedral in Porto or the Monastery of Alcobaça, often only charge a small fee, while others are completely free to enter.

Outdoor activities such as hiking in Peneda-Gerês National Park, strolling through the colorful streets of Porto's Ribeira district, or basking on the Algarve's stunning beaches, won't cost you anything. In cities, you'll often find free walking tours where guides work on a tip basis. These tours can be an excellent way to learn about the history and culture of the place from a local perspective.

Also, don't underestimate the charm of simply soaking up the atmosphere in a local café, watching the world go by in one of the country's many beautiful squares, or catching a sunset from a miradouro (viewpoint) in Lisbon. These experiences are all part of the beauty of traveling in Portugal and can be enjoyed at minimal cost.

Navigating Portugal Affordably:
Public Transportation Tips

Public transportation in Portugal is extensive, reliable, and affordable, making it a great option for budget travelers. Major cities like Lisbon and Porto have a network of metro, bus, and tram routes that can take you around the city for a fraction of the cost of a taxi. Purchasing a day pass can be a more economical option if you plan on taking multiple rides in a day.

Trains are an excellent way to travel between cities. They're comfortable, scenic, and often cheaper than buses. If you're planning on doing a lot of intercity travel, look into getting a rail pass which can offer unlimited travel over a certain period. Buses are also widely used, especially for routes where trains don't operate. The national bus company, Rede Expressos, serves most towns and cities throughout the country. For shorter distances, walking or cycling can also be feasible, healthy, and cost-effective options, with many cities offering bike rental services.

Thrifty Shopping:
Affordable Souvenirs and Goods

While it's natural to want to bring a piece of Portugal back home with you, souvenir shopping doesn't have to be a budget-buster. Traditional products like cork accessories, ceramic tiles known as "azulejos", or canned sardines make for unique and reasonably priced souvenirs. You can often find these at local markets, where haggling is a part of the shopping experience.

For affordable fashion, look for sales at the end of each season when many shops offer significant discounts. Portugal is also known for its high-quality textiles, such as towels and linens, which can be found at a bargain in department stores or textile outlets.

When it comes to food, local supermarkets offer a range of Portuguese wines, cheeses, and cured meats at lower prices than most specialty shops. And, of course, a bottle of the famous Port wine or a box of Pasteis de Nata could also serve as delightful, budget-friendly reminders of your Portuguese escapade.

Travel Insurance:
Saving from Unexpected Expenses

Travel insurance is a critical component of any budget travel plan. While it might seem like an unnecessary expense initially, it can potentially save you from exorbitant costs in case of unforeseen circumstances such as illness, injury, trip cancellations, or loss of belongings.

There are various plans available, so take the time to research and choose one that best suits your needs. A good travel insurance plan will cover emergency medical expenses, repatriation, luggage loss or damage, and trip cancellation or interruption. It's advisable to get your insurance at the same time as you book your trip to ensure that you're covered if you have to cancel.

Also, check your existing insurance policies and credit card agreements. Some already include basic travel insurance coverage. Remember, the goal is to have peace of mind while exploring and enjoying Portugal to the fullest.

Off-Peak Travel:
Experiencing Portugal Without the Crowds

Traveling to Portugal during the off-peak season, generally from October to April, can offer substantial savings and a different kind of experience. Flight and accommodation costs are often lower during this period, and you're likely to encounter fewer crowds at popular tourist spots.

The weather, while cooler and potentially wetter, is generally mild and still pleasant enough for sightseeing. Also, since there are fewer tourists, you'll have more opportunities to interact with locals and gain a deeper understanding of Portuguese culture.

That said, some attractions may have shorter opening hours or be closed during the off-peak season. Always check the schedules beforehand. Also, pack suitable clothing for the weather. Layers are key for Portugal's often unpredictable climate.

Volunteering Opportunities:
A Different Way to Experience Portugal

Volunteering can be an enriching and affordable way to travel. In exchange for a few hours of work a day, you often receive free accommodation and meals. This can significantly cut down on your travel costs and provide an opportunity to immerse yourself in the local culture.

Portugal offers numerous volunteering opportunities. From working on organic farms through organizations like WWOOF, helping out in hostels, teaching languages, to participating in environmental conservation projects, there's likely to be something that matches your skills and interests.

Not only does volunteering provide an affordable way to travel, but it also allows you to give back to the communities you visit. It can be a truly rewarding experience, offering unique insights that typical tourism rarely affords. As always, ensure you're working with a reputable organization that values and respects its volunteers.

Portuguese Budget Cuisine:
Eating Cheap but Tasty

With a diverse and tasty cuisine, Portugal offers a plethora of options for travelers who are keen on enjoying local delicacies without stretching their budget. The culinary culture of Portugal is founded on simple, fresh ingredients that create a symphony of flavors in your mouth, and luckily, experiencing this doesn't have to come with a hefty price tag.

One of the best ways to eat well on a budget in Portugal is to venture beyond the well-trodden paths. Local markets, traditional 'tascas' (taverns), and small family-run eateries often provide authentic meals that not only satiate your taste buds but also introduce you to the true essence of Portuguese cuisine. These places tend to be inexpensive, serving generous portions that can be enjoyed without worrying about your budget.

The 'prato do dia' (dish of the day) is a common feature in Portuguese eateries and is typically a hearty, well-rounded meal. It often includes a soup or salad starter, a main course, a beverage, and sometimes even a dessert, all for a very reasonable price. These meals reflect the local fare and vary from region to region, offering you a chance to taste a variety of dishes during your stay.

The Portuguese are also renowned for their sandwiches, like the 'Bifana'—pork steak in a roll—or the 'Prego'—beef steak in a roll. These filling sandwiches are usually affordable and make for a quick, easy meal on the go. Another economical option is the traditional soup 'Caldo Verde' made with potatoes, collard greens, and chouriço sausage—a comfort food that is light on the pocket yet rich in taste.

Then there is the unmissable 'Pastel de Nata', the famous Portuguese egg tart pastry. This sweet treat is not only mouth wateringly delicious but also surprisingly affordable, perfect for a budget dessert or snack.

For those who enjoy cooking, local markets are treasure troves of fresh produce. From seasonal fruits and vegetables to local cheeses and freshly baked bread, these markets provide high-quality ingredients at lower prices than conventional supermarkets.

Final Thoughts:
How to Make the Most of Your Budget in Portugal

Discovering Portugal on a budget is far from a limiting experience. In fact, it opens up avenues for more intimate and authentic encounters with the country's culture, history, and of course, its culinary delights.

A journey to Portugal is filled with hidden gems that can be enjoyed without splurging. Remember, the best experiences come from exploring local life, savoring regional cuisines, and connecting with the welcoming Portuguese people, and these rarely require a hefty budget.

Here are some key tips to keep your budget in check while enjoying the best of what Portugal has to offer:

- Plan your trip during the off-peak season. This is when airfares and accommodations tend to be less expensive. Plus, you'll get to enjoy the destinations without the large crowds.
- Explore options for budget accommodations. Portugal offers a range of hostels, guesthouses, and vacation rentals that are comfortable yet economical.
- Discover the local cuisine at small, family-run establishments and markets. Not only will this save you money, but you'll also get to taste authentic Portuguese food.
- Make the most of the numerous free or discounted attractions and cultural events. Many museums and sites have specific days or hours when entry is free or reduced.

- Utilize public transportation. It's generally reliable and much cheaper than taxis or renting a car. For shorter distances, consider walking or biking.
- Shop at local markets and independent shops for unique and affordable souvenirs.
- Consider investing in travel insurance to protect you from unforeseen costs. This could save you a significant amount of money should any unexpected incidents occur during your trip.
- Look into volunteering opportunities. These can be a great way to immerse yourself in the local culture and give back to the communities you visit, all while reducing your overall travel expenses.

Ultimately, traveling is about experiencing new cultures, connecting with different people, and creating memories that last a lifetime. Portugal, with its rich history, warm hospitality, and diverse landscapes, offers all this and more, even for those traveling on a budget. So embrace the adventure, dive into the experiences, and let the charm of Portugal capture your heart. It's an incredible journey that shows the most valuable aspects of travel are indeed priceless.

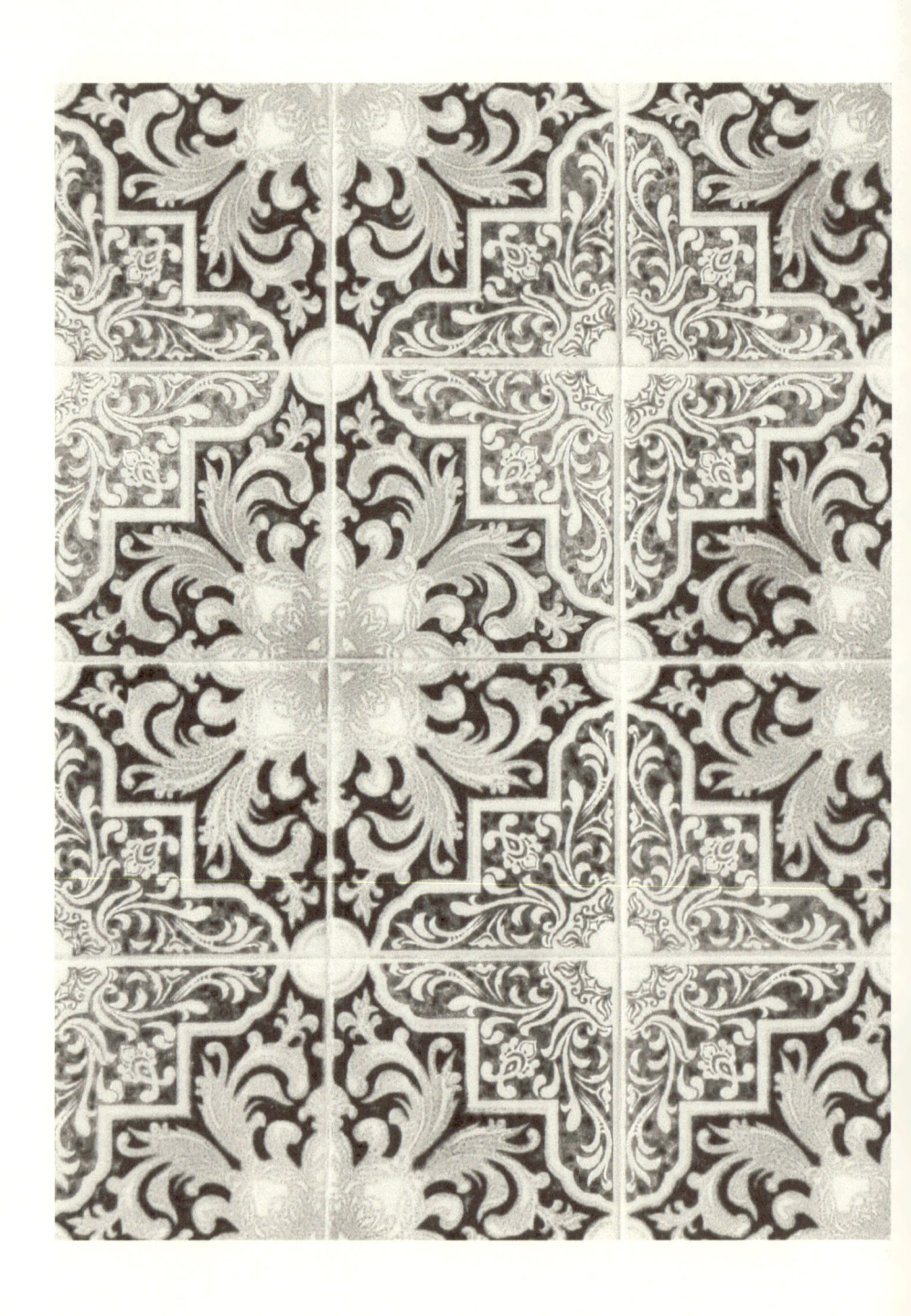

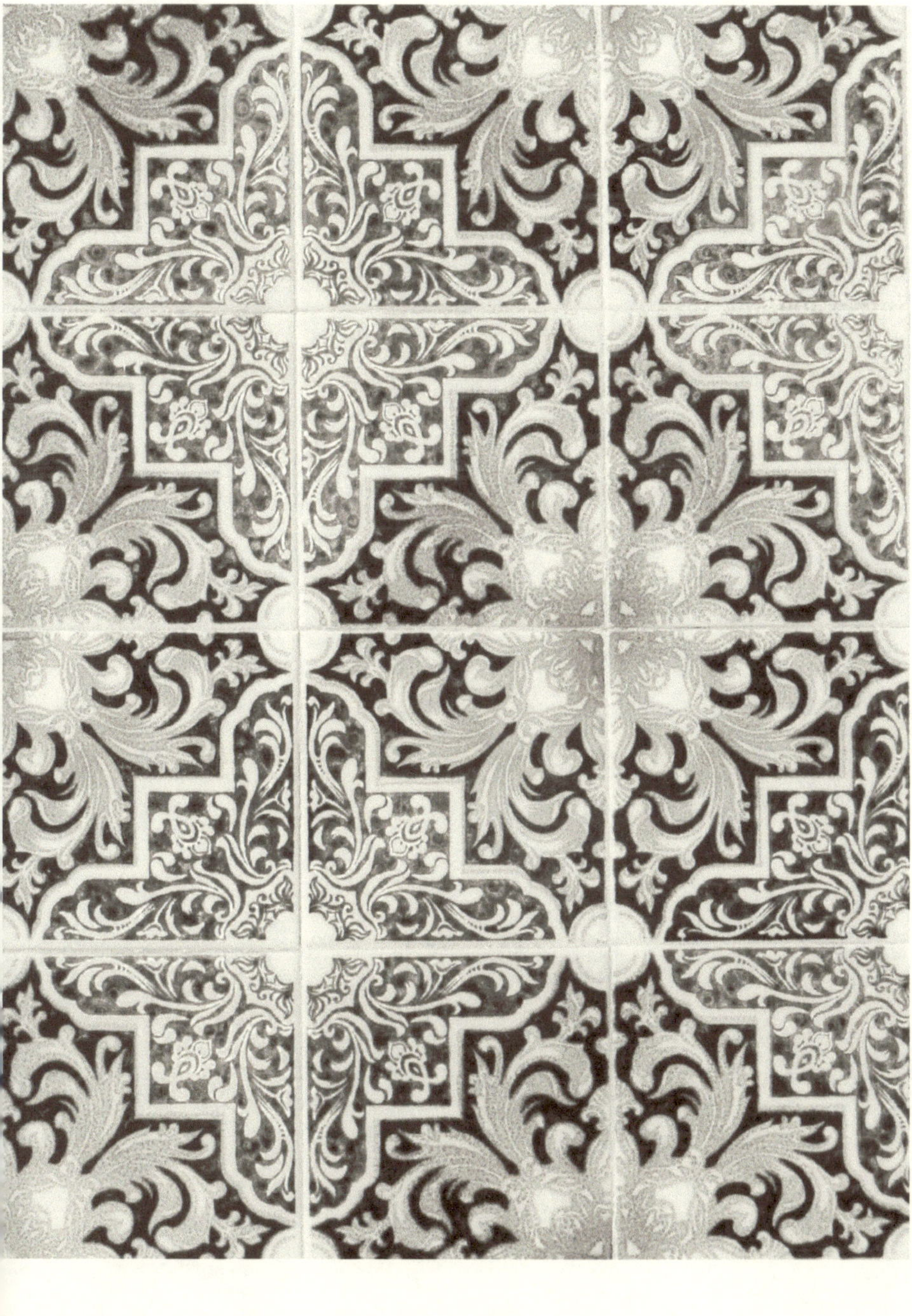

CHAPTER 12:
10 Cultural Experiences You Must Try in Portugal

As we reach the end of this comprehensive guide, we find ourselves stepping into the realm of cultural experiences that shape the soul of Portugal.

This country, renowned for its history, culinary prowess, and stunning landscapes, is also a cradle of rich and fascinating cultural experiences that invite travelers to delve deeper and engage with the local way of life. Exploring Portugal doesn't just mean visiting its monuments or tasting its food—it also means experiencing its traditions, learning its crafts, and engaging with its people.

Each region of Portugal has its unique cultural charm that reflects centuries of tradition and heritage. From the soul-stirring melodies of Fado in the alleyways of Lisbon to the joyful festivals in small towns; from the art of Azulejos that colorfully adorn city walls to the age-old wine-making traditions in the Douro Valley; each experience serves as a thread in the vibrant cultural fabric of Portugal.

In this chapter, we invite you to embark on a journey beyond the typical tourist routes. Here, you'll find a collection of cultural experiences that offer a deeper insight into the Portuguese way of life. These aren't just activities; they are invitations to participate, learn, and connect. They're opportunities to try your hand at a traditional craft, understand the nuances of the Portuguese language, sway to the rhythm of local dances, and so much more.

So get ready to immerse yourself in the soul of Portugal through these 10 cultural experiences. Whether you're a solo traveler seeking an authentic connection or a family desiring to make lasting memories, there's something here for everyone. Each experience not only enriches your understanding of Portugal but also leaves you with a piece of this enchanting country in your heart.

Dive in and embrace the joy of discovering Portugal through its culture. As the Portuguese saying goes, "A vida não é para ser entendida, é para ser vivida". Life is not to be understood, it's to be lived. So, let's live it the Portuguese way.

1 - Fado Performance:
Feeling the Soul of Portugal

Nothing captures the essence of Portugal quite like a Fado performance. Originating in the working-class neighborhoods of Lisbon, Fado is a traditional form of Portuguese music characterized by melancholic tunes and poignant lyrics. Fado performances are intimate, almost like a conversation between the singer, the guitarists, and the audience. They are typically held in 'Fado houses', small, intimate venues that add to the soulful atmosphere.

To truly experience Fado, visit a Fado house in the Alfama or Mouraria neighborhoods of Lisbon, or the Ribeira district of Porto. As the lights dim and the first chords of the Portuguese guitar resonate, you'll find yourself immersed in the raw emotion that Fado embodies. Remember, it's customary to maintain silence during the performance as a sign of respect for the performers.

2 - Portuguese Cooking Class:
Learning to Cook Like a Local

Engage with Portuguese culture through its rich and diverse cuisine by enrolling in a local cooking class. Not only will you learn to cook traditional Portuguese dishes, but you'll also get a deeper understanding of the regional ingredients and cooking techniques that define Portuguese cuisine.

Most cooking classes begin with a visit to a local market where you'll source fresh ingredients for your cooking session. Then, under the guidance of a local chef, you'll prepare classic dishes such as 'bacalhau à brás' or 'pastel de nata'. The experience usually concludes with everyone sitting down to enjoy the prepared meal together, often paired with local wines.

You can find cooking classes in major cities like Lisbon, Porto, and Faro, as well as in some smaller towns and rural areas. It's advisable to book in advance, especially during the peak tourist season.

3 - Traditional Azulejos Workshop:
Creating Your Own Piece of Portuguese Art

Azulejos, the beautiful ceramic tiles that adorn numerous buildings throughout Portugal, are one of the most distinctive features of Portuguese architecture. Attending an Azulejos workshop is a fantastic way to understand the history, significance, and process behind this traditional craft.

In a typical workshop, you'll learn about the evolution of Azulejo design and techniques over the centuries. Then, guided by a master artisan, you'll get to create your own tile, from sketching and painting to the final glazing and firing process.

Workshops are offered in several cities, including Lisbon and Porto, and vary in length from a few hours to a full day. Not only do you leave with a unique handmade souvenir, but you also gain a deep appreciation for this art form that is so integral to the Portuguese cultural landscape.

4 - Douro Valley Wine Tour:
Exploring Portugal's Wine Tradition

If you're a wine enthusiast, a visit to the Douro Valley is a must. Renowned as one of the world's oldest wine regions and a UNESCO World Heritage site, the Douro Valley offers a unique opportunity to delve into Portugal's winemaking tradition.

Wine tours in the Douro Valley usually involve visits to several quintas (wine estates), where you can explore the vineyards, learn about the winemaking process, and of course, sample a variety of wines. Most notably, you'll get to taste Port, the fortified wine that the region is famous for, as well as some excellent still wines.

Wine tours can be booked from major cities like Porto or you could stay in the valley itself for a more immersive experience. Remember to pack comfortable shoes for walking in the vineyards, and don't forget your camera for those breathtaking vineyard views.

5 - Walking Tour of a Historic City:
Stepping Back in Time

Portugal is blessed with numerous historic cities, each one steeped in history and brimming with architectural treasures. Whether it's Lisbon's vibrant Alfama district, Porto's UNESCO-listed Ribeira, or the well-preserved medieval town of Óbidos, taking a guided walking tour is one of the best ways to explore these places.

Guided tours not only bring you to the city's iconic sights but also to the less-touristy corners that you might otherwise overlook. Your guide will provide you with insights about the city's history, culture, and local life, enriching your understanding of the place.

You can find guided tours in almost every city in Portugal. Most tours are in English, but other language options are also available. Wear comfortable shoes, carry a bottle of water, and don't forget to tip your guide if you enjoyed the tour.

6 - Attending a Portuguese Festival:
Reveling in Local Traditions

To truly feel the pulse of Portugal, plan your visit around one of the many local festivals or festas that take place throughout the year. These events offer a lively and colorful glimpse into Portuguese culture and traditions.

Festivals range from religious processions, like Lisbon's Festas de Santo António or Porto's Festa de São João, to music festivals, gastronomy fairs, and historical reenactments. They're a great opportunity to witness traditional customs, enjoy local food and music, and mingle with the locals.

Before your trip, check the local tourist office's website or social media pages for information on upcoming festivals. Be prepared for large crowds and book your accommodation in advance if you plan to attend a popular festival. Most importantly, dive in and enjoy the festive atmosphere!

7 - A Visit to a Portuguese Market:
Immersion in the Local Culture

Markets are the beating heart of local life in Portugal, making them an ideal place to immerse yourself in the culture. From bustling food markets, like Lisbon's Mercado da Ribeira or Porto's Mercado do Bolhão, to weekly flea markets and artisanal craft fairs, there's a market for every interest.

These are places where you can sample a wide array of Portuguese delicacies, buy fresh produce, or discover unique souvenirs. It's also a great opportunity to observe the day-to-day life of the locals and engage in some friendly haggling.

Remember to bring a reusable shopping bag and cash, as many vendors don't accept credit cards. Be respectful of the vendors and their products, and always ask before taking photographs.

8 - Portuguese Language Class:
Speaking Like a Local

Portuguese is a beautiful language, steeped in history and culture. Taking a language class during your stay is a great way to dive deeper into the Portuguese way of life and communicate better with locals.

You can find language schools in all major cities offering courses for all levels, from beginners to advanced. Some schools even offer cultural immersion classes, which combine language learning with activities like cooking, wine tasting, or city tours.

Don't worry if you can't master the language. Even learning a few basic phrases can greatly enhance your travel experience, and locals will appreciate your effort to speak their language.

9 - Portugal's Coffee Culture:
Savoring a Bica in a Local Café

Coffee is a way of life in Portugal, and understanding its coffee culture is a must for any visitor. Start your day the Portuguese way with a bica (espresso) at a local pastelaria (pastry shop), or enjoy a meia de leite (latte) during a leisurely afternoon break.

Portugal is full of historic cafés, like Lisbon's Café A Brasileira or Porto's Majestic Café, which offer a unique setting to enjoy your coffee and perhaps a pastel de nata. But you'll also find local coffee shops in every neighborhood, each with its unique atmosphere.

Remember, Portuguese coffee is usually enjoyed in small quantities but full of flavor. And when you order, be sure to specify how you like your coffee. A bica, for example, is a shot of espresso, while a garoto is an espresso with a little milk. Enjoy the experience and take your time, sipping coffee in Portugal is not a rushed affair.

10 - Portuguese Traditional Dance Class:
Swinging to the Rhythms of Portugal

Portuguese traditional dance is an expressive reflection of the country's diverse cultural heritage. From the lively folk dances of the Minho region to the seductive Fandango, each dance tells a story about Portugal's past and its people. Enrolling in a traditional dance class is a fun and immersive way to understand these cultural nuances better.

Dance schools in Portugal offer classes in various traditional dance styles. You don't need prior experience to join. It's about enjoyment and expression, not perfection. In Lisbon and Porto, some schools offer open community classes or 'bailes' where everyone is welcome.

Participating in a dance class is not just about learning the steps, it's also an opportunity to meet locals and fellow travelers. Don't be shy, just put on your dancing shoes, embrace the music, and let the rhythm of Portugal move you.

Final Thoughts:
Immerse Yourself in the Vibrant Portuguese Culture

As we've journeyed through these experiences, one common thread emerges – the vibrant, rich, and diverse culture that defines Portugal. From the melancholic strumming of a Fado guitar to the joyful steps of traditional dance, the soul of Portugal beats in every experience. Each offering is an opportunity to delve deeper into the country's heritage, to feel its pulse, and to connect with its people.

Partaking in these cultural experiences allows you to travel not just in space but also in time – to understand Portugal's past, appreciate its present, and envision its future. It's more than sightseeing; it's about understanding, participating, and immersing.

As we reach the end of this chapter, remember that the best way to truly understand a culture is to dive in, head first, and let it envelop you. So, whether you're strumming a guitar to the melancholic notes of Fado, shaping a piece of azulejo with your own hands, or dancing to the vibrant rhythms of Portuguese folk music, let yourself be carried away.

Embrace the experiences that await, for they are not just paths to discovery, but bridges to understanding and appreciation. And in this understanding, you'll find that Portugal is more than a destination – it's a feeling, an experience, a way of life. So go forth, explore, immerse, and above all, enjoy the vibrant Portuguese culture. Your journey is only just beginning. Boa viagem!

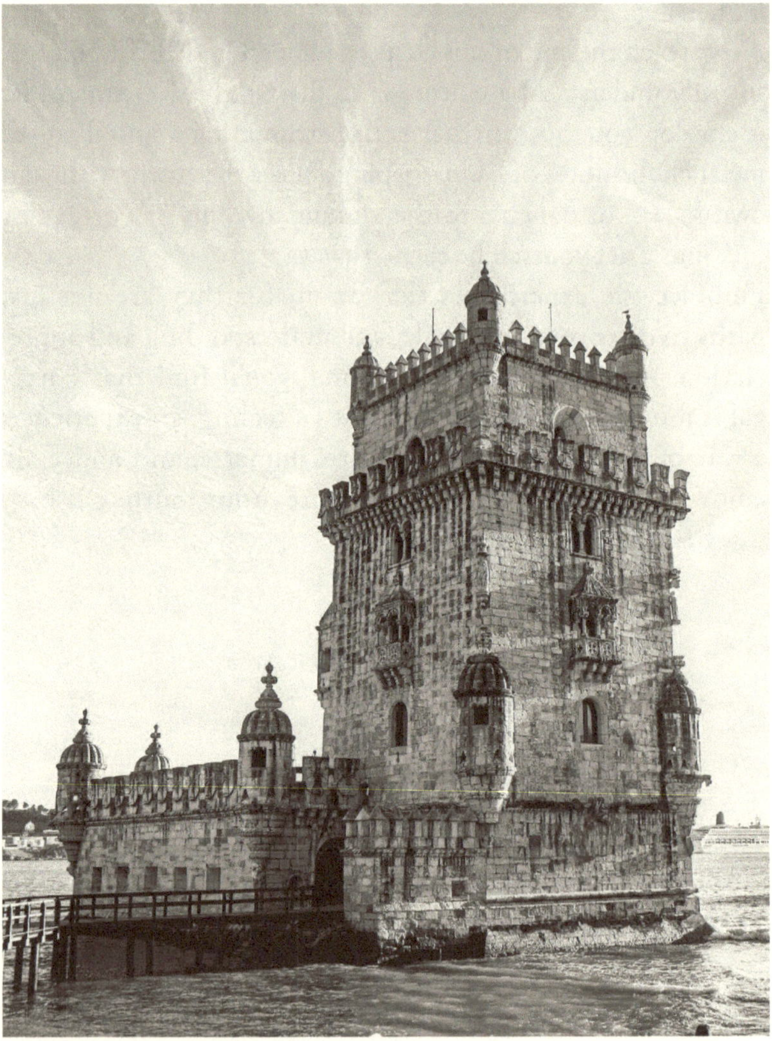

Conclusion

As we close the final chapter of this book, we take a step back and look at the journey we've embarked on together. We've traversed the length and breadth of Portugal, from the sunny beaches of the Algarve to the verdant vineyards of the Douro Valley, from the bustling metropolises of Lisbon and Porto to the tranquil villages in the Alentejo region. This journey has been an exploration not just of places, but of culture, traditions, gastronomy, and above all, the Portuguese spirit.

Portugal offers an unparalleled array of experiences, wrapped in its rich history and warm hospitality. This is a country that welcomes all - the solo traveler in search of self-discovery, couples seeking a romantic escapade, friends on an adventure, or families yearning for a memorable vacation. Each facet of Portugal presents a unique appeal, just waiting to be discovered.

For the solitary explorer, Portugal is a paradise of self-discovery. The country's diversity lends itself perfectly to those seeking both solitude and social interaction. Walking through the streets of Lisbon, you'll find yourself lost in time, steeped in history, yet very much in the present. Meanwhile, Portugal's vast natural landscapes, from the Peneda-Gerês National Park to the cliffs of Cabo da Roca, offer opportunities for quiet introspection amidst breathtaking natural beauty.

For couples, Portugal's old-world charm, coupled with its contemporary pulse, presents the perfect romantic getaway. Imagine a slow, serene boat ride on the Douro River, surrounded by terraced vineyards, or a candlelit dinner overlooking the ocean in Algarve. The quiet lanes of Alfama, filled with the haunting melodies of Fado, offer an ideal backdrop for those cherished moments of togetherness.

Friends embarking on a Portuguese adventure will find the country's vibrant nightlife and thriving arts scene captivating. From the buzzing bars of Bairro Alto to the street art of Lagos, Portugal pulsates with youthful energy and artistic expression. The country's festivals, like the Festa de São João in Porto or the Carnaval in Torres Vedras, promise unforgettable fun and camaraderie.

For families, Portugal provides a safe, welcoming environment filled with educational and recreational activities. Family-friendly museums, like the Oceanário de Lisboa, are as informative as they are entertaining. The many parks and open spaces, like the Parque das Nações, offer ample opportunities for relaxation and family fun.

The heart of the Portugal experience, however, beats in its culture and people. The Portuguese are known for their hospitality and kindness, always ready with a warm smile and an open heart. They are proud of their heritage, from the melancholic Fado to the intricacies of making Port wine. Engaging with them, learning from them, and sharing experiences with them can be the highlight of your visit.

As we've learned in our journey, language is a powerful tool that connects people, and Portuguese is no different. Even a basic understanding of a few Portuguese phrases can enrich your travel experience significantly. Here are some common phrases that you might find useful:

- 'Olá' (O-la): Hello. A simple greeting can go a long way in starting a conversation.

- 'Bom dia' (bong dee-a): Good morning. A bright start to your day!

- 'Boa tarde' (boa tarde): Good afternoon. This phrase can be used from noon until sunset.

- 'Boa noite' (boa noyt): Good night. Use this phrase to say 'Goodnight' before bed or to greet someone in the evening.

- 'Por favor' (por favor): Please. Courtesy is universal.

- 'Obrigado' (if you're male) or 'Obrigada' (if you're female) (o-bri-ga-doo/o-bri-ga-da): Thank you. A word of gratitude is always appreciated.

- 'Desculpe' (desh-cul-pe): Excuse me. For times when you accidentally bump into someone on a crowded tram in Lisbon or if you need someone's attention.

- 'Eu não falo português' (eyoo now falo portuguesh): I don't speak Portuguese. This can be helpful in situations where you need someone to speak English with you.

- 'Onde é o banheiro?' (on-deh eh o ban-yay-ro): Where is the bathroom? One of the most important phrases, you'd agree!

These are just a few of the many phrases you can use during your stay in Portugal. Learning a bit of the language not only eases your travel but also helps to connect more with the local people.

It opens up more authentic experiences and interactions, adding more depth and richness to your travel stories".

This information not only provides practical help to travelers but also enriches the conclusion by reminding them of the importance of engaging with the local culture in a respectful and meaningful way.

As we've learned in our journey, Portuguese cuisine is a delightful exploration of the senses. The diversity of flavors, from the sea-soaked dishes of the coastal areas to the hearty meals of the interior, mirrors the diversity of the land itself. The beautiful simplicity of Portuguese food, paired with world-class wines, is a testament to the country's rich agricultural tradition and innovative culinary arts.

Portugal's offerings go beyond the typical travel guide. It's in the intimate moments, like sharing a joke with a friendly local at a Lisbon café, admiring the skill of azulejos artisans, or simply watching the sunset over the Atlantic Ocean, that you truly connect with the country. These experiences define Portugal's unique character and charm.

As we conclude, let's remember that traveling to Portugal is not just about ticking off a list of attractions. It's about immersing oneself in the Portuguese way of life, understanding its past, being a part of its present, and looking forward to its future. Portugal is a country where every visitor can find a piece of themselves, a place that feels like home, and memories to last a lifetime.

Our journey in this book may be ending, but the adventure that awaits you in Portugal is just beginning. Armed with the insights and knowledge you've gained from these pages, you're now ready to create your own unique Portuguese story. Portugal is a tapestry of experiences, waiting for you to weave your thread into it.

So, here's to you, the future traveler. Here's to the experiences you'll have, the people you'll meet, and the memories you'll make in Portugal. The country awaits with open arms and a warm heart, ready to welcome you into its rich tapestry of life. Boa viagem – have a great journey. Your Portuguese adventure awaits!

Made in United States
Troutdale, OR
07/04/2024